Why Not Load
Your Own!

BASIC HANDLOADING FOR EVERYONE

Published by Echo Point Books & Media
Brattleboro, Vermont
www.EchoPointBooks.com

ISBN: 978-1-62654-117-7

Cover design by Rachel Boothby Gualco,
Echo Point Books & Media

Editorial and proofreading assistance by Christine Schultz,
Echo Point Books & Media

COLONEL TOWNSEND WHELEN

Why Not Load Your Own!

BASIC HANDLOADING FOR EVERYONE

FOURTH EDITION
Revised and Enlarged

E P B M
ECHO POINT BOOKS & MEDIA, LLC

The little bench in the Author's attic on which he has handloaded approximately 50,000 rounds of ammunition between 1925 and 1949.

FIT

From the beginnings of firearms, throughout all the years of muzzle loading guns, up to seventy years ago, every hunter, every soldier, every target shooter loaded his own ammunition, every round of it. He measured out the powder charge and poured it into his rifle or pistol barrel, seated the bullet on the powder, and primed the lock. How well his weapon shot depended partly on its quality, and partly on the quality and skill of his loading.

It still does. The load, the cartridge, is quite as important as the weapon. The load must *fit* the weapon.

Then came the machine age, the breech loading rifle and pistol, and the ready-assembled cartridge made in quantity in a factory. A manufacturing tolerance was unavoidable in both weapon and cartridge. Every cartridge had to be small enough to go into the smallest weapon of its caliber. *Exact fit* of the two machine products was no longer possible. Many men forgot, and more do not know, that there was and is such a thing as handloading, particularly handloading to fit a particular weapon.

But a few remained who did, and who also remembered the accuracy of the muzzle loader in the hands of an Old American who appreciated accuracy and who knew what the word "fit" meant. And these few kept the art of handloading alive. As their old tools wore out, and the art threatened to die, these riflemen persuaded an old retired sergeant of the Regular Army to make reloading tools, to design new and better ones for modern cartridges, and they also helped him to write an *"Ideal Handbook"* telling how to load cartridges.

And so it is proper that I should dedicate this book, which brings the art of handloading up to date, to a personal friend of mine of long, long ago:

JOHN H. BARLOW
Sergeant, Company H, 14th Infantry

Colonel, U. S. Army, Retired.

v

ACKNOWLEDGMENTS

I practically grew up with handloading. Many of the processes I mention herein I developed myself, and gave to riflemen in my articles in many sporting magazines and in my books.

I have received, and still receive, much assistance from articles and books published by other riflemen and handloaders. And I must not fail to mention the many fine workmen at Frankford Arsenal, where I was in command from 1919 to 1922, who instilled in me many of the important principles of loading small arms ammunition.

There are three riflemen to whom I am particularly indebted. The late Dr. Walter G. Hudson. The late J. Bushnell Smith. Mr. A. H. Barr of the Technical Staff, National Rifle Association.

TOWNSEND WHELEN.

Washington, D. C.
1949

CONTENTS

PREFACE TO FOURTH EDITION

Since the first three editions of this work were published there has been a truly remarkable growth in interest in reloading, and in the number of persons who regularly handload their rifle and pistol cartridges. Intense study has been given to the technique of loading. Many new methods have been developed and many new tools are now offered. Particularly, the National Bench Rest Shooters Association has considerably improved methods of loading for greater accuracy. I have endeavored to incorporate all this new material in this new edition in a manner that can be easily understood by any reader.

Also, during the past three years the National Rifle Association, in conjunction with the H. P. White Company, has undertaken a study of velocities and breech pressures of many handloads for most modern cartridges. This study has been of considerable help in assuring that the various loads I give in Part IV do not exceed permissible safe breech pressures, and also that certain of my loads giving increased velocity do not exceed sane pressures. Thus I believe my tables of loads given here are safer than any previously published. We are greatly indebted to the NRA for making this study, for equipment for taking breech pressures is so costly as to be beyond the means of individuals and small companies.

I practically grew up with handloading, having been at it steadily since 1899. Many of the processes and methods I mention were developed by me, and I gave them to shooters in articles in various sporting magazines and in my books.

I have received, and still receive, much assistance from articles and books by other shooters and handloaders, particularly those articles in *The American Rifleman,* the publication of the NRA, which every handloader should read. And I must not fail to mention the many fine workmen at Frankford Arsenal, which I commanded from 1919 to 1922, who instilled in me many of the important principles of loading small-arms ammunition.

I am particularly indebted to four riflemen: the late Dr. Walter G. Hudson; the late J. Bushnell Smith; the late A. H. Barr; and Captain M. D. Waite of the Technical Staff of the National Rifle Association.

T. W.

January, 1957

I
GENERAL INFORMATION
ADVANTAGES OF HANDLOADING

1. **Superiority.** American factory loaded cartridges are a wonderfully developed and satisfactory product; standardized, dependable, sure-fire and safe. However, it is possible to hand-load cartridges, or to reload fired factory cases, so that they will be more accurate in a particular weapon, or more suitable for a particular purpose than are the standard factory cartridges. Mass production rifles, pistols, and their ammunition must of necessity have certain manufacturing tolerances. The largest and heaviest loaded cartridge of a certain size must fit into the smallest bore and chamber of any factory rifle of that caliber and be perfectly safe in it even if that weapon is dirty and rusty, and the combination must be safe in tropical heat or arctic cold. Such tolerances are incompatible with the finest accuracy.

However, the handloader can use a cartridge case that has already been expanded, by being fired in his individual rifle or pistol, to a perfect fit in that chamber. He can use a selected factory or handmade bullet that fits the particular bore of that weapon perfectly. And he can use a powder charge weighed to 1/10th grain. By choosing his components, which can be varied at will, the handloader can produce ammunition which will give more accurate results in a certain rifle than any other load.

As a rule the ammunition factory manufactures but one type of cartridge for one type of weapon. Thus for big game rifles they make cartridges suitable only for big game. For small game rifles, cartridges suitable only for certain species of small game. For target rifles, cartridges suitable only for target shooting. But for his big game rifle the handloader can produce cartridges exceedingly suitable for long range varmint shooting, for shooting small game where he does not wish to destroy meat or pelts, or for economical target practice.

2. **Economy.** When a factory cartridge is fired, the brass

(1)

case remains. This is the most costly of all the components that make up the factory cartridge. This brass case can be reloaded many times, and the cost of all the other components which are used to reload it is a small fraction of the cost of the factory cartridge. The following cost of reloading certain typical cartridges, the fired case being available by salvage, is based on the retail price of factory loaded cartridges and components as of 1957, and on the assumption that the handloader does not charge for his labor. Handloading is such an interesting, instructive and profitable hobby that I know of none who regard it as "labor."

In the calculations below I have added $1.00 a hundred rounds to the cost of loading to cover the approximate express charges on the components from the retailer to the handloader. Costs of all are per 100 rounds.

Case 1. .30-06 rifle cartridge loaded with 180 grain jacketed bullet at M.V. 2,700 f.s., suitable for big game hunting or mid and long range target practice.

Cost of factory cartridges....................		$21.50
Cost of components:		
Primers	$0.95	
Powder	1.50	
Bullets	6.00	
Express	1.00	9.45
Savings per 100 rounds....................		12.05

Case 2. .30-06 rifle cartridge loaded with 154 grain cast lead bullet at M.V. 1,500 f.s., suitable for inexpensive target shooting to 200 yards, and for small game hunting. A cartridge of this type cannot be bought factory loaded. It is assumed that the handloader buys his lead and tin, and moulds, sizes and lubricates the bullets himself.

```
Cost of factory cartridges.....................  $21.50
Cost of components:
    Primers  .......................  $0.95
    Powder .........................   .90
    Lead, tin, fuel, etc., approx........   .80
    Express  .......................  1.00      3.65

Savings per 100 rounds....................         17.85
```

Case 3. .257 Roberts cartridge reloaded with a super accurate, custom-made bullet to high velocity.

```
Cost of factory cartridges....................  $20.00
Cost of components:
    Primers  .......................  $0.95
    Powder  ........................  1.30
    Bullets  .......................  5.00
    Express  .......................  1.00      8.25

Savings per 100 rounds....................         11.75
```

Case 4. .38 S&W Special revolver cartridge, Match Type, loaded with a wad cutter, lead alloy bullet cast, sized and lubricated by the handloader.

```
Cost of factory cartridges....................  $ 8.60
Cost of components:
    Primers  .......................  $0.95
    Powder, approx.  ...............   .25
    Lead, tin, fuel, approx............   .70
    Express  .......................  1.00      2.90

Savings per 100 rounds....................          5.70
```

There are many small custom handloaders throughout the United States who specialize in furnishing lead alloy bullets, either with plain base or with gas check, ready cast, sized, and lubricated, at a cost running from $2.50 to $5.00 per 100 bullets. The names and addresses of a number of them are given in the Appendix. In many cases it may pay the handloader to use these bullets instead of casting his own, as he then does not have to invest in the equipment for casting, sizing, and lubricating bullets, nor does he have the time-consuming labor of making his own bullets.

The .38 S & W Special cartridge seems to be the only one where it is hardly possible for the handloader to quite excel the factory product in accuracy and dependability. Practically all of our leading revolver shooters use factory loaded cartridges in important competitions, but at other times, and particularly for practice, they use hand loads. In fact if one desires to really excel in revolver marksmanship he must practice to the extent of thousands of rounds annually, and the economy of handloading becomes imperative. As a consequence more .38 S & W Special cartridges are handloaded annually than any other caliber.

Of course an actual saving does not occur until enough cartridges have been reloaded to make the saving therefrom offset the initial cost of the loading tools. Thus if the original cost of the tools is $30.00, and the saving is $5.00 a hundred rounds, a real cash in the pocket saving does not result until 600 rounds have been reloaded. That is, you start with 100 rounds of factory cartridges, you reload each of the fired cases six times, and then, your tools having paid for themselves, your real saving starts.

3. **Suitability for various purposes.** Factory cartridges are usually suitable for one particular purpose only. Thus most factory cartridges for the heavier rifles are good for big game shooting only. But it is possible to reload these cases with other loads suitable, and in many cases eminently satisfactory, for any of the following uses:

Varmint shooting, often to extended distances.

Small game shooting where you want to preserve meat or skins.

Economical target practice.

Thus the shooter can make one rifle do for many purposes.

4. **Marksmanship.** Basic marksmanship can be, and very often is learned from shooting a small bore rifle using the economical .22 Long Rifle cartridge. But if the shooter wants to use his centerfire rifle for acquiring this basic skill, then gen-

erally speaking, he will fire upwards of a thousand rounds, and the economy of handloading becomes almost a necessity.

5. **Knowing your rifle.** It has been my experience that knowing your rifle, its zero adjustments, its elevation for all distances, trajectory, wind allowance at various distances, value of sight adjustments, accuracy, peculiarity of grouping its shots, etc., so that you can use it for competitive target shooting or successful game shooting, requires the expenditure of at least five hundred rounds in careful and recorded target practice. Here again the economy of reloading becomes very desirable. Also there is no way you can so thoroughly learn the sciences of interior and exterior ballistics as by handloading. In fact, handloading is essential in the study of those sciences.

6. **Effect on the arms industry.** At first glance one would think that reloading and handloading would have a detrimental effect on the sale of factory loaded cartridges, and therefore on the business of the large arms companies. Actually the effect is just the opposite.

The average American sportsman who shoots a center fire rifle or revolver and who does not handload buys about forty rounds of factory ammunition a year. He uses twenty rounds for sighting in his weapon and the other twenty rounds for hunting. If he is a small game hunter and uses a rifle like the .22 Hornet he probably buys not more than 150 rounds of factory cartridges a year.

But the reloader almost invariably becomes an enthusiast, and on an average he can be counted on to purchase about the following from the ammunition industry each year:

> 100 rounds factory cartridges.
> 100 rounds primed cases.
> 1000 primers.
> 500 bullets.
> 5 pounds powder.

Also as the years go on he very probably purchases a rifle of another caliber for hunting or for experiment, and makes similar purchases of cartridges and components for it.

The ammunition companies understand this, and encourage hand loading. But there is a decided nuisance factor involved in handling so many small components, and so the ammunition companies sell components only to dealers. All purchases of such components should be sent only to dealers. (See Appendix.)

SAFETY

7.   A certain amount of danger would seem to attend the handling of explosive powder and primers. It would be extremely foolish and unsafe for anyone to attempt handloading without first studying a good instruction manual or handbook, and then using it constantly as a reference. Personal instruction is not sufficient for an instructor is only human and may forget or neglect some safety precaution.

All the necessary safety precautions are given in this book, and are emphasized in *italic* type. I believe that anyone who follows the instructions carefully will reduce danger to the zero point. *However, I do not assume any responsibility.*

But I can say that I have never heard of any accident resulting from handloading where the handloader followed a good manual that was not due to sheer carelessness. I know of no successful lawsuit arising from handloading. So far as I can estimate there are over three hundred thousand shooters handloading in the United States. I have never had an accident myself. But handloading is not for the man who is habitually careless, or who cannot follow plainly written instructions, or who thinks he knows more than the experts.

THE SCHEME OF THIS BOOK

8.   This book tells in precise and clear detail how to load or reload a cartridge for use in a rifle or pistol. First, each step in the process of loading is given and described in sequence, beginning with the fired or empty cartridge case, and ending

with the complete, loaded cartridge. Then bullet making is described. Specific instructions for loading all the more important and commonly used cartridges follow, and the most useful and best loads that have been developed for each particular cartridge are given. Finally there is an Appendix that gives all the tabulated data and work tables that are necessary.

The paragraphs throughout the book are numbered for easy cross reference. A notation such as (P 38) means a cross reference to that particular paragraph.

9. **What cartridges can be reloaded.** Only centerfire rifle and pistol cartridges can be reloaded. It is not possible to reload rim fire cartridges. In this country it is difficult to reload foreign makes of cartridge cases. Most use the Berdan primer, which is not readily procurable in America. All American centerfire cartridge cases use the American (Boxer) primers which are sold everywhere.

I do not include instructions for reloading shotgun shells because that involves a very different technique and requires its own handbook. However, one wishing to reload shotgun shells should refer to the *Ideal Handbook* published by the Lyman Gun Sight Corporation (see Appendix).

RELOADING TOOLS

10. This book is written so that the instructions apply to all standard makes of reloading tools. The method of operating each make of tool differs, but is fully described in the manufacturer's instructions. It has been my experience that entirely satisfactory, in fact top notch reloading, can be done with any of these standard makes of tools. It is entirely unnecessary to purchase the most expensive or the latest models of tools. If you seemingly fail to load well with one tool (provided it has no obvious defects) don't rush out and buy some other tool. Usually a little more care in using the tool will solve the problem. Some tools are more convenient than others, and some are faster than others. I should purchase more for convenience than anything else, and this makes a choice a matter of personal preference. Some manufacturers produce a basic

tool for loading one cartridge, and then you can purchase as extras the various dies and holders for loading any other cartridge in that tool. As most handloaders end up in loading for many different cartridges, either for themselves or friends, I think it is often wise to choose this type of basic tool.

For years I did satisfactory loading with the old Ideal tong tool, but I do believe it is best to buy a good, heavy bench tool at the start because it will do better work, do it faster, and is much more convenient. I also advise purchasing this tool to use the standard ⅞″ x 14″ seating and resizing dies because they are, as a rule, better than the others, and can be had of many makers, are all interchangeable, and can be had for all rifle and pistol cartridges. Thus you can use any bench tool to load any number of different cartridges, and all that is necessary is a set of dies for that cartridge, and a shell holder for that particular case. Many cartridges have the same size of head and use the same shell holder.

I have not found that it is much of an advantage to have the bench tool fitted with any automatic primer feed. My experience has been that it takes longer to fill the automatic feed, all primers faced the same way, than it does to feed the primers with the fingers, one at a time, into the priming arm. Also, I am not convinced of the advantage of the multiple turret tools, where the head of the tool holds two or more dies. They are much more expensive than the single die tool. Only one operation should be done at a time in order to inspect the product of that operation before proceeding to the next, and it takes only a few seconds to remove a resizing die, and insert one for bullet seating.

For individual handloading, not for profit, I think it is best to purchase a tool which does one operation at a time, except the operations of decapping and neck resizing which are almost always done in one operation. This enables the handloader to inspect each cartridge as it passes through each operation. I think that such step by step inspection is quite necessary for the best results, and it eliminates the chance of ever finding a defective cartridge among the batch you have loaded. Moreover I have found the "one operation at a time" tools just as fast as those designed for faster and quantity production.

In addition to the reloading tool proper, a powder scale for weighing the powder charge, and a powder measure for expeditiously throwing the charges into the cartridge cases are necessary.

In addition to the above, certain small accessories which add almost nothing to the cost are quite desirable, such as: Two small funnels, one for .22 and .25 caliber, and one for larger, used to guide the powder into the case. Two loading blocks. A case-mouth chamfering tool. A jar of anhydrous lanolin for lubricating cases. A machinist's micrometer calipers, capacity 1 inch, reading to thousandths of an inch is also very desirable.

If you want to make your own lead alloy bullets then a bullet mould, a melting pot, dipper, a lubricating and sizing tool, and some make of furnace or burner for melting the lead alloy are necessary. For making metal cased (jacketed) bullets a set of bullet forming dies and a uniform weight case forming die, both of which are used in the Super-Pacific or Hollywood reloading tool, are necessary.

A workbench or table on which to secure and use the tools, and shelves on which to store tools, accessories, and components are desirable. The modest little bench on which I have done all my handloading for twenty years is shown in the frontispiece. Much ingenuity can be employed in arranging convenient and comfortable working conditions. On the other hand special facilities and rooms are unnecessary. I have seen several portable bench rests for shooting arranged so that they also formed a loading table, that could be transported in the luggage compartment of a car and set up anywhere.

A list of all the standard and better known makers of reloading tools, reloading accessories, and components for handloading, with their addresses, will be found in the Appendix. Consult the test and advertising columns of *The American Rifleman* (monthly magazine of The National Rifle Association) for new tools that might be offered after the publication of this book.

CHECK LIST OF TOOLS AND EQUIPMENT

The following is a rather complete list of the loading tools and equipment that a well informed handloader would probably consider adequate and workmanlike for hand loading three sizes of cartridges.

1 Reloading Tool (possibly Pacific, R.C.B.S., Lyman Tru-Line or Hollywood) for .30-06 U. S. Cartridge, including:

    1 Seating Die to seat pointed bullets without crimp.*
    1 Neck Resizing Die.*
    1 Expander for metal cased bullets.*
    1 Expander .311" for lead alloy bullets.
    6 extra Primer Ejecting Pins for expanders.
    1 Priming Cup and Arm for large size primers (will also serve for .22 Varminter, .257 Roberts, .270, etc.).*
    1 Shell Holder .30-06 (also does for all other rimless cases having same size head).*

*All of the above are included in the price of a complete tool.

Additional for .22 Varminter cartridge. Will fit in the above basic tool.

    1 Seating Die, .22 Varminter, to seat pointed bullets without crimp.
    1 Sizing Die, .22 Varminter (usually for neck sizing only).
    1 Expander, .22 Varminter, for .224" bullets.

Additional for .222 Remington cartridge.

    1 Seating die, to seat pointed bullets without crimp.
    1 Neck Resizing Die.
    1 Expander, for .224" bullets.
    1 Priming Arm and Cup for small primers.
    1 Shell Holder, .222 Remington.

1 Chamfering Reamer for each caliber.
1 Powder Measure with both .30 and .22 caliber tubes.
1 Powder Scales (Pacific or Redding).

2 Loading Blocks for each cartridge.

1 Case trimming tool (Wilson).

1 small jar Anhydrous Lanolin for lubricating outside of cases (any drug store).

1 small jar finely powdered graphite for lubricating inside of case necks (any hardware store).

2 Screwdrivers filed to proper size for scaping powder fouling from corners of large and small primer pockets, or else the standard primer pocket cleaners (Pacific).

1 boxwood or steel rule for measuring lengths.

1 machinist's micrometer.

Several screwdrivers of assorted sizes, wiping rags, etc.

In addition, should the handloader desire to cast his own lead alloy bullets he will require about the following:

1 Bullet Mould for each bullet he desires to cast.

1 Melting Pot (Ideal) or Electric Furnace.

1 Dipper (Ideal).

1 Old tin pan for dross.

1 Pair old gloves.

1 Apron.

1 Wood mallet or club.

1 Lubricator and Sizer with dies for each diameter of bullet, and a separate top die for each different bullet point.

A sturdy work bench (suggest 4x4″ legs and 2″ plank top) is very desirable, and a large machinist's vise, hammer, files, etc., always come in handy.

COMPONENTS FOR RELOADING

11. In addition to the tools above, one must also have the components for reloading, that is the primers, powder, and the bullets. The large ammunition companies, as a rule, do not sell components for reloading to individuals, but instead sell them in quantities to dealers. There are a large number of dealers who specialize in selling components to handloaders. The addresses of most of them are given in the Appendix.

These dealers not only sell the primers and bullets made by the large ammunition companies, and du Pont and Hercules smokeless powders of all kinds, but often as well sell other components, chiefly bullets, made by certain small custom makers. The handloader will probably wish to purchase from the nearest component dealer and thus save transportation.

REQUESTS FOR INFORMATION

12. Requests for information on handloading (except for catalogs of tools, or prices on tools and components) should not be made to the arms and ammunition companies, nor to the makers of reloading tools or dealers in components. These firms have no facilities or time to answer letters of inquiry, and in most cases they do not have the information, or it may be biased. Such correspondence is a continual handicap to these organizations and firms, reduces their profits and the service they can give to their customers, and eventually increases the cost of their product.

All letters requesting special information on handloading or other matters connected with rifles and pistols should be addressed to the Technical Staff, National Rifle Association, 1600 Rhode Island Avenue, N. W., Washington 6, D. C. They have the experience, facilities, funds and time to answer such inquiries, and their replies are unbiased. In writing letters of inquiry, make them brief but exact, come quickly to the point.

You must be a member of the NRA to avail yourself of this source of information. As a matter of fact, every handloader should join the NRA. Its official magazine, *The American Rifleman,* continually publishes helpful articles on handloading.

It may interest the writers of letters of inquiry to learn that five per cent of such letters cannot be answered, and that about fifteen per cent of the remainder very greatly increase the time and cost of replying *because the name and address of the writer was not clearly printed on the letter. On the envelop. is not sufficient.*

II

HANDLOADING—STEP-BY-STEP
THE OPERATIONS INVOLVED

13. The various operations involved in reloading a brass cartridge case that has been fired in a certain rifle, for use in that same weapon again, are as follows:

(a) Chamfering the mouth of the case.
(b) Decapping—pushing out the fired primer.
(c) Resizing the neck of the case. (Operations (b) and
    (c) are usually done at the same time.)
(d) Repriming the case, and inspection.
(e) Charging the case with powder, and inspection.
(f) Seating the bullet.
(g) Final inspection and labelling.

In the above sequence each of these operations will be described in detail for cartridges in general, and certain departures from the general rule will be mentioned. Specific instructions for loading all of the more popular and commonly used cartridges, together with the best powder charges and bullets for them will be found in Part IV of this book.

The making of cast alloy bullets and metal cased bullets, for those who wish to make their own bullets, is covered in Part III.

CARE AND LIFE OF FIRED CASES

14. You save the cases you fire in your rifle or pistol for future reloading. Try not to let them fall in the dirt or sand where they might gather grit, and when you get home wipe each case off outside only with a slightly oily rag. Particularly wipe the powder smudge off the outside of the neck. It is best to decap (P22) the cases as soon as possible to prevent any possible corrosion in the primer pocket, but practically, in a dry climate, no harm will result if they are left a month or two without decapping. Better place these fired cases in a cigar box, and include a slip of paper showing in what rifle they

RIMLESS, NECKED RIFLE CARTRIDGE

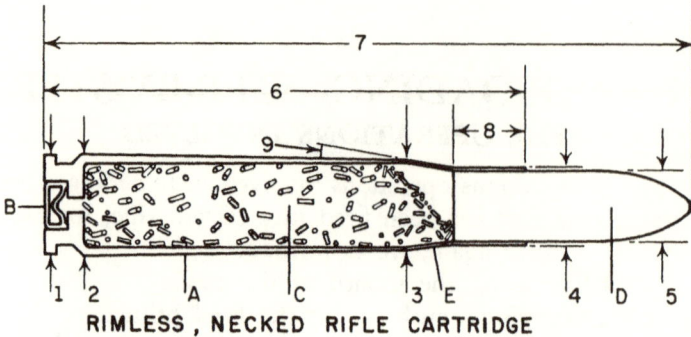

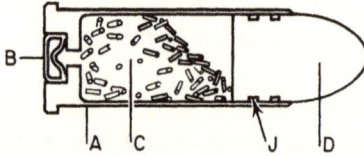

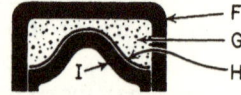

RIMMED, STRAIGHT
RIFLE OR PISTOL CARTRIDGE

AMERICAN
PRIMER
ENLARGED

Nomenclature of Metallic Cartridges

A. Case.
B. Primer.
C. Powder.
D. Bullet.
E. Shoulder of case.
F. Primer cup.
G. Priming mixture.
H. Foil.
I. Anvil.
J. Lubricating groove.

1. Diameter of rim.
2. Diameter at base.
3. Diameter at shoulder.
4. Diameter at neck.
5. Max. diameter of bullet.
6. Overall length of case.
7. Overall length of cartridge.
8. Length of neck.
9. Angle of shoulder.

were fired, and any other desirable data. The paper cartons in which cartridges are purchased are convenient, but they often absorb moisture and cause the cases to corrode. Wood or cigar boxes are better.

15. Life of cases. Many cases can be reloaded an almost unbelievable number of times. I have frequently reloaded .30-06, .270, and .257 Roberts cases at least twenty five times without noting any deterioration. Thin revolver cases that have to be crimped every time they are loaded do not usually last for more than ten reloads. .220 Swift cases also have a rather short life as will be explained later (P40).

Cases wear out chiefly because a crack develops in their neck, because the primer pocket enlarges so it will no longer hold the primer tightly, and because the mouth of the case gets ragged and thin. Whenever a case shows any of these defects throw it away.

16. **Season cracking.** When cases get very old the brass is liable to change its grain structure and become brittle. Then the case may develop a crack or split, usually a longitudinal split in the neck. This crack may occur in the loaded cartridge, in the case while loading, or when the cartridge is fired. Usually this is not at all dangerous unless the split occurs down close to the base of the case (which it hardly ever does), but of course a cartridge that cracks before firing is unserviceable, and one that cracks during firing usually means that the bullet does not hit the bullseye. Cases seldom crack in this manner until they are about ten years old, and this is about the only way that cartridges deteriorate with age. In the days of black powder we had to wash our cases after every firing because the fouling would corrode the brass badly. But the smokeless powder fouling inside a case does no harm to it, and it is neither necessary nor desirable to wash fired cases before reloading them. In fact washing cases rather predisposes to season cracking.

CHAMFERING MOUTHS OF CASES

17. Factory loaded cartridges have the mouth of the case crimped into a cannelure in the bullet to hold it firmly in the case, and when they are fired some of this inturned crimp remains. New primed cases that have never been loaded or fired have a square edge, almost a scraping edge, at their mouth. In both instances, if we try to seat a bullet in a case, the base of the bullet, instead of entering smoothly inside the neck, often tends to hang up on this sharp inner edge of the mouth,

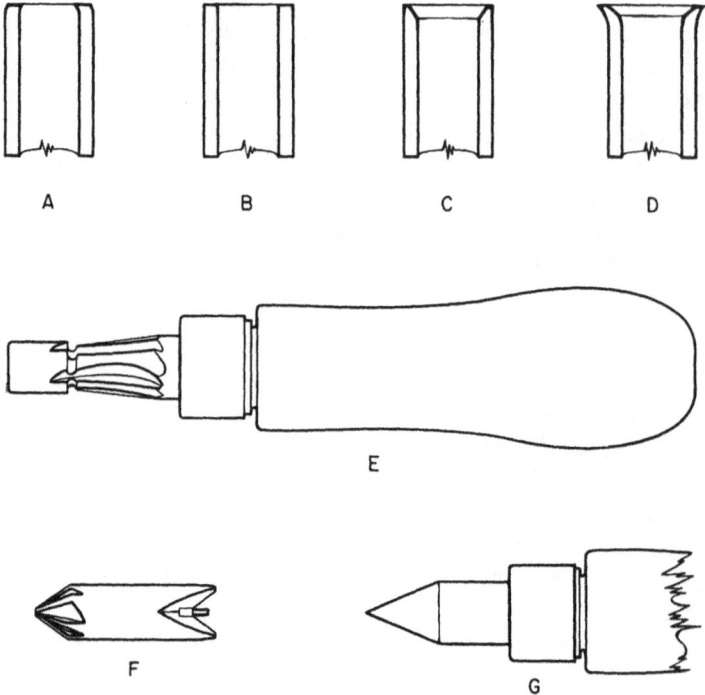

PREPARING THE MOUTH OF THE CASE

A. Fired factory case showing remains of crimp.

B. New primed case showing square mouth.

C. Chamfered mouth ready for reloading for bolt action and single shot rifles.

D. Bell-muzzled mouth ready for reloading for tubular magazine rifles and revolvers.

E. Chamfering reamer with pilot for one particular caliber of case.

F. Universal chamfering reamer for all calibers. The right end is for smoothing the outside of the mouth when necessary.

G. Plain smooth steel cone for bell muzzling.

and the pressure crumples the neck of the case, ruining it. To avoid this we should slightly bevel or chamfer the inside of the mouth before reloading it for a bolt action or single shot rifle. This is easiest done with a small chamfering reamer furnished by most makers of loading tools as an extra to their outfit. The reamer is simply run into the mouth of the case, turned around about two revolutions, and the job is done. Do

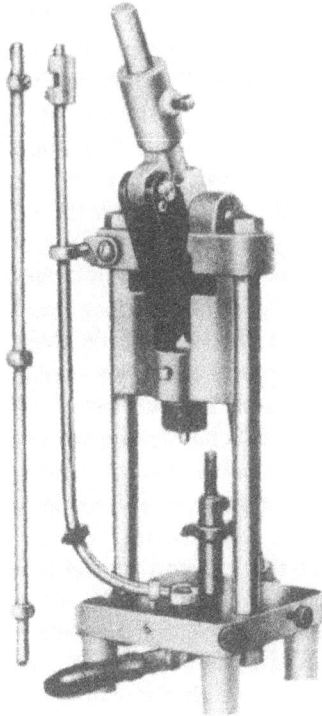

Ideal 310 Tru-Line loading press with automatic primer feed attached.

not overdo it, you want just a barely discernible bevel. Or the job can be done by a careful man with a sharp jack-knife. After chamfering each case tap the mouth of the case lightly on the loading bench to see that no small shavings of brass remain inside the case.

This chamfering of such cases for use in bolt action and single shot rifles, where the case is never going to be crimped again, has to be done only once before it is first handloaded. It is well to do it as soon as convenient after the cases have been fired, and then to note on the slip of paper in the box that contains those cases the word "Chamfered." A typical slip in one of my boxes of fired cases says, "Fired in Rifle No. 1320, chamfered, necks resized for metal cased bullets."

18. Cases for lever action rifles and revolvers. When cartridges are handloaded for rifles with tubular magazines the cases must be crimped onto the bullets each time to prevent the bullets being driven deeply into the necks of the cases by spring pressure plus recoil as they lie in the tubular magazine. Revolver cases must be crimped on the bullets to prevent them moving while the cartridges lie in the cylinder during firing, and also to offer sufficient initial resistance to cause the quick burning powder to generate proper gas pressure. If we were to chamfer or ream the mouths of these cases each time we handloaded them, pretty soon we would have a knife-sharp edge to the mouth, and then we would gradually wear the case shorter. So instead of chamfering or reaming the mouths of these cases we slightly bell-muzzle them with a smooth cone-pointed tool which can be easily made. Or when we use the neck resizing die we screw it just a little farther into the tool so the shoulder at the top end of the primer ejecting rod will slightly bell-muzzle the case as we resize its neck. The bell-muzzling should be done after the case has been neck resized (P 23) and before the powder charge is placed in it, and should be done only enough so that it can just barely be felt by the fingers. Then when the bullet is seated in the case, the crimping shoulder in the bullet seater (P 90) reverses this bell-muzzle and turns it into a crimp on the bullet.

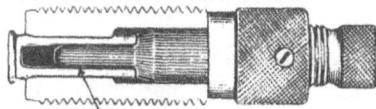

Shell Ironer.

19. Ironing revolver cases. The Pacific Gunsight Company furnishes an Inside Shell Ironer. This is an inside expanding die, which is run into a pistol case after it has been neck resized. It expands the inside of the case to exactly the right diameter to hold the bullet, smooths up the inside of the neck, and properly bell-muzzles the mouth of the case. It contributes considerably to the preparation of accurate and dependable handloaded revolver ammunition.

20. **Automatic pistol cases.** The .38 Colt Automatic Pistol, and the .45 Colt Automatic Govt. Pistol use straight rimless cases. These cases have no shoulder as do bottle-necked rifle cases to hold them to the proper depth in the chamber and to give them proper headspace. Instead they depend upon the square mouth of the case abutting against the square end of the chamber to hold them in the proper headspace position, and against the blow of the firing pin. Therefore the square mouth of these cases should be left as it is and never disturbed by chamfering or bell-muzzling. Simply neck resize the case and then expand it inside to hold the bullet friction-tight.

Lead alloy bullets for these cartridges should have their base very slightly beveled so they will enter the case without hanging up or shaving.

DECAPPING AND NECK RESIZING

21. The second and third operations on the fired case are decapping and neck resizing. Many reloading tools do these two operations with one throw of the operating lever, or one passage of the case through the die. But it will be clearer to describe the two operations more or less separately.

22. **Decapping** is usually done in the resizing die of the reloading tool. There is a primer punch inside the die and when the case is forced into the die during the resizing operation this punch enters the case and punches out the old primer. Or it is easy to make or buy a decapping punch and a base that can be used separately from the reloading tool.

Take a piece of steel drill rod about 5 inches long that will just enter the neck of the case freely. Drill a small hole in one end and drive in a blunt pointed steel pin about .06″ diameter so it projects about a half inch beyond the rod as shown. A slightly blunted phonograph needle makes a fine pin. Make a base to hold the head of the case when you drive

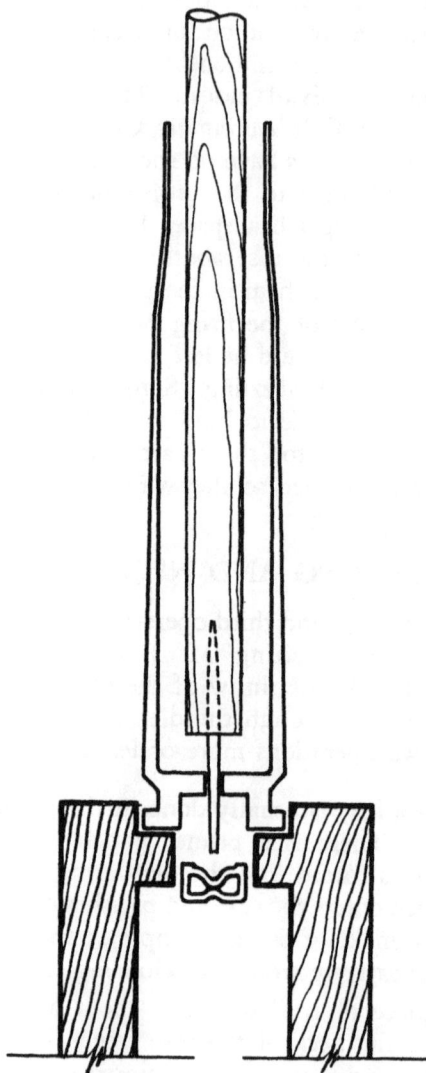

A simple decapper. Simple bullet seaters are also made on the same design, a bullet seating plunger replacing the primer pin stem.

the primer out. A cylinder of brass or hard wood, countersunk slightly to take the head of the case with a 1/5″ hole drilled clear through it in the center of the countersink is fine. Place this base on the loading bench, place the head of the case in the countersink, insert the decapping punch in the mouth of the case, feeling carefully so the pin enters the flash hole. Tap the end of the rod with a hammer, and the primer will be driven out and fall into the hole in the base. When the hole in the base is filled with primers, dump the old primers into the waste basket.

This simple method of decapping is convenient to use in the field away from tools, and may also be desirable when you have not decided whether you wish to resize the necks of those cases for metal cased or lead alloy bullets. These two types of bullets require the necks of the cases to be expanded to a slightly different diameter (P24).

23. **Neck resizing.** When a cartridge is fired in rifle or pistol its neck expands to the diameter of the neck of the chamber in the weapon, which is usually about .003″ larger than the neck of the loaded cartridge. As a consequence the neck of this fired case is so large that the new bullet, if seated in it, would not remain firmly in the neck but would either fall out or would fall down inside the neck on top of the charge of powder. So the neck must be resized smaller by forcing it into a resizing die.

The inside diameter of the neck of the resized case is very important because for good accuracy the bullets should be held with a certain uniform tension. Powder gases build up to a high pressure in a cartridge when the bullet is tight in the neck, and to a lower pressure when the bullet is held loosely, and the accuracy suffers. Brass cartridge cases are drawn in dies during manufacture, and not turned accurately in a lathe, and consequently the thickness of the neck walls is not uniform. Therefore we cannot get a uniform inside diameter by simply resizing the outside of the neck of the case. For this reason the best practice, for which almost all tools are adapted, is to

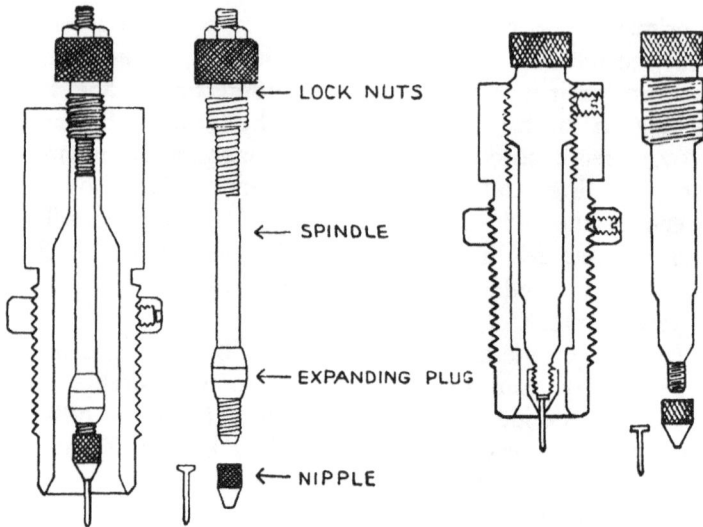

← LOCK NUTS

← SPINDLE

← EXPANDING PLUG

← NIPPLE

Resizing die.

resize the necks of the cases in a die which makes them about .002 inch smaller inside than necessary, and then expand them to the exact inside diameter by pulling or forcing an expanding plug through the inside of the neck.

A cross section of the usual rifle and pistol resizing die is shown in the accompanying cut. The die has a combined decapping pin and expander screwed into the center of its cavity. Let us say that our case is one of .30 caliber, and that it has been expanded by firing so that it measures about .311" inside neck diameter. We wish to resize and then expand this neck to about .307" inside so that it will hold a normal .30 caliber bullet measuring .308" in diameter. To do this we use a decapping rod inside the die which has an expander plug or swelling on it that measures about .308". This expander passes through the resized neck as we withdraw the case out of the die, and enlarges the neck to .308". The case springs back slightly after the expander has passed through it, so that the neck then measures about .307", just what we wanted.

Now let us see how the die shown in the accompanying

cut works. Suppose we force a fired case into this die by means of the lever and the case holder of the reloading tool. The case slips freely over the decapping rod-expander because its inside neck diameter is slightly larger than the rod. The case slides on until its mouth enters the neck at the upper end (or bottom) of the die. As the case neck is forced into the die neck it is reduced in diameter. At the same time the decapping pin has entered the flash hole of the case and has driven out the fired primer.

Now reverse the motion of the lever of the reloading tool and the case is drawn out of the die. Its neck has now been sized down so it is smaller than the expanding plug, and as it is drawn over this plug the neck is expanded to its correct inside diameter.

For pistol cartridges with straight cases, like the .38 S&W Special, .44 S&W Special, .45 ACP, and .45 Colt Revolver cartridges, three dies are advisable. The first straight resizing die resizes the fired case to correct outside dimensions. Then it is run into a resizing and neck expanding die which expands the inside of the neck correctly for the diameter of the bullet, a shoulder on the upper part of the expander plug slightly bell-muzzles the mouth of the case to permit seating the lead bullet without shaving, and the old primer is ejected. The third bullet seating die seats the bullet and crimps the case on it.

24. Adjusting resizing dies. At the start of the resizing operation it will be necessary to adjust the die correctly in the reloading tool. Screw the die part way into the tool. Try forcing a lubricated case into it. If the die does not resize the neck its entire length keep screwing the die farther into the tool until it does. You can easily tell how far down the neck the die is resizing by the marks of the lubricant on the neck. Never screw the die into the case so far that the die will compress or shorten the shoulder of the case. That would reduce the headspace dimension of the case and might introduce a dangerous condition (P 34). The die usually has a stop collar on it. When the die has been correctly adjusted screw this stop

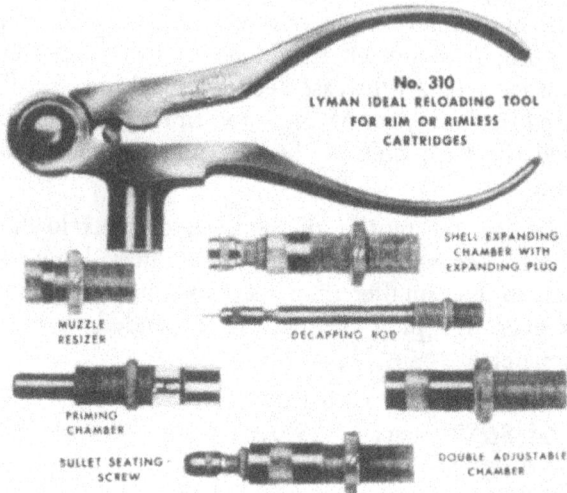

No. 310
LYMAN IDEAL RELOADING TOOL
FOR RIM OR RIMLESS
CARTRIDGES

SHELL EXPANDING
CHAMBER WITH
EXPANDING PLUG

MUZZLE
RESIZER

DECAPPING ROD

PRIMING
CHAMBER

BULLET SEATING
SCREW

DOUBLE ADJUSTABLE
CHAMBER

This is the oldest type of reloading tool, and has given excellent results for the past sixty years. Light and portable. One tool (handle) will serve for cases having similar heads such as the .250-3000, .270, and .30-06 series, but different dies must be purchased for each cartridge. The various dies and chambers also fit the Lyman Ideal Tru-Line junior press.

collar down until it touches the frame of the tool, secure it, and thereafter merely screw the die on to the tool up to the stop collar and it will be in adjustment.

25. Ordering neck resizing dies. Further on in Part IV of this book where specific information is given for reloading certain cartridges you will find the normal diameter of both metal cased and lead alloy bullets for that particular cartridge. If you are going to handload cartridges with metal cased bullets only, order your reloading tool for the particular cartridge you wish, and specify a "neck resizing die and expander to resize case necks to hold metal cased bullets friction tight." If, in addition you are going to load lead alloy bullets order "an extra decapping rod and expander to expand case necks to - - inch inside to hold lead alloy bullets friction tight." This second expander will be from .001" to .003" larger in diameter than the one for metal cased bullets.

26. **Lubricating cases.** You must never try to force a dry case into a resizing die. If you do the case will "freeze" in the die, you can not get it out, and the die will have to be sent back to the reloading tool maker to have the brass case removed. Always lubricate the outside of each case before it is forced into the die. The inside of the case neck must be lubricated also so it will slide easily over the expander plug.

On the outside of the neck you can smear on a light coat of oil or grease, not too heavy or it will cause the neck to buckle or dent. The best lubricant I have found for this purpose is anhydrous lanolin. You can buy a small jar of it from any drug store for a few cents. Four ounces will suffice for many thousand cases. Or some loading tool makers supply their own grease that I don't know is any better.

My own method of applying lubricant to cases is the easiest and most convenient I have seen any handloader employ. I have the jar of lanolin and the pile of cases on the bench to the left of the loading tool. I annoint the thumb and forefinger of my left hand with the lanolin. Then I take a case in my right hand and rotate the outside of the neck through my lanolin-covered thumb and forefinger, thus smearing a light coat on it. If the case is to be neck resized only the grease need be smeared on only down as far as the shoulder. But if you are using a full length resizing die the grease must be smeared over the case almost down to its head or it will soon stick in the die. Then I run the case through the resizing die with my right, ungreased hand.

Now once in about every five cases, as you smear the neck

with lanolin, draw your forefinger squarely across the mouth of the case, resulting in smearing a very small edging of grease on the inside edge of the mouth of the case. This will keep the neck expanding plug lubricated enough so that the case will slide easily over it as you withdraw it from the die. If you get just a slight suspicion of grease on this inner edge of the mouth it will be sufficient for the purpose. If you get too much on you will have the inside of your case necks greased, and you will have to wipe them out afterward with a small rag on a stick, for you don't want any grease here when you come to pour the powder in and seat the bullets.

Instead of the above method, Wilkins & Schutz have a little gadget called the "Sure Mark Case Graphiter," a small can filled with a graphite lubricant of their own. In the canter of the can is a post with a washer the diameter of the inside of the neck on it. The case is run down over the washer so as to just get a little lubricant on the mouth. Then when run in the die, the lubricant spreads over the neck, and this insures a very slight amount getting inside the neck to lubricate the expander. This has become very popular, and is particularly good for .22 caliber cases.

In neck resizing, it is not necessary to resize the full length of the neck of the case. In fact, it is better to resize the neck only down as far as the seated bullet extends down, as often better accuracy is obtained in this manner. You adjust for this according to how much you screw the resizing die into the reloading tool.

When all the cases have been resized in the above manner, take a rag and wipe all the grease off the cases. The cases are now ready for the next operation of repriming, unless enough fouling has accumulated in the primer pockets to make it necessary to clean them.

27. **Cleaning primer pockets.** A hard residue of primer fouling tends to accumulate in the bottom corner of the primer pocket. Enough may gather to prevent the new primer being

seated to the correct depth; that is, clear to the bottom of the primer pocket. Then the primer would extend out beyond the surface of the head of the case and it might be struck and ignited in handling, or the rifle bolt might crush the primer, either causing it to fire, or possibly powdering the priming pellet so it would not fire properly. Or the fouling might cushion the primer against the blow of the firing pin, causing a misfire or a hangfire.

Watch this accumulation of fouling in the bottom corners of the primer pocket and if it causes any difficulty whatever in seating the new primer clean it out. I personally have had but little trouble from this source and have not had to clean primer pockets oftener than about once in five loadings, but it is a condition that must be watched.

Primer pockets can be easiest cleaned with the little Wesnitzer Primer Pocket Cleaner sold by the Pacific Gun Sight Company. It looks like a small round broom with wire bristles. It can be placed in a drill press or motor or rotated by hand inside the primer pocket and promptly scrapes out all the residue. Or use a screwdriver, the blade of which has been filed to exactly fit the bottom of the pocket, and with a scraping edge. Don't scrape so hard as to remove any of the brass.

28. Flash holes. When reloading fired cases for the first time examine the size of the flash holes in the bottom of the primer pockets. If the hole appears to be appreciably larger or smaller than normal, destroy that case. These flash holes are made the exact size to properly ignite the powder. If larger or smaller than standard the result will be poor ignition and poor accuracy, or more serious, blown primers and gas blowbacks. Therefore never attempt to alter the size of flash holes. It is interesting to note that one of the causes of misfire in factory ammunition is a case with no flash hole at all. I don't believe I find more than one flash hole defect in ten thousand cases, but it is one of the things to watch in trying to load superaccurate and dependable ammunition.

29. Crimped in primers.   .30-06 military cartridges

(Ball cartridges, Caliber .30 M1 and M2 and armor piercing cartridges) loaded in Government Arsenals, or loaded by commercial ammunition companies under Government contracts, have the primers crimped in the primer pockets so there will be no danger of their popping out and clogging the mechanism of machine guns and automatic weapons. It often happens that handloaders fire these cartridges in practice, or they may pick up a supply of them on Government target ranges, and wish to reload them.

The primers in these cases are very hard to punch out. Trying to do so with the standard primer extractor pins usually bends the pin. A much stronger pin is necessary. Also when the primer has been removed the primer pocket has much of the crimp remaining in it, and a new primer cannot be inserted until this crimp has been removed. There are special tools for removing these crimped in primers and primer pocket crimps, and it pays to buy them. Some of the tools for removing the crimp in the pocket ream it out, and some press it out. I rather think that the latter is the better practice.

FULL LENGTH RESIZING

30. So far we have considered only *neck* resizing of cases to be used again in *the same bolt action or single shot rifle in which they were originally fired*. It is best to resize the necks only of such cases because their bodies and shoulders have been accurately expanded to fit the chamber of the rifle in which they are to be used again. But there are two types of fired cases which need full length resizing to restore their original outside dimensions and shape.

First, cases that have been fired in rifles other than the one in which the reloaded cartridge is to be used. The chambers of various rifles of the same caliber differ slightly in their dimensions, and a case fired in one rifle may not exactly fit another.

Cases collected from various places should be segregated according to make (stamping on the head) because cases of the same caliber but of different makes do not always have the same wall thickness or inside capacity. The pressure and velocity will differ slightly in each make, and they may not shoot to the same center of impact with an identical load.

Second, cases that have been fired in lever or pump action or semi-automatic rifles. There is a slight spring back to the breech block when these rifles are fired which permits the case to expand in length. This expanded case, if reloaded without full length resizing, probably could not be again loaded into the rifle which fired it without using prohibitive force to close the breech. As a consequence these cases have to be full length resized even for use in the rifle in which they were originally fired.

31. Different types of full length resizing dies. Considerable force has to be applied to push a case into a full length resizing die, and to pull it out of the die. There are certain light models of reloading tools with which this force cannot be applied. If you have this type of tool you will have to buy a separate full length resizing die which is operated by hand and not in the tool. Other stronger models of tools have full length resizing dies which fit in the tool and are operated in exactly the same way as neck resizing dies. Because of this difference I explain full length resizing with each type of die.

32. Resizing with separate die. This consists of a cylinder of hard alloy steel bored and chambered inside to the correct dimensions and shape. A case forced into it will be resized practically to the same outside dimensions as the case of a factory loaded cartridge. A punch to drive the case out of the die is also furnished. To use this die the case must first be coated outside *its full length* with a light coat of anhydrous lanolin (P 25) and it is then inserted in the die. Stand it on a firm bench with the case head up. Place a block of hard wood on the head of the case, and strike the block with a hammer or mallet, driving the case fully into the die, head of the case flush with the head of the die. Then reverse the die and hold it in the hand, insert the punch in the open end of the case, and while holding the die in the hand, strike the end of the punch with the hammer and thus drive the case out of the die. It is then necessary to neck resize and expand this fully resized case so that it will hold the bullet friction tight, and with proper uniform tension (P 23). It is best to neck resize at once while the case is still lubricated.

Personally I do not like this method of hammering the case in and out of the die, and instead I usually place the re-sizing die with the case stuck in it between the jaws of a large machinist's vise, jaws with copper covers, and squeeze the case into the die, then insert the punch and similarly squeeze the case out of the die.

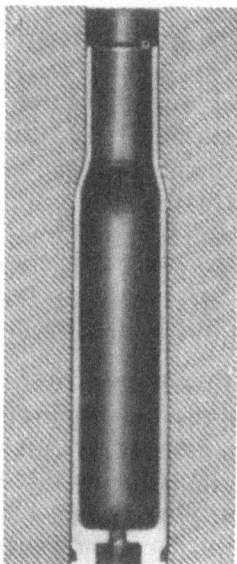

A separate Ideal full length resizing die.

33. Full length resizing in heavy tools is done in ex-actly the same manner as neck resizing (P 26), the die being similar in adjustment and construction. Of course here also the case must be full length coated with anhydrous lanolin as described in the preceding paragraph.

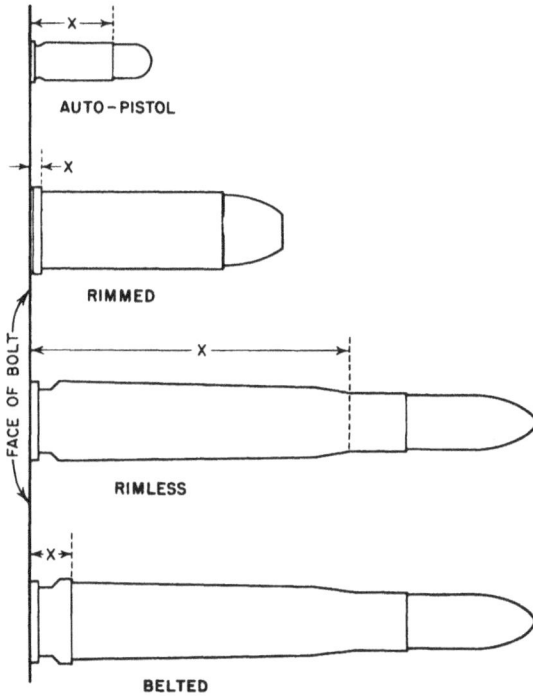

In the sketch shown "X" is the headspace dimension. *With rimmed and belted cases* it is the distance in the rifle from the face of the bolt to the shoulder in the chamber against which the rim or front of the belt on the head of the case rests. In a cartridge it is the thickness of the rim or the thickness of the belt. This dimension depends upon the tolerance allowed in the manufacture of the cartridge cases.

Generally speaking the minimum headspace is the maximum allowable head or bolt thickness in the case, and the maximum allowable is about .004" greater than this. We seldom or never run into any headspace difficulty with rimmed or belted cases. All you have to do is to screw the full length resizing die into the reloading tool, resize a case in it, compare that case with a standard factory loaded cartridge, and adjust the tool until the shoulder of the resized case appears in exactly the same position as the shoulder on the factory case. When it does try the resized case in your rifle. If it requires quite a tug on the lever or bolt handle to close the bolt on the head of the case the die should be screwed just a little tighter into the tool until it requires just a barely perceptible tug or pressure on the lever or bolt handle to seat the case in the chamber and close the bolt. Then screw up to the stop collar on the die and go ahead and resize your lot of cases.

One very important precaution must be taken in full length resizing. The resizing die must be screwed into the tool exactly the right distance so that it will resize the case to exactly the right headspace dimension (P 34). If the die is screwed too far into the tool it will press the shoulder of the case back, giving a shortened case that would cause excessive headspace. And if the die is not screwed in far enough the case will be too long, head to shoulder, and probably will not fit into the rifle.

Some makers manufacture their heavy reloading tools, and the dies that they furnish for them, so that when the case holder is at its topmost position, the full length resizing die should be screwed into the tool to meet the case holder, then the cam action of the press over dead center takes out the spring of the tool, and the case is resized just enough, including resizing, to correct headspace.

So, full length resizing in the reloading tool brings up the matter of headspace for consideration.

But before we leave this paragraph, remember that after you have full length resized a case you still have to neck resize it to get the correct neck dimension to hold the bullet friction tight.

HEADSPACE

34. Headspace measurement applies to both rifle and cartridge, and it must be maintained correct in both or there will be trouble. Headspace in a rifle is the distance between the face of the bolt or breech block and the stop in the chamber that prevents the cartridge from going too far into the chamber. Headspace in a cartridge is exactly the same—the distance from the head of the case to that part of the case that strikes the stop in the chamber. In both cases the measurement is one of length, not diameter.

If the headspace in the rifle is too short, or the headspace in the cartridge is too long, you cannot get the cartridge into the rifle and close the breech without using prohibitive force, and that's all there is to that.

But if the headspace in the rifle is too long, or the headspace in the cartridge too short, then a number of very undesirable things may occur. First, the cartridge may seat so deeply in the chamber that the firing pin will not strike the primer, or will not indent it sufficiently, and a misfire or a hang-fire may occur. Second, if the cartridge does fire, the cartridge case expands and stretches lengthwise abnormally. It sometimes stretches so much that the brass case ruptures, allowing the hot powder gas to come back outside the case, against and through the bolt. If this happens a primer may blow, a flash of gas may come back through the bolt and into your eyes, the case may separate (split in two just in front of the head) and the front portion may stick tightly in the front part of the chamber and be difficult to remove. Or the escaping gas may enter and distort or destroy the magazine or carrier and splinter the stock, or the rare and worst thing that may happen is that the whole breech mechanism may shatter and destroy the rifle.

Therefore in handloading you must take pains to see that the cartridge headspace is always correct. There is scarcely any chance of making it incorrect except when we use a full length resizing die in a reloading tool, which is why we have to bring the matter of headspace up at this stage of handloading.

35. With rimmed and belted cases headspace is the distance in the rifle from the face of the bolt to the shoulder in the chamber against which the rim or front of the belt on the case rests. In a cartridge it is the thickness of the rim or the thickness of the belt. This dimension depends on the tolerance allowed in the manufacture of the cartridge case. Generally speaking the minimum headspace in a rifle is the maximum allowable rim or belt thickness in the cartridge, and the maximum allowable headspace in the rifle is about .004″ greater than this. We seldom or never run into any cartridge headspace difficulties with rimmed or belted cases. If there is

trouble it is usually due to the rifle which should be returned to its maker for correction. All you have to do is to screw the full length resizing die into the reloading tool, resize a case with it, and compare that case with a standard factory loaded cartridge, adjusting the tool until the shoulder of the resized case appears in exactly the same position as the shoulder of the factory cartridge. When the two appear the same, try the resized case in your rifle. If it requires quite a tug on the lever or bolt handle to close the breech then the die should be screwed just a little tighter into the tool, until it requires just a perceptible tug or pressure to seat the case and close the breech, but not enough so it would bother you in rapid firing. Then screw up the stop collar on the die and go ahead and full length resize your lot of cases.

As a matter of fact in resizing a rimmed or belted case, even if the die sets the shoulder (in rear of the neck) back quite a little it would not necessarily make the cartridge unsafe. The case would still be held to correct headspace by its rim or belt, and the gas pressure, if not abnormally heavy, would just swell the neck and forward part of the body out to fit the chamber. This is exactly what is done in fire-forming many rimmed or belted wildcat cartridges. See under ".219 Donaldson Wasp". There is a limit, however, to the amount of this pressure expansion that can be done. If the brass is expanded too much, or if the brass is poor and brittle, the case may crack or split. Even then the consequences are not likely to be serious with a rimmed or belted case.

36. With rifles using rimless cases headspace in the rifle is the distance, determined only by a standard headspace gage, from the head of the bolt to a point on the shoulder of the chamber. With the cartridge it is a similar distance from the head of the case to the shoulder. Standard headspace gages are made for a few of our rifles and cartridges by certain manufacturers (see the Appendix for their names). If gages are available, place the minimum gage in the reloading tool and then screw in the full length resizing die until it makes

firm contact with the gage when the handle of the tool is closed, and then screw down the collar and clamp the die. If no headspace gage is available then proceed to adjust the die with respect to the shoulder of the case as described in the preceding paragraph for rimmed or belted cases, but adjust the die so it takes a little more of a tug or press on the lever or bolt of the rifle to close the breech on a resized case (P 33).

37. Allowable headspace with rimless cases. It cannot be stated how much headspace over the minimum is allowable because this depends on the breech pressure and the quality of the brass. The bolts on the .30-06 Springfield Army rifles are individually fitted so that the bolt will just close on the minimum headspace gage, which is known as the "1.940" gage. Then the rifle is proof fired by firing two proof charges in it, and after that the rifle must not accept the "1.943" gage; that is, the headspace must not be over .003" longer than minimum. Rifles that have been cleaned and repaired at arsenals and then issued must not accept the 1.946 gage (.006" above min.). At the annual inspection of rifles, when a rifle is found that will accept the 1.950 gage it is withdrawn from service and sent to an arsenal for repair or destruction.

But we are not prepared to state that .010" headspace above the minimum is safe with any rifle or cartrdige. It depends upon many things. With a combination of poor brass in the case, a fold, or dirt laminated into a case, a relatively high breech pressure, an oily chamber, and a day hotter than normal, the stage might all be set for a serious accident with a headspace .010" above minimum. In this connection the reader is referred to the chapter on headspace in that most excellent work, *Hatcher's Notebook,* by Major General Julian S. Hatcher.

38. With auto pistol cases headspace in the pistol is the distance from the face of the bolt to the shoulder at the front end of the chamber, and with the cartridge it is the distance from the head of the case to the square mouth at the front end of the case. The square mouth of the case abuts against the shoulder at the front of the chamber and holds the case back against the bolt face, supporting the head of the case and the primer against the blow of the firing pin. Auto pistol cases are simply resized for outside diameter, and the interior of the case is expanded for bullet fit, usually by simple neck resizing. They are not chamfered or resized for length, although after repeated loadings and firings, they may lengthen slightly and have to be trimmed for length (P 39). Simply compare the neck resized case with a factory cartridge to see that its length from head to mouth is practically identical.

TRIMMING FOR LENGTH

39. As cases are continually resized, reloaded and fired they tend to lengthen a little, and get longer than normal from head to mouth. In the normal centerfire rifle, and in the cylinder of most revolvers, there is a shoulder at the extreme front end of the chamber where the chamber itself ends and the lead and bore proper start. The total length of the chamber from the face of the bolt to this shoulder is usually about .05" to .10" longer than the overall length of the normal case, so that the case can expand or lengthen slightly when fired without coming into contact with this shoulder in the chamber. But after repeated use its overall length may increase until finally it may abut hard against this shoulder, or the shoulder may sort of crimp the case onto the bullet, and the case and bullet may thus cause a serious constriction at the mouth of the chamber. This might result in a considerable increase in breech pressure, perhaps a dangerous increase, and accuracy would also probably suffer.

The avoidance of this condition is simple. When you have completed resizing a batch of cases compare a few of them for overall length—head to mouth—with a new standard factory cartridge. If they appear to have lengthened noticeably they must be trimmed for length; that is ground, reamed or filed off to standard length before loading again. A number of tools for this operation are available, some work in the regular reloading tool, some work separately.

My own experience has been that when using the better grade of bolt action rifles which have quite accurately cut chambers, this lengthening of cases seldom occurs to any appreciable extent and when it has with me it is usually because the cases have been fired twenty or thirty times, and I simply throw them away. But the rifle chamber, particularly with lever action rifles, may cause cases to lengthen much faster, and this condition must always be watched for.

40. **The .220 Swift.** Here is a case where unusual precaution has to be taken. The breech pressure and the angle of the shoulder are such that the brass of the case seems to flow or be extruded forward into the neck. The case lengthens and the wall thickness of the neck increases, so that often after the case has been reloaded about three times the increased length and thickness take up all the available space in the neck and front end of the chamber, and a serious and dangerous constriction is liable to occur. So with .220 Swift cases that have been fired with full charges I make it a rule, after they have been reloaded three times, to ream the neck of the case to standard wall thickness, and to trim to standard length before reloading again. This is done with a neck reamer and trimmer. It should be done again after about three more firings, but I think it is best to limit these cases to six firings, with reaming and trimming after three. The .220 Swift is known as a "semi-rimless" case, and it is headspaced by its shoulder like a rimmed case.

40.5. **Forming wildcat cartridges:** The method of forming cartridges for various wildcat rifles differs with each wildcat rifle, and generally speaking, you should take the advice of the gunsmith who makes the rifle. It is perhaps easiest of all with the .219 Improved Zipper cartridge. Simply fire standard .219 Zipper factory loaded cartridges of Winchester or Western make in your Improved Zipper rifle, then they are all ready for reloading when you have run them through your Improved

Zipper resizing die to resize and expand the necks to hold your bullets friction tight.

Forming cases for the .22-250 Varminter rifle is also easy and simple. Simply run new .250-3000 Savage cases into your Varminter resizing die, thus sizing down and then expanding the case neck to hold your bullets properly.

Forming .35 Whelen cases is also easy. Simply take new .30-06 cases and run them into the R.C.B.S. .35 Whelen expanding die that expands their necks to about .35 caliber. Then run them into the .35 Whelen expanding and resizing die which sizes the inside of the neck to hold the bullet. There is no change in the shoulder of the case at all.

Some of the heavier wildcat cartridges of large power capacity use cases with the same belted head as the .300 H&H Magnum and .375 Magnum cartridges. The Norma Company can furnish empty cases without primers (they use American .210″ primers) that are cylindrical in form, and not necked down at all. Neck these cartridges down in appropriate dies. If you are necking these cases down as small as .30 caliber or smaller you will probably have to use two expanders in your die, one to neck them halfway down, the other to complete the necking to the desired caliber. A little anhydrous lanolin should be used on these expanders to keep them from sticking inside the cases. If your wildcat case is much shorter than these Norma cases it may be necessary to trim them to almost, but not quite, the desired length, before necking them down, then afterward, when completed, trim them to the exact length. If you neck these Norma cases down to small caliber you will naturally crowd a lot of brass into the walls of the neck, and the wall thickness of the case may be too tight for your chamber when you seat a bullet in it. Consult L. E. Wilson, Cashmere, Washington, about this. He makes a reamer to be used in his case trimming tool which will ream out the inside of the necks of cases that are too thick in wall thickness, to the desired thickness. After these cases have been thus necked down they should be run into the expanding die for the particular wildcat cartridge to make the neck the desired size, then trimmed to exact length, and the mouth of the case should be chamfered. Then fire them in your rifle to expand them to exact chamber shape and form the shoulder properly, using a powder charge several grains lighter than the normal charge, and with a normal bullet. They are then ready to be loaded with the charges which the maker of your wildcat rifle advises.

Fire-forming a case for use in a wildcat rifle cannot be done properly with a light powder charge. You should use a powder charge, say, only about two to five grains less than the normal charge for the cartridge. If this case to be fire-formed is rimless, then you must load the bullet far enough out of the case to surely contact the lands when you load it into your rifle, so as to surely hold the head of the case into firm contact with the bolt face. Otherwise, when it is formed the case head may have been forced a little forward, and that case will be formed with deficient headspace.

Best results are almost always obtained with cases that have been completely formed as above, and then have been fired at least once in the rifle to expand them to correct chamber fit, after which they should be trimmed for length if necessary, resized and expanded in the neck resizing die, and the mouth of the case chamfered. They are then ready for loading for maximum accuracy.

The .219 Donaldson Wasp cartridge is perhaps the most tedious to form. It is formed from the .219 Zipper empty case, preferably of Winchester or Western make. First of all, the case is lubricated and then run into a Wasp resizing die which forms the shoulder backward to approximately right location, and these dies are usually made so that when the case is driven into them up to the head, a portion of the neck of the case projects out of the top of the die. This projecting top is then cut off with a fine hacksaw, and at this point some reloaders run a reamer into the neck of the case while it is still in the die to ream the neck to the desired wall thickness. Then the case is removed from the die, loaded for fire-forming, and then fire-formed in the rifle to expand its body below the shoulder to the desired increased diameter, and to form the shoulder exactly. From then on it is treated just exactly like a normal fired case. As all this takes considerable labor with special tools, many shooters prefer to buy their .219 Donaldson Wasp cases already formed from the maker of the rifle, thus avoiding the expense and labor, and saving that much wear on the barrel of the rifle. Such cases need only to be fired once in a rifle to expand them to the exact chamber; then they can be loaded for maximum accuracy.

PRIMING

41. The fired case has now been wiped clean, chamfered, resized, neck expanded, decapped, inspected, and is now ready to be actually reloaded with primer, powder and bullet. The first process in the actual reloading is priming—inserting a new primer in the primer pocket of the case.

42. **Choosing the proper primer.** As will be seen from the accompanying table, there are three sizes of primers, measuring in diameter .175″, .204″ and .210″. As the .204″ size it suitable only for the .45 Colt Auto Pistol cartridge made by Frankford Arsenal, you would be almost correct in saying that there are only two sizes of primers. The .175″ primers are called "small primers," and the .210″ "large primers."

In each size two different strengths of primers are made. Pistol primers give a smaller flash, and have thinner metal cups easily indented by the weaker mainsprings of pistols and revolvers. Except in certain special cases they are suitable only for pistol and revolver cartridges. They might be punctured by the heavier blows of rifle firing pins, and they might not ignite rifle powders properly. *Rifle* primers emit a larger flash, and have thicker metal cups, and they in turn are suitable only for rifles, might not be properly indented and fired in a pistol, and their strong and hot flash might over-ignite pistol powders.

TABLE OF PRIMERS

MAKE	LARGE RIFLE No.	Diam.	SMALL RIFLE No.	Diam.	LARGE PISTOL No.	Diam.	SMALL PISTOL No.	Diam.
Federal......	210	.210	200	.175	150	.210	100	.175
Frankford...	.30	.210			.45*	.204		
Peters.......	12	.210	65	.175	20 X	.210	15	.175
Remington...	9½	.210	6½	.175	2½	.210	1½	.175
Cascade.....	200	.210	400	.175	300	.210	500	.175
Western.....	8½	.210	6½	.175	7	.210	1½	.175
Winchester...	120	.210	116	.175	111	.210	108	.175

* For use in .45 A.C.P. cases of Frankford Arsenal make only.

43. Primers can be purchased from dealers in reloading components (see the Appendix). They come packed in boxes of 100, and in cartons of ten boxes (1,000 primers). Not less than 100 can be sold to a purchaser, and it is cheaper to buy them by the thousand. They cannot be mailed, but must be shipped by express. Store them in a cool, dry place, never in an attic that might become over-heated in summer. You can always tell the size primer a case takes, whether .210″ or .175″ by measuring the diameter of the primer pocket, or indeed by just looking at it. It is desirable, although not absolutely essential, that you use the same make of case and primer. That is if you are using Remington cases use Remington primers, and thus you may avoid a slight misfit of primer in primer pocket, although such misfits seldom occur.

44. **To prime the cases.** Arrange the reloading tool for repriming according to the instructions that accompany it. Insert the empty case in the tool, and insert the new primer in the seat provided for it, or in the priming stem or arm, or balance it on top of the primer pocket of the case, according to the way the tool works. Close the tool and press the primer into the primer pocket. It should go in easily without using any force at all. Just a little practice will give you the skill to insert it smoothly and easily. Be sure you continue the gentle pressure on the lever of the tool until you feel the primer seat right down to the bottom of the pocket. Then reverse the lever and take the primed case out of the tool.

Occasionally, as you start to press a primer into its pocket, you will feel the primer hang-up on the edge of the pocket. Don't try to force it in. Reverse the lever, turn the case around in the tool about half a turn and then almost always

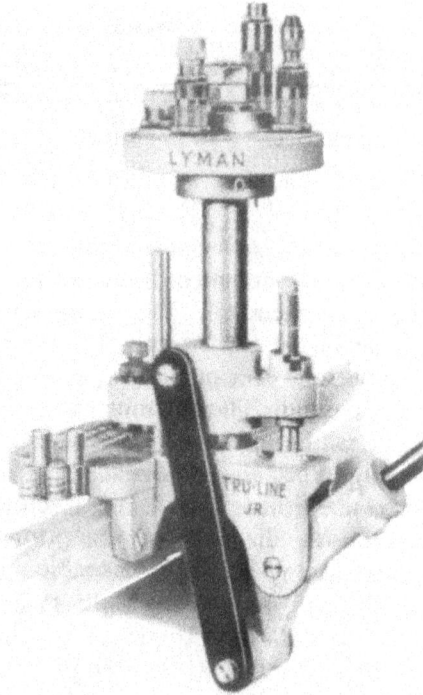

The Lyman-Ideal Tru-Line Junior press uses the same dies as the Lyman Ideal No. 310 reloading tool. Different shell holders are supplied for cases with different heads so that the press is adaptable to any cartridge.

the primer will seat easily and smoothly. If you have extreme difficulty in seating a case and primer discard them.

I have found it very convenient to have a small pan with an edge to it, like the top of a pressed-top tobacco pan. Turn down a portion of the edge about an inch wide so it forms a lip of the same height as the surface of the pan. Secure this pan on a block of wood so it will lie firmly on the loading bench. Pour out your primers onto this pan. Shuffle the pan, and ninety per cent of the primers will turn cup-side up. Turn the remainder cup side up with the fingers. Then, when wishing to insert a primer in the priming arm of the tool, place the forefinger of your left hand on top of a primer, drag it along the top of the pan to the lip, where it slides into and is grasped by forefinger and thumb, when it is easily inserted in the cup of the priming arm with the same left hand. Almost right away one gets to feel with his fingers that the primer is inserted correct side up in the priming arm. This gadget makes inserting of the primers in the primer cups very easy and saves a lot of time.

Sometimes you may wish to remove live primers from primed cases to insert another type of primer. This is always attended by a certain small risk, but with commercial cases (where the primer is not crimped in) it can be done by exercising care. Press the primer out slowly so as to avoid any suspicion of a blow that might ignite the priming mixture. Keep the face away from the tool in the unlikely event that the primer might ignite and cause an alarming flash-up. Destroy the ejected live primers as they will not be sure-fire.

But under no circumstances should any attempt be made to force live primers out of Government cases in which they are crimped as there is great danger that the effort will cause the primer to flash. Snap these primers in an old rifle, and then drive them out.

45. **Inspection.** As you remove the case from the tool draw your finger over the head. After a few trials you will be able to tell by feel whether the primer is seated fully down in its pocket, with the cup of the primer just barely below the surface of the head of the case, or whether it projects too far, or has been seated crookedly.

46. **Safety Precautions.** *When you start to handle primers stop smoking. Never under any circumstances attempt to prime a case that contains powder. Never strike the primer a blow with the reloading tool punch to try to force it into its pocket. Use gentle firm pressure only. If primers drop on the floor pick them at once—they might get stepped on, explode, and cause an injury or fire. WIPE ALL OIL AND GREASE*

*FROM THE HANDS, cases, and tools when handling primers,
for grease or oil on primers kills them.*

47. Automatic primer feeds.   Some reloading tools
have automatic primer feeds, either a part of the tool or procurable as an extra.   A long tube is filled with primers, all
faced in the same direction, and this tube carries each primer
in turn into position to be pressed into the primer pocket
simply by the movement of the tool lever.   Thus each primer
does not have to be handled individually with the fingers.
Sometimes a funnel shaped pan is provided to funnel the
primers into the tube, but it is still necessary to turn the primers
right side up on the pan so they will all go into the tube faced
in the right direction.   It is questionable whether an automatic primer feed actually expedites the operation of priming
unless one is loading in very large quantities.   Often the difficulty and time taken in filling the tube with say fifty primers
all faced correctly, is as much as that taken in handling each
primer separately with the fingers.   By the finger method with
the Pacific tool I have no trouble in repriming about twelve
cases a minute.

48. After repriming set each case, mouth down, primer
end up, in the loading block.   This is simply a board drilled
with a number of holes in which cases can be inserted.   Its
principal purpose is to prevent cases upsetting on the loading
bench when filled with powder, and before the bullets are
inserted, and as the block is usually made to hold either twenty
or fifty cases it also serves as a counter.   Loading blocks can
be obtained from all dealers in loading tools.

After all the cases are primed and placed in loading blocks,
run your eye along the rows of cases to see that each and
every one has the primer completely seated, head of the primer
just barely below the head of the case, and that none is seated
crooked.   The cases are now ready for charging with powder

SMOKELESS RIFLE AND PISTOL POWDERS

49. Safety Precautions.   *Never smoke nor have any*

*matches around when handling powders. Never handle powder
in a room where there is a naked light—candle, lamp, or stove.
Read the following paragraphs relative to powder carefully
before ordering, buying, or handling powder.*

50. Assuming that black powder will not be used, we can
divide smokeless small arms powders into three general types;
(1) Shotgun Powders. (2) Rifle Powders. (3) Pistol and
Revolver Powders. Shotgun powders should never be used for
loading rifle or pistol cartridges as they are often exceedingly
dangerous when so used.

There are many different kinds of both rifle and pistol
powders, each being best for a particular type of cartridge or
use, but unsuited and perhaps dangerous for another use or
in some other cartridge. Be sure you use the right powder.
You cannot well go wrong if you follow the instructions later
to be given as to loading each of the different cartridges.

American powders are made for sale to handloaders by
E. I. du Pont de Nemours and Company, and the Hercules
Powder Company. These firms sell their powders to dealers
in hand-loading components. Handloaders order their powder
usually from the nearest dealer so as to lighten the transportation charges. See the list of dealers in Appendix III. Smokeless powder may be shipped by express, not to exceed ten
pounds in any one shipment, when the cans are boxed in a
wooden container. It usually comes in one pound or half-
pound tin canisters with screw-on top. Smokeless powder
may be safely stored in any dry place that does not become
excessively hot. Not, for example, in an attic that might
become very hot in summer, nor close to a stove, furnace, or
heat register. When the top of a canister of powder is un-
screwed to fill a powder measure, or to return unused powder
to the canister, always screw the top of the canister back on
again immediately. Examine the label on the canister every
time to be absolutely sure you are using the right powder, or
returning the powder to the right canister.

51. Burning of powder. Smokeless powder ignited in the open does not explode, but rather burns or blazes up with a hot flame which may endure for several seconds. For example, you can empty the small amount of powder contained in a rifle or pistol cartridge into a pile on a piece of paper and touch a match to it. The pile will flare up with a bright flame and a small "hiss" for perhaps two seconds, and while it will not ignite the paper on which it rests, it will scorch it. But do not try this with black powder which would explode. Black powder is far more dangerous to handle and store than smokeless powder.

When the powder within a cartridge is ignited by the hot flash of the primer it starts to burn, and as it burns it develops a very rapidly expanding gas which builds up pressure within the case, chamber and bore of the weapon. This gas, seeking a means of escape, pushes the bullet, the only movable item, out of its case and up and out of the barrel.

The larger the amount (charge) of powder placed in the cartridge the more gas will it generate, and of course the more gas, the greater the pressure. Also the more tightly the gas is stoppered by the bullet the greater the pressure. A heavier bullet, or one that fits tighter in the bore will cause a higher pressure. If the case and chamber were stoppered completely so that no gas could escape, the powder would explode rather than burn, or perhaps detonate, and would blow up the weapon unless it was remarkably strong.

Smokeless powders are formed in small grains which may look like perforated cylinders, washers with or without a central hole, flakes, small balls, or small irregular lumps. Generally speaking the finer or smaller the grains the faster will the powder burn, and the more gas will it generate for a given weight of charge. Pistol powders are designed to burn more rapidly than rifle powders because they have to generate the necessary gas and pressure to drive the bullet at the required velocity up a very short barrel in which they do not have much time to burn.

Besides being of different granulation, various smokeless

powders are made of different ingredients and proportions of those ingredients. Some of these burn faster than others. In this way the powder companies make up a large number of different powders, each designed to burn and generate its gas in a certain manner best suited to a certain cartridge and weapon. Let us take a few general examples.

52. Use the correct powder. A pistol powder may be designed so that a proper charge will burn and generate just enough gas to drive the bullet through the short 6″ barrel of a pistol and have the bullet come out the muzzle at a velocity of, say, 1,000 feet per second. This powder in various charges may also be used in other pistol cartridges to give muzzle velocities of from 800 to 1200 feet per second. But if we used this powder in larger charges in an effort to get, say, 1,600 f.s. in a certain pistol, the large charge and the resulting high pressure might burst the pistol which was not designed to stand anything like the high pressure that this charge will give.

Again, this same fast-burning pistol powder used in a light charge in a rifle would all burn close to the breech of the barrel, and the bullet would leave the muzzle with a very low velocity, or it might even stick in the barrel. On the other hand if we used more of this fast burning pistol powder in the rifle in an effort to get higher velocity, the powder burning very fast would set up a high and unsatisfactory chamber pressure without enough continuing push through the entire bore to give the muzzle velocity we wished. And if we used still more powder the pressure would rise very fast to a dangerous extent, probably blowing out the primer, rupturing the brass case, or even demolishing the breech action of the rifle. So we can see that this pistol powder is utterly unsuited for, and indeed often dangerous when used in rifles.

Other powders are designed for use in the older cartridges formerly loaded with black powder and lead bullets, to give moderate velocities under about 1,600 f.s., and for use in reduced loads and mid-range loads in certain more modern rifle cartridges with either lead alloy or metal cased bullets. These powders are designed to burn at a low pressure and at a cool temperature. If we load larger charges of them in a rifle cartridge in an effort to get higher velocity, we get an extremely high and perhaps a dangerous pressure. Also the gas from this excessive charge may be so hot that it burns or erodes out the breech of our rifle barrel in a few hundred rounds, or if we were using a lead alloy bullet it might start the lead bullet melting while it was in the bore and we would get no accuracy. On the other hand, in a few specific cases it is possible to use these low pressure rifle powders with fair success in certain revolver cartridges.

Certain other powders are designed to give high velocities in rifle cartridges with metal cased bullets. Some of them are designed to burn well at pressures of from 30,000 to 45,000 pounds per square inch and produce standard velocities in certain rifles, often in lever action rifles. Others are designed to burn best at 40,000 to 55,000 pounds pressure in certain other cartridges to give standard higher velocities, perhaps in the stronger bolt action rifles. These powders are strictly high velocity powders, and cannot be used in much smaller charges to give reduced velocities for short range loads because they would not burn correctly at these low pressures, and indeed the primer might not properly ignite the powder. Some of these powders are made for the smaller rifle cartridges with light bullets, and others are made for use in much larger cartridges with heavier bullets.

So you can see the high desirability, in fact the absolute necessity of using the right powder for a certain cartridge and bullet. And likewise the very unsatisfactory results, and often the very great danger that comes from using the wrong powder, or even the wrong amount of the right powder. There is, however, no danger in any of this if you will follow the instructions in this book. If you are about to load a certain cartridge you should turn to Part IV of this book where specific instructions are given for the loading of that cartridge. There you will find a list of all of the powders that are suitable for use in that cartridge with bullets of various kinds and weights, together with the velocities that the various charges will produce, and much other pertinent information.

53. Rifle powders. The following are the American rifle powders available for handloading as of April, 1949, together with the general class of cartridges and loads for which they are suitable:

54. DuPont I.M.R. No. 4227. For small-capacity cartridges with metal cased bullets, like the .22 Hornet, .22 Bee, 2R Donaldson, .25-20, .32-20, .38-40 and .44-40. Not for the .222 Remington. It is a fine-grained, fast-burning powder, and measures very evenly in powder measures.

55. DuPont I.M.R. No. 4198. For the smaller-sized high-power cartridges like the 2R Donaldson, .219 Zipper, .222 Remington, .22 Savage H.P., .25-35, .30-30, and .303 Savage. Also suitable in some of the larger-sized cartridges for reduced and mid-range loads.

56. DuPont I.M.R. No. 3031. For small, medium, and fairly large rifle cartridges from .25-35 to .30-06, and also for some of the older large-bore cartridges such as .405 Winchester, .45-70, and .45-90. In the larger cartridges it is usually best with light bullets. Best for the .30-06 with 125 or 150 grain bullets.

57. DuPont I.M.R. No. 4064 and No. 4320. I class these two powders together because they are very alike in their characteristics and adaptability, although they differ in grain size. They usually, but do not always, require the same grain weight of charge. They have been used successfully in cartridges all the way from .220 Swift to .375 H&H Magnum, always with rather full loads. But in cartridges from .257 Roberts up, when heavy bullets are used, I.M.R. No. 4350 usually gives better velocity and accuracy.

58. DuPont I.M.R. No. 4350. This is the slowest-burning of du Pont canister powders and is generally adapted to the larger bottleneck cartridges with heavy bullets. It has become very popular because of the fine accuracy and high

velocity it gives with moderate pressures, particularly in the
.257 Roberts with 100 and 117 grain bullets, in the .270 Winchester with 130 and 150 grain bullets, and in the .30-06 with
180 and 220 grain bullets. It is not suitable for reduced loadings, and should be used with near maximum loads. In some
loads the powder charge fills the case to the base of the bullet.

59. **DuPont S.R. No. 4759.** For short and mid-range
loads with either lead alloy or metal-cased bullets in a large
variety of cartridges. A very excellent and clean-burning powder
for reduced loads, particularly in the .257 Roberts, .270 Winchester, and .30-06 with either gas check or metal-cased bullets.
No attempt should be made to attain high velocity with it, as
with heavy charges it gives very high pressures, and is erosive.

60. **I.M.R. No. 4895.** A military rifle powder sold to
members of the NRA by the Director of Civilian Rifle Practice
at a moderate price. Also sold by B. E. Hodgdon, Merriam,
Kansas, to handloaders generally. It is suitable for high-power
cartridges from .219 Donaldson Wasp up to .30-06. In characteristics it seems to be midway between 3031 and 4320
powders. But different lots of it may differ considerably in their
rate of burning, so that it has not been possible in this book to
give exact charges for it. The handloader should start with
the grain weight of charge that has been recommended for
3031 powder, and exceed this charge with caution. In some
cases one to two grains heavier than the charge for 3031 can
be used. I.M.R. No. 4895 powder obtained from Hodgdon
consists of many lots blended together, and once a charge has
been established for it, it is safe to repeat it with the Hodgdon
powder. In some cartridges it gives exceptionally fine accuracy
with light and medium weight bullets.

61. **Hercules HiVel No. 2.** For full and mid-range loads
in many medium-size rifle cartridges with metal-cased bullets.
A very fine powder that gives exceptional accuracy. The best
powder for 300-meter loads in the .30-06. In large charges,
however, it is liable to be rather erosive.

62. **Hercules No. 2400.** A fast-burning powder designed
for small cartridges like the .22 Hornet, .218 Bee, and .25-20.

Should positively not be used in the .222 Remington. It is also one of the best powders to use in magnum pistol loads to obtain the higher velocities.

63. **Hercules Unique.** A fast-burning powder for use in small and medium calibers for reduced loads with lead or metal-cased bullets. Good for medium heavy loads in some revolver cartridges. The recommended charges should never be exceeded.

64. **I.M.R. No. 4831.** A slow-burning powder for medium and large cartridges with heavy bullets, supplied at moderate cost to handloaders by B. E. Hodgdon, Merriam, Kansas. It is very similar in characteristics to du Pont No. 4350 powder; in fact, it has sometimes been known as "4350 Data Powder" because one can use the same grain weight charge of it as is prescribed for 4350. Actually it takes from one to three grains more of 4831 to equal the velocity given by 4350. So loaded, it has given me the same velocity and accuracy as 4350, with greater economy. It has become a very popular powder among handloaders.

65. **I.M.R. No. 4676.** A powder recently introduced to handloaders by Hodgdon, who supplies it. Its characteristics are somewhat similar to du Pont No. 3031, and in fact it may be used with the same grain weight of charge as is recommended for 3031. In velocity such charges will run slightly lower in small-capacity cartridges, but tending to give the same velocity as 3031 in larger-capacity cases. Hodgdon publishes tables of charges for it.

66. **Hercules Bullseye.** The powder most used for standard and slightly reduced target loads in pistol and revolver cartridges, giving fine accuracy and almost no fouling. The charges required are very small, and care must be taken not to get two or more charges in the same cartridge. Do not attempt to get velocities higher than standard with it.

67. **DuPont Pistol Powder No. 5066.** Very similar in all its characteristics to Bullseye, except a very slightly greater charge of it must be used to give the same velocity as Bullseye. The same precautions should be exercised to avoid getting a double charge in a cartridge.

68. **Western Ball Powder Type C.** At the time of going to press Hodgdon is supplying a lot of Ball Powder made by the Western Cartridge Company. As yet very little is known of its characteristics, although apparently it is giving some fine results in cartridges for which 3031 is a suitable powder. Because of the small ball shape of its grains it loads in very uniform charges when thrown in powder measures. By the time this book is published handloaders can probably obtain more information on it from Hodgdon.

69. **Canister lots of powder.** The above powders are known as "canister lots of powder," that is they are put up in one pound or half-pound tin canisters or cans for sale to handloaders. They are the only powders that handloaders can buy at the present time, and they are the only powders about which definite handloading information is available. Certain details about them must be understood so you will not confuse them with the lots of entirely different powder which the ammunition companies use in loading factory cartridges.

Powder is made in lots of many thousand pounds at a time. Each lot of the same general kind of powder has its own characteristics, its rate of burning, and the proper charge for each cartridge for which it is suitable For a given lot these characteristics cannot be absolutely determined in advance. Therefore each lot of powder differs at least slightly in its characteristics from other lots of the same powder.

Let us suppose the general type of powder is similar to DuPont I.M.R. No. 3031. Many different lots of this powder have been and are being made, each differing more or less slightly in its characteristics. One of these lots has been set aside as a *canister lot,* has been called DuPont No. 3031, and its characteristics have been made known to handloaders. Many other lots of this kind of powder have been manufactured, each having slightly different characteristics from 3031, and therefore these lots have been given different numbers. These lots are sold only to the ammunition companies who use them in loading their factory cartridges, and the ammunition companies determine the proper charge for each cartridge and bullet, and control the loading with their chronographs and pressure guns.

When the supply of canister lot No. 3031 nears exhaustion on the market, the DuPont Company sets aside another lot of this same kind of powder which has characteristics so close to that of the original No. 3031, that it is practically identical, and this becomes the new canister lot and is known again as No. 3031. Thus, while No. 3031 has been on the market for many years, the present No. 3031 is practically identical with that original lot. This applies to all powders mentioned above, all being canister lots, except 4895.

70. Powder in Factory Cartridges. As explained above, the ammunition companies do not load their factory cartridges with canister lots of powder. They give their specifications for powder for a certain cartridge to the powder companies who turn them out a lot of powder, possibly many thousand pounds, as close to those specifications as they can. The ammunition companies then determine the proper charge of this powder for all the cartridges in which they wish to load it, controlling its loading to give standard velocities with pressures within their safety limits.

Thus if you open up a certain factory cartridge and look at the powder, and it looks like 3031, beware! It is not 3031, and the amount or weight of that powder is no good guide as to the amount of 3031 to use in handloading that cartridge to get results similar to those of this factory cartridge. *Thus neither the amount nor the appearance of the powder found in any factory cartridge must be taken as a guide for handloading.*

It is only common sense that if you have a supply of old .30-06 Government ammunition, with 150 grain metal cased bullet, and find that it is loaded with 45 grains of a certain powder, that you can salvage that powder, and use it again in a 45 grain load to handload a fresh batch of .30-06 cases with 150 grain metal cased bullets. It might even be safe to assume that if you wished to load 180 grain bullets in your new batch of ammunition that you would be safe in using, say, 41 grains of this identical powder. But further than that it is not safe to go. It would not be safe, for example, to use that powder in loading the .270 Winchester cartridge unless you had a chronograph and pressure gun to determine the load, or unless you started with a very small charge, and worked the load up a grain at a time, watching for indication of excessive pressures (P 179).

71. **Proper charges of powder.** While all of the above explanations are necessary to prevent beginners from doing dangerous things with powder, no reader need be confused about modern smokeless powder. The proper kinds of powder, and the proper amount of that powder which can be used with satisfaction and safety in loading a certain cartridge with a certain weight of bullet is given in Part IV of this book. Simply look up there the cartridge you wish to hand-load, and you will find complete information.

CHARGING CASES WITH POWDER

72. Your cases are now all chamfered, sized and primed, ready to be charged with powder. You are going to load your cartridges with a certain weight and kind (lead alloy, lead alloy with gas check, or metal cased) bullet. So you turn to Part IV of this book where you will find a table of powder charges for your cartridge, and for the different kinds and weights of bullets as well as for the powders that are suitable. Sometimes two or more charges of powder are given for a certain bullet, the heaviest charge being the maximum safe charge which should be used only when everything about rifle, case, and bullet are excellent and normal, and you verify your powder charge by weighing it on scales, or verify the charge thrown by the powder measure with scales.

From this table you select the charge you are going to load; that is the kind of powder and the weight of the charge in grains. Note the number of grains you will use on a sheet of paper. Close the book and open it again, and again carefully refer to the table to see that you selected the correct charge the first time. Long experience in handloading has shown that it is very desirable to check the load twice. Anyone is liable to make a mistake in reading a table, reading the wrong line or column, and I have known of a number of mistakes being made in just this way.

73. **Powder is measured by grains.** Charges of powder are indicated by grain weight, which is the foundation of all systems of weights used in the United States and Great Britain except the metric system. There are 7,000 grains in one pound, or 437½ grains in one ounce, Avoirdupois.

74. **Ways of measuring the charges.** There are three ways of measuring the charge to be placed in each cartridge case. (1) By dipping the charge out of a reservoir of powder with a small dipper which holds just the right amount. (2) By mechanically measuring each charge with a special powder measure. (3) By weighing each charge on an accurate scale. The most practical method is a combination of (2) and (3).

75. **Dipping Powder.** A powder dipper is easily made by filing off a cartridge case until it holds just the right amount of powder as verified by an accurate scale, then soldering a short wire handle to this dipper. Dippers can also be bought at nominal price from some dealers in loading tools (Ideal). The powder should be poured out of the canister into a can or box in which it will bulk up in a pile at least two inches deep. The dipper is inserted down into the bottom of the pile, then turned mouth up, and brought up to the surface of the pile so that the powder will fill the dipper each time with the same pressure. Keep the pile at the same uniform depth. The dipper will now be full to overflowing with powder. Take a card (postal or visiting card) and gently scrape it across the mouth of the dipper to level off the powder just even with the top of the dipper. Place a small funnel in the mouth of the cartridge case, and pour the powder

from the dipper into the cartridge case, taking care that no powder is spilled.

This method is crude and not very accurate, and its sole recommendation is that you don't have to buy a powder measure or scales. Dipper charges will vary from dip to dip about one to three grains, depending on the weight of charge and the kind of powder being measured. Therefore if this method is used your charge should be at least two grains lighter than the heaviest charge given in the table for the bullet you are loading.

The Ideal powder measure.

76. Charging by powder measure. A number of different mechanical measures for measuring power are available

—Ideal, Belding & Mull, R.C.B.S., Redding, etc. A table comes with each which shows where to set the measure to cause it to throw a certain number of grains of a certain powder. You first fill the reservoir of the measure almost to the top with powder. Then set the scale at the proper graduation, hold the empty cartridge case under the tube opening at the bottom of the measure, pull down the handle of the measure, and the charge of powder in the receptacle will fall into the cartridge case. Then lift the handle of the measure and the receptacle again fills with powder ready to charge another case. There is often a little knocker on the side of the measure and when you have lifted the handle you should flick this knocker up, thus jarring the measure slightly and settling a uniform amount of powder into the receptacle. Also the reservoir should be kept at least half full of powder at all times to give a uniform reservoir pressure which will further assure a uniform charge settling into the receptacle.

These measures do not throw an absolutely accurate series of powder charges. With most of them successive charges will vary plus or minus about .2 grain with the finer powders, and about .4 grain with the coarser grained powders. The greatest variation from lightest to heaviest charge in loading 100 cases with coarse grained powder would thus be about .8 grain. Also you cannot be quite certain that the measure set at the graduation given in the table accompanying it will throw the corresponding charge of powder. There may be an error of one or two grains either way. Thus if you set the measure by the table to throw, say, 36 grains of a certain powder, it may actually average 37½ grains or perhaps 34½ grains. Also, if it averages 37½ grains of a coarse grained powder, some of the charges may weigh 37.1 grains, and some 37.9 grains. Therefore if you wished to load a maximum charge of 36 grains it would not be safe to use the measure in this way. In fact if you set the measure by the table that accompanies it you should not approach within about 1½ grains of any maximum charge given in the table of loads in Part IV of this book.

Many powder measures have tubes projecting from the bottom of the measure that funnel the powder into the cartridge case. Two of these tubes are usually furnished, one for cases of .25 caliber and larger, and one for .22 caliber. When using coarser grained powders in the .22 caliber tube the grains will occasionally "bridge" in the tube, making an obstruction past which no powder, or only a small amount of powder drops into the cartridge case. The tube thus fills with powder, and at the next throw it may dump a charge and a half or a double charge into the case. This is an exceedingly dangerous matter that must be watched for constantly, but the system of inspection given below will always discover it. Also, by looking into each case after the powder has been loaded to see that it stands at a uniform level, any failure to deliver the correct charge will be instantly detected.

These little troubles are mentioned merely as cautions. There is almost never any trouble at all except in the unavoidable slight variation in successive charges, and these measures are very efficient.

77. The Belding and Mull powder measure operates on a slightly different principle. The measuring receptacle is entirely separate from the reservoir. You set the receptacle for a certain charge, place it under the bottom opening of the measure, and when the handle is operated the receptable fills with powder. You then place a small funnel over the mouth of the cartridge case, and pour the powder from the receptacle into the case, and as you see every grain go into the case there can be no accidental variation other than the very small variation in the receptacle content. The B & M measure is thus slightly slower to operate than the other measures. You can perhaps charge about ten cases a minute with it as compared with about 15 cases with the measures that dump directly into the cartridge case.

78. The best procedure is: Have a loading block containing all the primed cases, mouths down and primer up. Take a case from the block, fill it with powder, then return the filled case to its hole in the block, or to another block, mouth of the case up so it will not be knocked over and no powder will spill out. When all cases in the block have been charged with powder, take the block into a good light, run the eye along the rows of cases, and see that the powder stands at a uniform depth in each and every case. Or the SURE-MARK Charge Gauge (see Wilkins & Schultz in Directory) can be inserted in each case and shows visually if any charge is short or over.

79. Charging by measure and scale. This is the method used by practically all experienced handloaders. The powder measure is set as before (P 76), but instead of throwing the first charge into a case it is thrown on to the pan of the powder scale which has been previously set to weigh the exact charge desired. If the charge as thrown by the measure does not balance correctly on the powder scale, the setting of the powder measure is changed just slightly, and this is continued until the measure throws at least two consecutive charges that balance and weigh correctly on the powder scales. Thus you really set the powder measure by means of the powder scales and not by the scale on the measure. Then you can go ahead and throw directly from the measure into the cartridge cases. As an added check it is well to throw every 25th or 50th charge on the powder scale to see that there has been no slip or variation.

In this manner you are quite certain of filling the cases with the correct charge of powder within the slight unavoidable variation of the measure, which, as stated above, practically never varies more than .4 grain above or below the normal charge. Such slight variation in the charges occasions less of a variation at the target than the unavoidable errors of aim with iron sights or low power hunting scopes.

80. Weighing each powder charge. This method of charging the cases, while it is, strictly speaking, the only really accurate method, is nevertheless so slow that ordinarily it is used only in loading cartridges for 1,000 yard target shooting, for target matches that are to be hotly contested, and

for certain experimental firings. Each powder charge is weighed out separately on the scale before it is funnelled into its cartridge case. Usually only about three or four cases a minute can be thus charged.

Set the powder scales at the exact charge desired. Set the measure at about 1½ grains less than the charge desired. Throw from the powder measure on the pan of the scale (usually taking the pan off the scale and holding it under the measure so that the powder piles up in the center of the pan and does not spill, then place the pan on the scale again). Then have a cartridge case (of a caliber other than the one you are loading to avoid any possible confusion) filled with powder, and holding it over the pan, tap it lightly with the finger and thus flick a few grains of powder onto the pan, until the scale just balances. Then lift the pan off the scale, and pour into the cartridge case through a funnel.

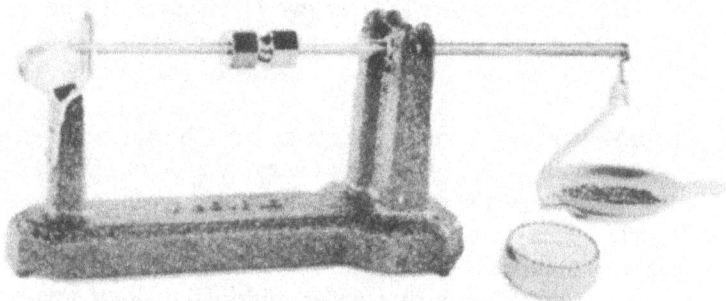

Pacific powder and bullet scales.

There is also a rather expensive electronic powder scale made by the Gunderson Instrument Company which will weigh powder charges in about seven seconds in 0.1 grain steps, accurate to plus or minus .05 grain.

Truth compels us to say, however, that innumerable tests have shown conclusively that powder charges thrown from a good measure result in just as good accuracy as where they are individually weighed to within one-tenth grain or less variation. Thus there is no real necessity for going to the time-consuming operation of weighing each individual powder charge. At first thought this does not seem reasonable, but the variation in ignition of each individual primer, plus the slight but unavoidable variation in powder capacity of each individual case, plus the slight variation of tension of the bullet in the case neck, plus slight variations in each individual bullet, make an algebraic sum which is not materially reduced by an absolutely uniform weighed powder charge.

81. **Powder scales** are sold by almost all makers of reloading tools. The more common makes are the Pacific and the Wa-Master which have separate weights and are the least expensive; and the Redding, Brown and Sharp, and Fairbanks which have graduated beams and counterweights and are most convenient and faster. With care they are all accurate to within about 1/10th grain. Take care that their trunnions do not get dulled, keep a bullet of precisely known weight with them to verify them from time to time, and when using them see that they are levelled on the loading bench.

82. **Economy.** If one has to economize in the purchase of his tools it is suggested that probably the best plan would be to purchase a Pacific Powder Scale (the cheapest of the scales) and dispense with the powder measure. However this means that only about three or four cases a minute can be charged, and probably sooner or later the handloader will add a powder measure to his outfit to save time.

83. **Compressed charges.** In almost all cases the powder charges recommended for various cartridges and weights of bullet will not completely fill the cartridge case with powder up to the base of the seated bullet. Usually even the maximum charges recommended for rifle cartridges will only fill the case to within ⅛ to ¼ inch of the base of the bullet. With mid and short range rifle loads and pistol loads often the powder does not fill the case more than about half full. All this is entirely normal. Heavier loads of that powder might give

excessive and dangerous pressures. There must be this air space for safety in these loads. Powder should not fill the case full, nor be compressed in seating the bullet.

However, there are exceptions to every rule. Some charges of 4350 and 4831 powder may fill the case almost to its mouth, and when the bullet is seated the powder will be compressed, and yet the charge, if a recommended one, will give normal pressure and good results. Indeed, an occasional proper charge of these powders may fill the case and overflow. To get such a charge into the case and seat the bullet, pour the powder into the case very slowly through a funnel with a long tube. The grains will settle themselves more compactly in this manner and you can get the whole charge in the case.

But be cautious when you first begin to fill your cases with powder. If you find that the charge fills the case right up to the base of the bullet, or overflows the case, check your load in the table, and also check your powder measure and scales to be certain that you have not made a mistake.

84. **Emptying the powder measure.** When all the cases of the lot being loaded have been filled with powder, do not empty the powder remaining in the measure back into the canister from which it came. It is usually best not to disturb the measure or the scales until you have seated the bullets into the charged cases because a case does get knocked over now and again. If the measure and scales have not been disturbed it is easy to fill that case with powder again. But when you are through loading a batch of cases always empty what powder remains in the measure back into its proper canister, for powder left for any great time in the open tends to dry out, and does not give exactly its normal burning pressure. But be sure you return the powder to the proper canister—look at the label— for there is a chance of an accident here.

SEATING BULLETS

85. The various kinds and types of bullets as well as bullet making are described in Part III of this book. All the

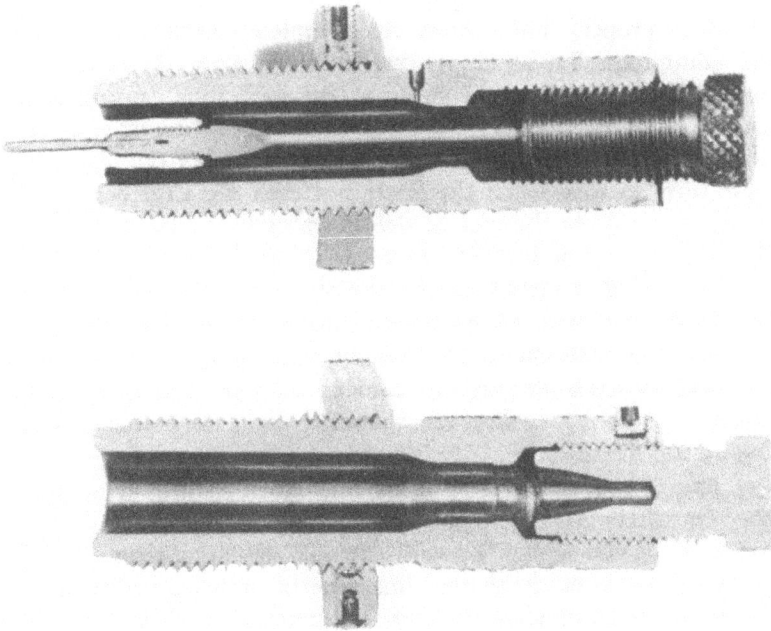

Universal resizing die (top) and bullet seating chamber. These dies, as well as the Pacific dies, will fit in many different makes of reloading tool frames.

cases having been charged with powder, and placed upright in the loading block, the next and final step in handloading our cartridge is to seat the bullet evenly, straight, and to the correct depth in the neck of the case.

To seat the bullets, the bullet seating chamber is first screwed into the loading tool. We will suppose you have not seated bullets before in your tool, therefore the bullet seating chamber must be correctly adjusted. If you examine a bullet seating chamber you will see that it is composed of two parts —the chamber into which the case fits, and the bullet seating stem in which the bullet fits. This last part pushes the bullet down into the case neck. (Sometimes there is a third part, the crimping stem or ring, which we will deal with later.) First screw the bullet seating stem almost out of the bullet seating chamber proper. Then screw the complete chamber into the reloading tool. Try an empty case in it, and screw the chamber until, when you close the lever of the tool, thus causing the case to enter the chamber, the case can be felt coming up against the end of the chamber. Then screw the chamber out about a half turn so that when the lever is closed the case does not come up to quite the end of the chamber by perhaps 1/32". Then screw down the clamping collar on the outside of the chamber until it comes against the shoulder of the tool, and clamp it there with its set screw, thus retaining the chamber in proper adjustment in the loading tool.

Always screw the die or chamber into the reloading tool until it comes up against the clamping ring, no matter what bullet you are seating.

The next problem is to screw the bullet seating stem into the die proper so it will seat the bullets into the cases to the exact depth you wish. We will first take up the seating of the bullet to the same depth that that type of bullet is seated in a factory-loaded cartridge. In Part IV, under each cartridge, you will find the "standard cartridge length." This is usually the standard overall length of the cartridge when it is loaded with the heaviest bullets that are generally used with it, and it is also the longest length that will operate through the magazine of standard rifles. However, there are some cartridges that the factories load with short, light bullets, and these cartridges have a shorter than standard overall length.

Suppose, for example, you wish to seat a 150 or 180 grain pointed bullet to standard overall length in a .30-06 case. The easiest way to seat the bullet seating stem is to take a factory cartridge loaded with a 150 or 180 grain pointed bullet (they are all the same seating length), place its head in the shell holder of the reloading tool, operate the handle and raise the cartridge all the way into the bullet seating die, then screw the bullet seating stem down against the bullet, and tighten the collar on the stem. For other seating depths you simply adjust the bullet seating stem accordingly, by trial and error.

Now you are ready to seat the bullets.

Take a case that is primed and filled with powder, and holding it upright, slide its rim into the rim slot in the cartridge case holder of the loading tool. Then take a bullet and place or balance it on the mouth of the case, base of the bullet centered in the mouth. If you rotate the base of the bullet just slightly as you place it on the case mouth, a little as you would start to cork a bottle, it will center there, and the bullet will stand upright in position to seat down into the neck of the case. There is a little knack of thus placing and balancing the bullet on the case mouth so it will slide into the neck smoothly and evenly when the bullet seating stem begins to press down on it. This knack is easily learned in three or four trials.

(Of course you cannot actually start the bullet into the mouth of the case with your fingers because the base of the bullet is slightly larger than the inside of the neck of the case, perhaps about a thousandth of an inch larger.)

The bullets should seat easily in the case necks—just a gentle pull-up on the handle of the tool—no force. If you feel a bullet apparently catch on the mouth of a case and refuse to start in smoothly, do not attempt to force it in. Lower the handle, thus withdrawing the case and bullet from the chamber, rotate the bullet slightly on the case mouth, thus giving it a more perfect and central fit in the mouth, and try again. If the bullet does not start to slide into the case neck easily this second time probably something is wrong. The case may be slightly deformed at the mouth, or the bullet may be too large, or you may be trying to force a bullet with a very square base into a case mouth that has not been chamfered. A little close inspection will show what is at fault. Trying to force a bullet in will crumple or mash down one side of the neck of the case, and distort the base of the bullet, ruining both.

86. For the finest accuracy it is highly desirable that the tension on the bullet in the neck of the case be as uniform as possible. This is called "bullet pull," that is the number of pounds of direct pull that it takes to pull the bullet out of a case. Before you have seated many bullets you will become aware of the gentle, quite uniform pressure on the handle of the loading tool necessary to seat the bullet. Whenever this pressure is markedly easier or harder, thus indicating lighter or greater tension on the bullet, lay that cartridge aside for a sighting shot or practice. All those seating with uniform pressure can be used for record firing, competitions or hunting.

87. Bullet seating stems are formed to just fit the point of the particular bullet you are loading. That is, the stem that fits over the bullet may be shaped to just fit a flat point, a round point, or a sharp point bullet. In recent years, however, practically all bullet seating stems have been made so that they will seat bullets with variously shaped points without deforming the point. But do not attempt to seat a sharp pointed bullet with an old type stem made for a flat or round point bullet or you will deform the sharp point of that bullet. Usually you should order bullet-seating dies with stems to seat sharp-pointed bullets. These will usually seat all bullets correctly. For tubular-magazine rifles, however, the stem should be ordered to seat standard flat-nose bullets, and pistol dies should be ordered with stem to fit the particular bullet you are going to load.

88. Seating depth of bullets. The depth to which a bullet is to be seated in the case depends on a number of factors. First, we may wish that the cartridge be short enough in its overall length so it will operate smoothly through the magazine of the standard rifle of that caliber. This standard overall length is given, for each cartridge, in Part IV. For example, for .30-06 and .270 W.C.F. cartridges it is 3.35", for .257 Roberts 2.75", and for .250-3000 Savage 2.52". Adjust the bullet-seating die so it seats the bullet to just this depth. Some rifles, however, have magazines that are longer than standard, and sometimes for these bullets can be seated to greater than overall length with advantage. See below. But generally, if the cartridge intended for a magazine rifle is seated to greater than standard overall length, then if loaded directly into the chamber, it cannot be extracted and ejected without firing unless the bolt is first withdrawn from the receiver. But of course such long cartridges can be used single-loading only.

It will be obvious that it will be impossible to seat very short, light bullets, like 110 and 125 grain .30 caliber bullets, to standard overall length, because not enough of the base of the bullet will be in the neck of the case for security. The base of .22 caliber bullets should always be inserted at least .18″ deep in the neck of the case for security, .25 caliber at least .23″, and .30 caliber at least .30″ deep.

When it can be done, it is sometimes desirable that the bullet be seated far enough out of the case so that when the cartridge is fully seated in the chamber of the rifle the ogive (curve of point) of the bullet just touches the lands of the

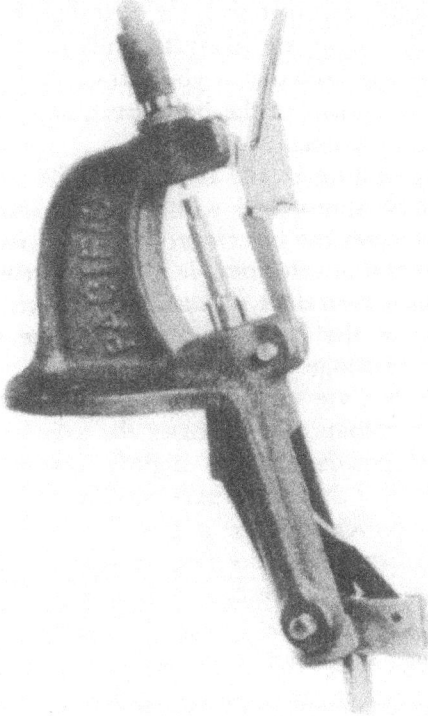

Super Pacific reloading tool, showing one die in place. This tool is also equipped with an automatic primer feed. This popular tool is much used in making .22 and .25 caliber metal cased bullets. See Part III.

rifling in the bore. This long seating sometimes results in greater accuracy. The bullet is trued up in the chamber and bore by the lands, and it does not have to jump through the bullet seat into the rifling, and likely slightly deform itself. A cartridge with bullet seated to make contact with the lands may not work through the magazine, but it can be handloaded singly into the chamber. Seating the bullet to thus make contact with the lands is done by adjusting the depth to which the bullet-seating die is screwed into the loading tool, and trying the cartridge in the chamber, until you get a length that, when you extract the cartridge, just shows a very slight mark or depression on the ogive of the bullet where the lands pressed into it. Do not seat to such a depth that the lands impress themselves deeply on the ogive, for cartridges loaded with such a long overall length are likely to press the bullet so deeply into the lands and bore that if you extract them without firing, the bullet may remain in the bullet seat, and the powder may be spilled in the action.

This long seating of the bullet to make contact with the lands should be approached with caution. Such long seating sometimes increases the breech pressure, and gives greater variation than normal in velocities. It is better to reduce the powder charge for such cartridges by one grain. Such reduction will usually result in the best accuracy. Note the remarks under .257 Roberts cartridge in Part IV.

When bullets are seated to greater than standard overall length, this automatically increases the powder capacity, and with standard powder charges slightly lowers both pressures and velocities. It is then sometimes possible, and safe, to increase the standard powder charge a grain or two, thus restoring standard pressures and velocities, or indeed, occasionally obtaining a few feet per second additional velocity. But such increases in powder should be approached with caution, watching for any sign of abnormal pressure.

89. **Seating depth and pressure.** Generally speaking the maximum loads given in Part IV of this book are for cartridges with bullets seated to standard depth or standard

The Universal Model B reloading tool made by the Hollywood Gun Shop
has a twelve position indexed turret head so that 12 different dies can
be kept adjusted to the tool. Universal, Hollywood, and Pacific tools
all use the same dies interchangeably.

overall length. If the bullet is seated deeper than this, thus decreasing the powder space and air space within the case, and giving greater density of loading, then the pressure is increased, possibly to the danger point. On the other hand if the bullet is seated to land-contact overall-length (particularly a light or short bullet) the powder and air space are increased, the density of loading is lowered, and the pressure is reduced. In such an event it may be possible to load a slightly greater charge of powder within pressure limitations, thus increasing velocity.

Example: The standard overall length of the .257 Roberts cartridge is 2.75". If we use a 100 grain Moffat bullet (a two-diameter bullet) seated to land-contact overall length the actual length of the loaded cartridge will be about 3.03". Loaded to this length it is practical to use a powder charge of 47 grains of du Pont No. 4350 powder which is within safe pressure limits. But if we seated this bullet, or any other 100 grain bullet to standard overall length (2.75") and then used 47 grains of 4350 powder we would have an excessive charge and probably dangerous pressure. A charge of 47 grains of this powder fills the .257 Roberts case full to the base of the 100 grain Moffat bullet seated to an overall length of 3.03", with no air space, giving what is termed 100 per cent density of loading.

90. Crimping the bullet. So far we have discussed only seating the bullet friction tight in the properly sized neck of the case. This is the common and best practice with all bolt action rifles and single shot rifles. However, this friction tight fit will not hold the bullet securely and satisfactorily in tubular magazine rifles, and revolvers. With tubular magazine rifles the mouth of the case must be crimped into the bullet to prevent the bullet being driven deeper into the case when the recoil of the rifle forces the column of cartridges in the magazine hard against the bullet. Also with tubular magazine rifles we must use flat pointed bullets so that the sharp point of the bullet of one cartridge is not against the primer of the cartridge ahead of it in the tubular magazine. The sharp point of a pointed bullet might set off the primer of the cartridge in front and cause an explosion in the magazine. Crimping revolver bullets is necessary to give enough initial pressure to make the relatively small powder charge with low density loading and considerable air space ignite and burn correctly. Also it is necessary to prevent the bullets of cartridges in the chambers from jumping farther out of their cases when the revolver recoils.

Many metal-cased bullets, particularly those for rifles with tubular magazines, have cannelures pressed into their jackets. If you are crimping the case on the bullet you naturally adjust to crimp in this cannelure. But if you are loading the bullet friction-tight in the case, you pay no attention to this cannelure, but just seat the bullet to the desired seating depth.

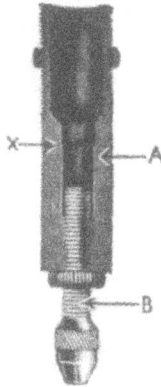

Ideal bullet seating chamber or die. X is the crimping shoulder. To crimp the case the die is screwed far enough into the tool so the shoulder crimps the case on the bullet. When not screwed in quite so far, the die seats the bullet without a crimp. B is the bullet seating stem which is screwed into the die deeply enough to seat the bullet to the desired depth. The end of this screw is formed inside to receive the bullet point.

91. Adjusting the crimping shoulder. It has already been seen (P 18) that when bullets are to be crimped in cases the mouth of the case is slightly belled. Most metal cased bullets that are designed for tubular magazine cartridges and most lead bullets designed for both rifles and revolvers have crimping cannelures or grooves in them.

To seat and crimp the bullet we must use a bullet seating

The newest Hollywood reloading tool. The large cylindrical pedestal insures alignment between the shell holder and dies. Pacific, Hollywood and Universal dies will fit. Extremely strong and suitable for swaging even the larger metal cased bullets with RCBS and Banta dies. The lever exerts power on the down stroke, making possible a light loading bench.

chamber that has a crimping shoulder or crimping stem. The bullet seating chamber is adjusted in the tool as before described (P 85) and both the crimping shoulder and bullet seating stem are then screwed in by trial and by degrees until the mouth of the case is crimped slightly but firmly in the crimping cannelure of the bullet. The bullet seating chamber, its crimping shoulder and the bullet seating stem are most easily adjusted by seating a factory crimped cartridge in the case holder of the loading tool, and then screwing down on it first the bullet seating chamber proper with its crimping shoulder, and then the bullet seating stem. Then try the cartridge case with its powder charge and the bullet balanced on the mouth of the case, and see if it seats and crimps the bullet properly. Adjust it until it does. It is easy to balance and fit the bullet on the mouth of a belled case because the bell mouth permits the base of the bullet to enter just slightly into the case mouth.

The accuracy of all cartridges depends greatly on the tension with which the base of the bullet is held in the case neck, so take pains to get these correct. It is just a matter of trial adjustments.

92. **Seating bullets in automatic pistol cases.** Here the flat mouth of the case abutting against the front end of the chamber provides the stop that prevents the rimless case from entering too far into the chamber, supports the case against the firing pin blow, and determines the headspace measurement. Thus the extreme edge of the mouth of the case must be quite square and even. The bullet is held friction tight in the case by having the neck of the case sized so that it measures several thousandths of an inch smaller inside than the diameter of the bullet. To have the bullet seat evenly and centrally in this case the bullet must be slightly rounded on the base. Bullets are seated to standard overall length, no crimp. Uniform tension of the bullets in the case necks is necessary for the best results. If bullets seat with less or greater pressure than normal use those cartridges for sighters or practice.

93. Packing. All of the cartridges having been completely loaded, it only remains to pack them properly and label them so as to identify the loading. While it is common practice to pack handloaded cartridges in the standard 20 round paper cartons in which factory cartridges are packed, these cartons are not ideal. If stored in a damp place the cardboard may absorb moisture and corrode the outside of the cartridges. It is better where one can conveniently do so, to pack handloaded cartridges in wood boxes, even in cigar boxes from which paper linings have been removed. Cigar boxes can be reinforced with tape to make them much stronger.

Then the box should be labelled to show the exact loading of the cartridges it contains. These data may be written on the outside of the box or carton, or they may be written on a label pasted on the outside, or they may be written on a card which is packed inside with the cartridges. All of the following data are usually desirable:

> For use in weapon No.....................
> Primer ....
> Powder, kind ....
> Powder charge; Grains...................
> Bullet.............. Grains............
> Bullet diameter ....
> Case necks expanded to...............inch
> Overall length ....
> Cases previously fired...............times
> Loaded (date) ....

No mistake can then be made with these cartridges next week or five years from their loading date.

94. Bullet pulling. A handloader sometimes wishes to pull the bullets out of loaded cartridges, and substitute other bullets or powder. Or he may wish to load the cases with some other load. Many of the reloading tool makers sell bullet pullers which are used in the reloading tool in place of the bullet seating and other dies. The cartridge is run into the bullet puller, the jaws of the puller are clamped on the bullet, the lever of the loading tool is reversed, and the bullet is pulled straight out of the case.

The case is then very much as though it had been fired. That is before it can have another bullet seated in it, it must be chamfered at the mouth (if it has previously been crimped), it must be neck resized and then expanded to the proper inside neck diameter for the new bullet.

Bullets that have been carefully pulled from cases in this manner are scarcely injured. They may not be quite good enough for fine target shooting, but they can usually be loaded and used again for ordinary practice or sighting shots.

A new "inertia Bullet Puller" has recently been introduced by Guns Products Division, 4114 Fannin Street, Houston, Texas. The one tool will easily pull all bullets from all cartridges, and it deforms both bullet and case less than other pullers. It is gradually replacing the clamp-on, older bullet pullers.

III

BULLETS AND BULLET MAKING

95. Importance of the bullet. The bullet is the most important part of the cartridge. Indeed today it is the most important part of both gun and ammunition. It is the bullet that hits the target and makes the bullseye or kills the game. All the rifle or pistol can do is to start the bullet correctly on its way to the target. Whether it hits in the X-ring, or strikes the game in a vital part depends on its perfection.

Formerly machine made rifles and pistols gave uncertain accuracy, due to the unavoidable tolerances in important parts. Today, thanks to the improvement in the last twenty years in machine tools, it is possible to regularly manufacture the vital parts of firearms to such close dimensions that fine accuracy is assured, provided that the stock of the weapon, and the ammunition, and most particularly the bullet, are what they should be. The best machine made rifles now have barrels approaching close to the ideal. Primers and powder have been greatly improved. Our factories and a few of our custom stockers now understand barrels and action bedding for fine accuracy and reliability. Many custom grip makers know how the grips of handguns should be made, and how their sights should be refined. On the rifle the modern telescope sight gives us errorless aim. Modern bench rest technique enables us to shoot the rifle with little human error. Therefore the greatest variable in the performance of the modern rifle and pistol lies in the bullet.

The twist of the rifling imparts a spin or rotation to the bullet as it flies through the air. Formerly it was thought that this rotation served only to keep the conical bullet flying with its its point to the front, and that the straightness of the barrel and its length was what made the bullet fly on a straight course to the target. However, we now know that this is not strictly true. Straightness of barrel is not what makes the bullet fly on a uniform trajectory to the target. When a conical bullet is launched into the air from a rifle or pistol, spinning rapidly, it becomes a gyroscope. A gyroscope launched into the air and unsupported, not only tends to keep flying on the same plane, travelling straight in the same direction in which launched, but it strongly resists all influences that tend to force it out of that plane and straight path. How accurately and consistently it travels depends on its perfection of form and balance, and the rapidity of its spin. A bullet that is formed unevenly, that is out of round, that has imperfections in point and particularly in base, that contains air pockets, or that has a core slightly loose in its jacket, or a jacket with uneven walls, is out of balance and is not a perfect gyroscope. It spirals or corkscrews through the air, and where these defects differ in a series of bullets, they do not start off from the muzzle of the weapon in the same straight line towards the target. The importance of bullet form and construction are apparent.

At present it is not practical to make perfect bullets in quantity by ordinary machine production. All have certain large or small imperfections, and all are more or less unbalanced. This is why we have never been able to shoot all bullets into the same hole at any considerable distance. Some factory bullets are better than others, and have established a reputation for accuracy. Some machines and some machine operators at certain times will turn out one lot of the same bullet better than others. At the turn of the century we considered that any bullet that would shoot consistently into 3 minutes of angle (3″ per hundred yards) was as accurate as could be machine produced. Today that still remains the standard of good accuracy with the average machine made bullets. But there are also some factory bullets, specially or more or less accidentally designed for fine accuracy, which will often average 1½ minutes extreme spread in good rifles and pistols. This is about the best average performance that can be relied on and should not be confused with occasional performance. Because a certain rifle and ammunition once made a lucky one minute group by no means entitles them to be considered a one-minute outfit. But when a rifle and ammunition makes ten small groups on ten different days we begin to take serious notice.

The very careful handloader has always been able to mould his own lead alloy bullets, and by discarding all bullets in any way imperfect, has been able to make series of lead alloy bullets that have always excelled the factory product. Recent experiences have indicated that the careful handloader can also make metal cased bullets which will equal the factory bullets in accuracy. Also that by using extreme care and with the best of hand tools, he can make metal cased bullets that will considerably excel the factory bullets in accuracy.

There is, however, one more bullet detail; the effect, the good killing effect on game, particularly on big game. With respect to metal cased bullets this has hardly been explored at all by handloaders, while the large ammunition companies have put very considerable time and research on it. We are here going to explain the various types of bullets, with notes on their particular spheres of usefulness. Afterwards we will describe the processes of making good bullets by hand.

96. Types of bullets. To understand and evaluate bullets in general it is necessary to divide them into a number of types according to shape and construction. First as to shape.

97. Short or light bullets (See 1 in the accompanying illustration). Bullets that are short, and consequently light in weight with respect to their diameter. They offer little resistance and friction in the bore and therefore develop less breech pressure with equal powder charges than longer and heavier bullets of the same diameter, and by using a larger powder charge with them than would be safe with heavier bullets, they can be given a higher muzzle velocity. But in prolonged flight their remaining velocity falls off much faster than with longer, heavier bullets because they do not overcome the resistance of the air as well; just as an arrow will maintain its flight much better than a baseball of the same weight starting out with the same velocity. Thus when a short, light bullet is shot at very high velocity it may have a very flat trajectory over a short distance, but the trajectory soon becomes much more curved, and the short bullet falls faster than a longer and

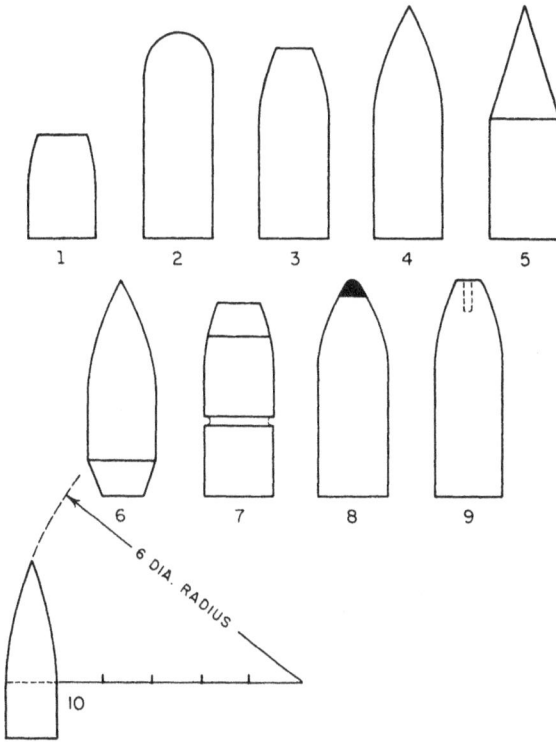

BULLET SHAPES

1. Short, light.
2. Long, heavy, round nose.
3. Flat point.
4. Sharp point.
5. Spire point.
6. Boat-tail or streamlined.
7. Soft point, maximum lead exposure.
8. Soft point, minimum lead exposure.
9. Hollow point or "Express."
10. Ogive formed on a radius of six diameters.

heavier bullet of the same diameter, even when the latter is projected at quite a little less muzzle velocity.

An example is the 110 grain .30 caliber metal cased bullet which in the .30-06 cartridge can be safely loaded to a muzzle velocity of nearly 3,500 f.s. At this velocity it has a very flat trajectory over 200 yards, flatter than that of any other heavier bullet with a safe load. But beyond 200 yards this short, light

bullet falls off so fast in its remaining velocity and develops
such a curved trajectory that we cannot hit small targets with
it at longer distances unless we know the distance accurately
and can allow for the very rapid drop of the bullet.

Short, light bullets also give less penetration than longer
and heavier bullets of the same diameter and construction, just
as a short piece of iron, say 1" x 6" will, with the same effort,
penetrate much less into earth than a long, heavy crowbar of
the same diameter. A short, light bullet at high velocity instead
of penetrating into solid substances tends to fly to pieces, to
disintegrate. It might thus be a good killing bullet on a small
animal like a woodchuck, but on a big game animal it might
fail to penetrate to the vital organs before it flies to pieces.

Short, light bullets can also be loaded in many rifle cartridges to give comparatively low muzzle velocities. This makes
them suitable for small game shooting at short distances where
you do not want to destroy meat or skins, or they may be used
for indoor target practice where penetration, destructiveness
and report are undesirable.

Short, light bullets are used practically to the exclusion of
all others in revolver and pistol cartridges. As they set up light
resistance and pressure in the chamber and bore they can be
given a comparatively high velocity. A small charge of quick
burning powder will give them roughly 700 to 1,400 f.s.m.v.
in handguns with the low pressure that is a necessity in these
light weapons. This velocity gives these light bullets a flat
enough trajectory over the short distances at which handguns
are used. It is almost impossible to fire long, heavy bullets in
a handgun because the velocity needed to give it a satisfactory
trajectory even at short distances would require a powder charge
that would develop a breech pressure that no handgun could
withstand.

A short, light bullet loaded to muzzle velocities over about
1800 f.s. must be jacketed or metal cased with copper, gilding
metal or mild steel because a base of plain lead would be melted
by the hot gases of the heavy powder charge required to give
higher velocities, and the bullet might possibly strip in the

rifling and not hold the grooves. Light bullets for automatic pistols are likewise metal cased because they operate more efficiently through the mechanism than soft lead bullets, and because expanding bullets are prohibited in warfare by the Hague Convention. For warfare plain lead bullets are now classified as expanding bullets. But for revolvers lead bullets are always preferred both because of their relative cheapness and because the serviceable and accurate life of the revolver is much prolonged when they are used.

These short, light bullets, even when made of soft lead, or with a hollow point, do not usually expand on animal tissue unless they are given a muzzle velocity in excess of about 1,300 f.s. Thus a pistol or revolver bullet, unless it is made with an extremely hollow point so that it is a mere shell, does not mushroom reliably, and has relatively poor stopping power on either game or man. To develop a fair degree of stopping power in a handgun a bullet should be both heavy (large diameter) and have a flat point, such as a 250 grain .45 caliber with flat point. The .357 Magnum High Velocity revolver cartridge was developed for police use to penetrate automobile bodies. If we used the same bullet at the same velocity (1,450 f.s.) in a .35 caliber rifle we would call it a small game load.

Finally, a short bullet will be spun more correctly and have better gyrostatic stability in a barrel having a much slower twist of rifling than a longer bullet. In .30 caliber, for example, a bullet of 100 grains weight will shoot very accurately in a rifling twist of one turn in twenty inches, but a 170 grain bullet in this rifling would have no stability and would not fly point on.

98. Long, heavy bullets (No. 2 in the illustration). In general these have just the opposite characteristics and behavior from short, light bullets. We refer in particular to a bullet of 170 grains or over as compared to a bullet of 120 grains or lighter in .30 caliber, and proportionately in other calibers. You cannot use as large a charge of powder or obtain as high a muzzle velocity with these bullets, within the limits of permissible chamber pressure, as you can with light bullets. But on the other hand, they overcome the resistance of the air much better than do light bullets, and except at very short distances they give flatter trajectory despite their lower initial velocity, and they also have longer extreme range. They penetrate much deeper in all substances than do light bullets, and if given a soft point, or a hollow point (or even a flat point with lead bullets) they mushroom much more reliably than do light bullets. Thus, except on the smaller animals they have much better killing power than light bullets. Because they fall off much less in their remaining velocity in proportion to their muzzle velocity, they are less deflected by wind than light bullets.

Long bullets because of their greater weight, and because their longer bearing surface in the bore causes greater friction, will develop a higher breech pressure than a light bullet with an equal powder charge. For this reason, in a given caliber, the longer and heavier the bullet is, the lower the velocity with which it can be fired, and the smaller the permissible charge of the same kind of powder. For example, in the .30-06 cartridge, using du Pont I.M.R. No. 4320 powder, the following tabulation indicates the approximate muzzle velocity that can be obtained in a 24 inch barrel with various weights of bullets, without exceeding the permissible pressure limit.

Weight of Bullet Grains	Powder Charge Grains	Muzzle Velocity f.s.
110	59.0	3400
150	54.0	3000
180	51.0	2700
220	49.0	2400

Thus a long, heavy bullet should be chosen for long range target and game shooting, and for satisfactory killing power on big game animals. How long should a bullet be with respect to its diameter? That depends upon many things. Referring again to .30 caliber bullets: because a 180 grain sharp point bullet at a M.V. of 2700 f.s. will buck the wind much better than a 220 grain round nose bullet at a M.V. of 2400 f.s., the former is preferred for long range target practice, and would be preferable on game at longer distances so far as *hitting* is concerned. On the other hand the penetration of the 220 grain bullet and its better mushrooming may make it a better killer on big game. However it is, and perhaps always will be debatable, whether a long, heavy bullet that mushrooms well but holds together, drills a 1½ inch hole through the animal, thus giving a good blood trail to follow, is a more efficient game bullet than a slightly lighter bullet at higher velocity, which expands much more quickly, often more or less "exploding" within the animal, and pulping the tissue in a large crater possibly three-fourths of the way through the animal. The killing power argument will probably be endless.

99. Flat point bullets   (No. 3 in the illustration). These were almost universal in black powder days, and also in the early smokeless, high power period when muzzle velocities ran from 1800 to 2100 f.s., because at these velocities the flat points expanded more reliably than round or sharp points. They are also still a necessity in tubular magazine repeating rifles to avoid any danger of the point of the bullet setting off the primer of the cartridge ahead of it when the rifle recoils and the whole column of cartridges in the magazine is driven rearward rather violently. But when velocities are increased to a M.V. of about 2,300 f.s. or over, flat point bullets tend to expand too quickly, and they sometimes lack the penetration desirable for the largest game.

For revolvers flat point bullets are preferred because, even though a soft lead flat point bullet when it is short and light will not mushroom well at a M.V. of 1,300 f.s., yet it will give better stopping power than round or sharp pointed bullets.

100. Round nose bullets   (No. 2 in the illustration) were designed because they would feed much more reliably into the chambers of rifles than flat point bullets which occasionally hang up on the flat rear end of the barrel just behind the chamber. This form of point was almost a necessity for sure feeding through bolt action rifles before pointed bullets were introduced. Also a round nose bullet may expand slower than a flat point bullet, and thus give better expanding results at velocities over 2,300 f.s.

Before World War II, Western Cartridge Company manufactured a .30 caliber 220 grain soft-point bullet, with round nose and boat tail, and having only a very small amount of lead exposed at the point. They loaded this bullet in their .30-06 cartridges to give a muzzle velocity of 2,300 f.p.s. This bullet had a very enviable reputation for killing well on larger game. Stewart Edward White used it extensively in Africa, and thought it killed better than any other .30 caliber bullet. Old sourdoughs also swore by it for shooting brown bear in Alaska. It was ideal for elk, moose and grizzly, but it would not expand enough to kill well on the softer bodies of deer, sheep and antelope. It also shot with exceptionally fine accuracy.

Because it gave poor killing results on smaller animals, Western discontinued its manufacture after World War II, but they now manufacture an almost exactly similar bullet of .30 caliber and 220 grains, with a flat instead of a boattail base, and load it to a muzzle velocity of 2,400 f.p.s. in their .30-06 cartridge; but they do not particularly feature this cartridge in their advertising, probably because they think it might be used on smaller game with poor results. Many of us think it is one of the very best killing .30 caliber bullets to be had for heavy American game, although it does not have the flat trajectory of the 180-grain bullets loaded to M.V. 2,700 f.p.s. However, except possibly for Alaskan brown bear, the Winchester-Western and Remington-Peters 180-grain bullets give ample killing power for all American big game. There is one thing, however, that this "tip of lead" bullet apparently does better than any other .30 caliber bullet. If, through lack of opportunity, the hunter has to shoot his heavy game through the hind quarters, this bullet, better than most others, will expand and penetrate through the animal's body clear up to the vital chest cavity.

101. Sharp pointed bullets (Nos. 4 and 5 in the illustration) were used to a small extent in the early days of conical bullets, and were finally adopted for military purposes about 1902 to 1905. The advantage for military purposes is that with a given weight and velocity the sharp pointed bullet overcomes the resistance of the air much better than flat or round pointed bullets, has a flatter trajectory, and hence a greater danger space. Also it is less deflected by wind. The effect in flattening the trajectory, however, is not very apparent at velocities less than about 2,300 f.s. For example, in the .30-06 cartridge if a 180 grain bullet be loaded to a M.V. of 2,700 f.s. its remaining velocity at 200 yards will be about 2,300 f.s., and its trajectory over 200 yards will not be appreciably different whether it has a very sharp or a very rounded point. But from 200 yards on the superiority of the sharp pointed bullet in better overcoming the resistance of the air, with consequent flattening of the trajectory will be quite apparent. Just recently the writer conducted a .30-06 drop test. Loaded to a M.V. of 2,700 f.s., and sighted in each case to strike the exact point of aim at 200 yards, a 180 grain bullet with a sharp ogive on a 6-diameter radius dropped 22 inches below the aim at 400 yards, and a round nose bullet of the same weight dropped 27.5 inches.

The degree of sharpness of the point is designated by the radius of the curve on which its point or *ogive* is formed. The illustration (No. 10) shows a bullet with a point having a "6 diameter radius," that is, the radius of the curve is six times the diameter of the bullet.

The penetration of these sharp pointed bullets is rather peculiar. One would ordinarily think that they would always penetrate very deeply, making only a small hole in the target with little destruction in animal tissue. This is exactly what usually happens when the striking velocity is below about 1,800 to 2,000 f.s. Fifty years ago small game hunters used sharp pointed lead bullets for squirrels and grouse in .25 caliber rifles because the usual flat point bullet destroyed too much meat.

The sharp pointed .25 caliber bullet did not make a more severe wound than the present .22 Long Rifle solid bullet. Also a great many hunters using .30 caliber rifles have used the 150 grain sharp pointed Government full jacketed bullet loaded to a M.V. of about 1,600 f.s. for small game including wild turkeys and the smaller fur bearing animals when destruction of meat and skins was undesirable.

The sharp pointed, full jacketed bullet, even at the highest velocities, usually gives deeper penetration in wood than bullets with blunter points. But with remaining velocities in excess of about 2,200 to 2,300 f.s. its behavior in animal tissue, either with or without striking bones, becomes quite unpredictable. Often it is liable to glance and change its direction considerably when it enters the game animal, and it does not surely penetrate in the direction in which it was fired. There have been innumerable cases where such bullets striking square on the side of a big animal have turned in their course so that they emerged from the back or under side of the animal, and others where the bullet tumbled end over end as it penetrated, "buzzing" as it were through the animal, and making a severe wound as though it had been a soft point or expanding bullet. If a sharp pointed, full jacketed bullet were always to turn over and tumble in this manner it would be most effective for big game, but unfortunately it also often penetrates straight through, making a small hole and a non-stopping wound, and the animal may escape to die several days later in agony. Thus sharp pointed, full jacketed (military) bullets are neither reliable nor humane for use on large game.

Hunters have sometimes used these bullets for big game, trying to make them surely expand or turn over by filing away the gilding metal jacket at the point just enough to expose a small portion of the lead core. Bullets treated in this manner do more often expand or tumble, but not always. Moreover the jacket is weakened, may rupture and the bullet may not reach the target, or the core may shoot through the jacket, leaving the latter lodged in the bore as an obstruction, and the next shot ruins or bursts the barrel. This process is not recommended, and our large factories at present are not attempting to do it, the great majority of their game bullets having round points or being only slightly pointed. American custom makers of metal cased bullets make many soft point, sharp pointed bullets, leaving just a small, sharp tip of lead exposed at the point. There are some objections to this type because the soft and sharp point is liable to be deformed and dulled in handling, or during recoil when the cartridge is in the magazine. Also sometimes this bullet does not expand at all, or expands too quickly and lacks the necessary penetration. Generally speaking these bullets in .22 caliber perform excellently on small animals such as woodchucks and foxes. But usually the jacket of these custom made bullets is hardly thick enough to keep the larger portion of the bullet intact enough to give the desired penetration to the vitals. One maker (Barnes) makes such a bullet with a heavy (strong) jacket, which usually seems to kill well, but generally we lack enough experience with these types of bullets to say that they are practically always certain on big game.

The large ammunition companies in the past have made their sharp pointed expanding bullets by forming a shallow hollow in the point (Western), or by placing a pointed copper wedge in the tip of the bullet, which on striking wedges the front of the bullet open (Remington), or by covering the lead core at the point with a very thin copper jacket which easily mashes (Winchester). It seems to me that the large companies, in their efforts to develop a pointed expanding bullet, have neglected one that they produced that was extremely successful. The .270 W.C.F. cartridge with 130 grain Winchester pointed expanding bullet has made an enviable reputation for quick and instantaneous kills on all American big game—more so than any other cartridge and bullet. This bullet had a very sharp point (6 diameter radius), the lead at the tip being covered with a very thin jacket of copper, also pointed. The base of the jacket, and the sides for about ⅝ths of an inch above the base were extremely thick. It is strange that this successful bullet is no longer being made. Perhaps its makers did not scan the reports from the game fields closely enough.

Other bullets with similar point construction but with thinner jackets at the base did not perform so well.

Probably the most accurate .30 caliber bullet for long-range shooting being made regularly today is the 180-grain boattail Sierra bullet, either the soft point or the full-jacketed "Match King" bullet. But it has been used so little on big game that as yet we have no reliable evidence of its killing power as compared with other bullets.

There are certain types of hunting in which deep and straight penetration is very desirable—elephant hunting for example. Mere destruction of tissue, even fairly vital tissue, will not always kill an elephant quickly enough to prevent its killing the hunter or escaping clear away. For this reason expanding bullets have not been found to be entirely reliable on elephant, and the preferred bullet for hunting them is the full jacketed bullet (English sportsmen call it a "solid" bullet) of .40 to .577 caliber weighing about 400 to 750 grains, driven at a M.V. of about 2,000 to 2,300 f.s. and having a round nose. If aimed right it will always penetrate well into the heart or lungs causing death in a few moments (not always instantaneously even in the heart) or it will break the spine thus "anchoring" the beast. If properly directed it will even penetrate through the great mass of skull bone to the brain, which a soft point bullet will hardly ever do.

The only shot that will invariably kill an elephant in its tracks is the brain shot. The beast must be facing almost side on to the hunter and the bullet must strike in a space about 6 inches in diameter, midway between the eyes and the orifice of the ear to reach the small brain. A fairly heavy and properly shaped full jacketed bullet of about .265 to .300 caliber, and driven at a M.V. of about 2,300 f.s. will make this brain kill on an elephant if it is properly directed just as well as the much heavier bullet from an elephant rifle. The small bullet should be round nosed and the extreme point should preferably be a little flat. The Western Cartridge Company used to make such a bullet in .30 caliber weighing 220 grains, but have now discontinued it. 300 grain bullets are now made in this form for

the .375 H & H Magnum cartridge. A few professional hunters in Africa have used these full jacketed (solid) bullets in
6.5 mm., 7 mm., and .303 caliber for brain shots on elephants,
mainly because the small, light rifles of these calibers were so
much handier, easier to carry, and more accurate than the heavy
12 to 16 pound large bore elephant rifles. But these men were
experienced hunters and cool shots, and moreover they were
backed up by an elephant rifle in the hands of their gunbearer.
These light bullets are decidedly not to be recommended to a
sportsman going to Africa for the first time. They have practically no stopping power on elephants except with a perfectly
placed brain shot.

Some custom made bullets have the point in the shape of
a pencil point or a *spire* instead of the ogive being on a curve
(illustration 5). Many such bullets have given excellent performance, but we are not prepared to state that they overcome
the resistance of the air materially better than those with curved
points.

I watch the performance of bullets day after day, season
after season on the rifle range. Although I have shot well over
a hundred big game animals of most American species, I have
always felt that my own experiences, or that of most hunters,
was not extensive enough to warrant any flat statements. I have
often read most positive statements recommending or con-
demning certain cartridges or bullets when I know for a fact
that the writer has done comparatively little hunting. But when
an old Yukon hunter has shot well over five hundred animals
with a certain bullet, and another Government hunter in Alaska
has shot well over three hundred with another bullet, both
being accurate observers and entirely truthworthy men, and
have reported the results to me, then I begin to sit up and take
notice. And at the present writing I would like to say that reports from the game fields on the type of bullets that have been
available to big game hunters since 1946 do not warrant any
statement that any one of them is any better than another,
caliber, weight, and velocity being nearly alike of course. Sportsmen should always give detailed reports of the performance

of their bullets on game because these, collated and tabulated, are extremely valuable alike to the manufacturer, the hunter, and the handloader.

102. **Boat tails or streamline bullets** (No. 6 in the illustration). These usually have a sharp point formed on about a 6 diameter radius, and the base or stern is tapered at an angle of about nine degrees. A good example is our .30-06, 173 grain boat tailed bullet which was the standard service bullet in our Army from 1925 until 1940, when it was abandoned in favor of a 154 grain pointed, flat base bullet loaded to a M.V. of 2,800 f.s. The muzzle velocity of the boat tailed bullet was 2640 f.s. The reasons for its abandonment were: (1) Its extreme range was not an important military necessity, and made it dangerous for use on many established rifle ranges. (2) It gave greater recoil than the lighter 154 grain bullet, and this imposed greater problems in marksmanship training. (3) It was an expensive bullet both in materials and manufacture. On the other side of the ledger it bucked the wind better than any bullet we have ever used, and in many lots it excelled all other .30 caliber bullets in long range accuracy except only the 180 grain pointed, flat based "Palma" and "International Match" bullets.

A boat tail bullet, shaped like and similar to a racing yacht, presents no material advantage in flight until its remaining velocity has been reduced to about the velocity of sound. Thus with two 173 grain pointed bullets, one with a flat base and the other a 9 degree boat tail, both with a M.V. of 2,640 f.s., up to about 500 yards the angle of elevation, and consequently the trajectory is identical. At 600 yards the boat tailed bullet begins to show slightly greater remaining velocity and a lower angle of elevation, and this superiority increases as the range increases. Finally the extreme range of the boat tailed bullet is about 5,500 yards, and the flat base bullet about 3,700 yards. Considering present day requirements the only real advantage of the boat tailed bullet is lessened wind deflection beyond 500 yards.

Accurate boat tailed bullets are more difficult to make than flat based bullets. Generally their form has to be more perfect, and they have to be swaged harder. All successful ones have usually been metal cased, and lead alloy bullets in this form have not been markedly successful. They seem to present no superiority as game bullets, although the old Western 180 grain open point boat tail bullet was a very successful big game bullet.

103. Expanding bullets. In black powder days practically all bullets were made of lead, slightly hardened with small additions of tin or antimony. In rifles these were shot at muzzle velocities of from 1,300 to 1,600 f.s. If these bullets were fairly long and were given a flat point they usually mushroomed quite uniformly on game. Sometimes more expansion was desired and some lead bullets had a hole formed in their points to make them expand easier, these being called "hollow point" or "express" bullets.

On the introduction of jacketed bullets for high power rifles about 1898, expanding bullets were made with the copper, gilding metal, or cupro-nickel jacket covering the base and sides of the bullet nearly to the point, but with the lead core exposed at the point, the point being either round or flat. Sometimes the core was exposed for as much as a quarter inch down from the point. Such bullets are termed "soft point" bullets. When such a bullet strikes game, normally the soft lead point expands to possibly twice its diameter, but the remainder of the bullet inclosed in the jacket does not expand, hence the bullet takes on the form of a mushroom, makes a wider wound in the animal, and is a more effective killer than the full jacketed bullet which does not expand.

It was soon found that if much lead was exposed the bullet might mushroom ideally on the relatively soft bodies of deer, but on larger animals like moose, elk, and grizzly there would be too much expansion, and the bullet would often fly to pieces and fail to penetrate deeply enough. So manufacturers began to make two types of soft point bullets, one with thin jackets and much lead exposed for deer, and the other with less lead exposed and thicker jackets for larger game. This caused some confusion because rifle hunters, unlike shotgun hunters, had not become accustomed to selecting their bullets (shot) according to the game they were hunting. The absurdity of the situation was reached one fall in the State of Maine (essentially a deer state) where the retailers were stocked up by their jobbers with heavy game bullets only, which shot clear through the deer without expanding, and the deer kept on going.

At the same time many bullets were made with the soft points covered with very thin jackets to prevent deformation in handling or with hollow points as already described. All these were more or less open to the criticism that on some game they would not expand enough, on others they expanded quite ideally, and on some others they expanded entirely too quickly.

About 1938 the larger ammunition companies designed new expanding bullets which they hoped would be equally effective on all sizes of big game. They were constructed generally with a point that expanded easily even on deer, but the rear two-thirds of the bullet had a much heavier or reinforced jacket. The point thus always expanded well, and the base usually remained intact to give deep penetration. Such bullets are now being produced almost exclusively for big game hunting, and are called by various names—"Core Lokt," "Belted," and "Silvertip." On the whole these bullets have performed well on all species of game, although even ten years after their introduction reports of their actual effect on game are too fragmentary to permit us to state that any one type shows a superiority over the others. Of course you have to consider the cartridge and the bullet made for it. The .30-30 cartridge with a bullet of any of these types would hardly be called an elk or grizzly bear load. There is still, and always will be need for reports on behavior of bullets on game, both the behavior of the game when struck, and the nature of the wound. So far as we can generalize on bullet effect on game, if the brain or spinal column is not struck, quick killing depends almost entirely upon the amount of vital tissue that is destroyed. A bullet that enters the chest cavity and destroys much lung tissue, and even penetrates the heart will usually kill quite promptly, but the animal frequently runs some little distance before dropping. Such a death rush should not be considered as a failure of the bullet in any sense.

LEAD ALLOY BULLETS

104. In black powder days (prior to about 1896) all bullets were made of lead, usually slightly hardened with a small percentage of tin or antimony to prevent their leading the bore. They were formed with grooves around their cylindrical bearing surfaces, and these grooves were filled with grease or wax to lubricate them and thus further prevent their leading the bore of the rifle. Lead bullets are still used almost universally (except for military purposes) in revolver cartridges, but in centerfire factory loaded rifle cartridges they have been almost entirely replaced by metal cased or jacketed bullets.

There are two reasons for this: (1) Because the demand has been for greater velocity, meaning larger powder charges that generate hotter gas which melts the bases of lead bullets while they are traveling through the bore. Given extremely high velocity lead bullets may strip in the rifling. (2) It is difficult to prevent a certain amount of deformation of the soft bullets during manufacture, shipping and use. Metal cased bullets stand up much better under handling and are not deformed so much when they jump from the case through the throat of the chamber into the rifling. They are more accurate for this reason.

However, lead alloy bullets still present many advantages to the handloader, perhaps the chief being economy. Metal cased bullets must still be bought from their manufacturer through retail dealers (See the Appendix for retail dealers) and cost from $2.00 to $6.00 per hundred depending on weight and caliber. But if the handloader has the necessary mould and accessories (which are not expensive) he can easily make his own lead alloy bullets for the cost of the lead alone, which brings their cost down to only a small fraction of metal cased bullets. It is just beginning to be possible for handloaders to make their metal cased bullets also, but while these are cheaper the economy is not as great as with lead bullets.

Lead alloy bullets are still very useful and in many cases highly desirable in rifles, while in revolvers they are a necessity. In rifles they can be used for target practice at short and mid ranges for both economy and to lessen the wear on rifle barrels, and for use on target ranges where the higher velocity metal cased bullet loads might be unsafe. They are also useful for reduced loads for small game shooting and for indoor gallery practice. The heavier lead alloy bullets may also be satisfactory for large game. In addition, of course, there are many of the old black powder rifles still in use, and for these lead bullets are a necessity.

105. Varieties of lead bullets.   The various reloading tool manufacturers can supply bullet moulds and other accessories for making hundreds of different calibers, weights and types of lead alloy bullets. These various bullets are illustrated and described in the *Ideal Handbook* (Lyman), the *B & M Handbook* (Belding and Mull), and the catalogs of the Modern Bond, Hensley & Gibbs, and Cramer companies. A few of these bullets will be described here, sufficient to illustrate the general principles.

106. Plain base bullets.   There are two general types of lead bullets for use in rifles. One type has a plain, unprotected base. Such bullets are used with the cooler burning powders and when loaded to not exceed a M.V. of about 1,600 f.s. If loaded with higher pressure powders and large charges in an effort to secure higher velocity the resulting hotter powder gases may melt the base of the bullet as it passes up the bore and the accuracy will be exceedingly poor. Plain base bullets are used in revolver cartridges to the practical exclusion of all others, even in factory cartridges, the gases from the smaller powder charges not being hot enough to melt the bases of these bullets.

107. **Gas check bullets.** The other type of lead alloy bullet is called a "gas check" bullet. A small hollow copper disc or cup is pressed onto the base of the lead bullet, the base being formed or shaped to receive it and hold it firmly in place. This cup or gas check protects the lead base of the bullet from being melted by the powder gases. Slightly larger powder charges can be used, and also hotter burning kinds of powder, thus making slightly higher velocities possible. Such bullets are used in rifles only, and in general can be loaded to muzzle velocities from about 1,800 to 2,300 f.s. They are suitable for use at longer ranges than plain base bullets, and some years ago were used very extensively in .30 caliber rifles for target practice up to 600 yards. They are also highly satisfactory for varmint shooting up to 150 to 200 yards, and the heavier of these bullets in the larger calibers and with flat points can also be used very successfully for deer shooting. The cartridges loaded with them wear the rifle barrel less than do higher velocity cartridges loaded with metal cased bullets. These gas check bullets are very easy to prepare and handload, and thus are much more economical than metal cased bullets. The gas checks, procurable from many reloading tool dealers, cost about $1.50 a thousand.

108. **Grooves and Cannelures.** Practically all lead bullets of either type have grooves formed around the circumference of their cylindrical diameters to hold the grease or wax necessary for their lubrication. This lubrication reduces friction in the bore and prevents the soft bullet leading the bore. Many bullets, particularly revolver bullets and those designed for use in tubular magazine rifles, have an additional groove called the "cannelure" into which the mouth of the case is slightly crimped to make the bullet more secure in the case neck. When such bullets are used in bolt action or single shot rifles the case is usually not crimped, and this cannelure also is filled with lubricant.

109. Wear on Barrels. It is not quite proper to state that plain base and gas check lead alloy bullets cause less wear on rifle barrels than metal cased bullets. It is the hot gases of the powder charges used with the high velocity metal cased bullet loads that cause wear and shorten the accuracy life of barrels by eroding or burning the bore just in front of the chamber. There are cases where centerfire rifles have been fired with lead bullets and cool burning powders for as many as 200,000 rounds with little or no wear on the bore, and likewise instances where similar cool burning powder charges with metal cased bullets have been used for upwards of 20,000 rounds with little or no wear.

With some of the ultra high velocity wildcat cartridges using very large powder charges the gases so erode the bore that the barrels become inaccurate after about 500 rounds have been fired. The most erosive factory loaded cartridge is probably the .220 Swift, the accuracy life of its barrels being about 1800 rounds when chrome molybdenum barrels are used, or about 2,500 rounds when the harder chrome rustless steels are used. .22 Varminter and .219 Donaldson Wasp barrels used with full loads usually go about 3,500 rounds before any falling off in accuracy is noticeable. .270 Winchester rifles are also about in this class. .30-06 barrels run about 5,000 rounds, and the other cartridges like the .30-30 and .35 Remington run well above 10,000 rounds of accuracy life. Of course this presupposes that the barrel is given perfect care and is not allowed to rust. Also it depends upon the rapidity of fire, as barrels used in rapid fire heat up to a much higher temperature than when fired more slowly. There is reason to believe that a single round fired from a cold barrel causes little or no erosion.

110. Fit for lead bullets. In black powder days it was quite common for lead bullets to be made with the diameter of their cylindrical bearing surface about .001″ to .003″ smaller than the groove diameter of the barrel. Black powder on being ignited gave more of a sudden blow to the base of the bullet than does smokeless powder, and this blow upset or immediately enlarged these slightly smaller bullets so that as they entered the bore they were expanded to completely fill the bore to the bottom of the grooves. However, I had considerable experience with black powder and lead bullet loading in my early days, and I always found it was best to use a bullet of exactly the same diameter as the groove diameter of the barrel.

But smokeless powder in its initial ignition gives more of a push than a blow to the bullet, and does not upset it so completely. It is very desirable to use lead bullets that have the same diameter as the groove diameter of the barrel, or even about .001″ to .002″ larger than the groove diameter. In .30 caliber a bullet diameter as much as .003″ larger than the groove diameter seems to work about as well as .001″ larger. But sometimes in an individual barrel a small change in bullet diameter within these limits will give better accuracy, possibly because the change has slightly affected the velocity or bore friction which has caused the bullet to leave the muzzle at the slowly moving end rather than the rapidly moving center of the barrel vibration.

Bullet moulds are usually made to cast bullets about .003″ larger than the common standard groove diameter of the barrels (see the Appendix for table of groove diameters of various rifles) and the reloading tool makers provide sizing tools, or combined lubricating and sizing tools which will size these bullets to the exact diameter desired.

111. **Measuring groove diameter.** With quantity produced factory made barrels a certain tolerance in dimensions was usual because of the wear on tools and the necessity for economy. Before about 1920 it was quite common to find rifle barrels that varied as much as .003″ from the standard groove diameter. Thus .30 caliber barrels which have a standard groove diameter of .308″ might be found measuring all the way from .3075″ to almost .312″. That was probably the reason why it was common to size lead bullets for these .30 caliber rifles to .311″. But a great improvement was made in machine tools

after about 1920, and today as a rule the best quantity produced factory barrels vary only .001″ in excess of standard diameter. Usually in sizing lead bullets for present day rifles we can take the standard groove diameter (as given in the Appendix) as being close enough to actual diameter. But occasionally it becomes desirable to actually measure the groove diameter of an individual barrel.

Have the barrel perfectly clean, and very lightly lubricated with a thin oil. Obtain or prepare a pure lead bullet or slug that is several thousandths larger than what you expect the groove diameter of the barrel will be. A satisfactory slug can often be made from a buckshot much larger than the groove diameter. Roll it between two hard boards until it assumes a conical or elongated shape about .003″ larger than expected groove diameter. Remove the bolt from the rifle and place the muzzle of the rifle on a soft pine board. Slightly moisten the slug with thin oil and drop it into the chamber. Take a strong steel cleaning rod or ramrod just large enough to run through the bore perfectly, and having a square, flat top. With the rod press the lead slug into the bore, and push it down until it comes to the soft pine board at the muzzle. Sometimes you can push the slug quite easily through the bore with a steady, firm, strong pressure which should not be stopped or varied. In this way it is possible, by noting the pressure on the rod, to feel whether there are any tight or loose places in the bore. But usually I have found that it is difficult if not almost impossible to start the slug into the bore, or to press it through. Instead it is usually necessary to tap with a hammer on the upper end of the cleaning rod, both to start the slug into the bore, and to gradually tap the slug up the bore. When the slug is started each tap with the hammer on the rod should move it about an inch.

When the slug reaches the board at the muzzle, that is when the point of the bullet is right at the muzzle about to emerge, reverse the rifle, hold the fingers of the left hand over the muzzle, and gently tap the base of the slug with the cleaning rod so that it slowly emerges from the muzzle. As it comes out ease it with the fingers, and catch it so it does not become deformed. Then measure this slug with a machinist's micrometer caliper reading in tens of thousandths of an inch. You measure across the diameter of the slug from one raised portion that entered one groove to the opposite raised portion that entered the opposite groove. This will give you the groove diameter of that barrel.

112. **Star gauged barrels.** Springfield Armory uses a micrometer measuring instrument called a "star gauge" for measuring the groove and bore diameters of their .22 and .30 caliber barrels. With this very expensive instrument it is possible to measure both the bore and groove diameters of a barrel for every inch of the barrel length from breech to muzzle. This star gauge has been made only for the type of rifling used at Springfield Armory. In the days when the manufacture of Springfield rifles was at its height (prior to 1939) all those rifles made specially for National Match use, as well as all .30 caliber sporting and Type T (bull gun) barrels were selected by star gauging. Only those .30 caliber barrels were designated as "star gauged" which proved to have a bore diameter of not less than .3000″ or more than .3005″ and a groove diameter of not less than .3080″ or more than .3085″, and that had no spots or pockets throughout the bore that differed more than .0002″ from average diameter. Star gauging presents no mysterious or particular advantage to the barrel. It simply means that the diameters of bore and grooves throughout the barrel are close to the ideal standard.

113. **Alloy for lead bullets.** It has already been stated that lead bullets are usually alloyed with a small amount of tin or antimony or both to make them slightly harder so that they will not lead the bore. The amount of tin or antimony used is designed by proportionate weight. Thus an alloy composed of ten pounds of lead to one pound of tin was called a 1 to 10 tin and lead alloy, or a 10% tin alloy. In black powder days most of the bullets used in center fire rifles were alloyed 1 to 16 or 1 to 20 tin and lead. Generally speaking the quicker

the twist of rifling the greater the proportion of tin used to make the bullet harder. Schuetzen riflemen using .32-40 and .38-55 black powder rifles experimented a lot with various tempers of bullets to get one that caused the most perfect bullet upset in the bore and thus gave the best accuracy.

Today it has been found that generally for lead alloy bullets, either plain base or gas check, for use in modern high velocity rifles having quick twists of rifling, the best alloy is a 1 to 10 tin and lead alloy, or an alloy of 90 parts by weight of lead, 5 parts of tin, and 5 parts of antimony. This 90-5-5 alloy is often called the Ideal Alloy, or Ideal Bullet Metal No. 2 because it was originally developed in conjunction with Ideal reloading tools by the Lyman Gun Sight Corporation. This corporation continues to sell Ideal Bullet Metal No. 2 (90-5-5) in six pound ingots to handloaders, and it is very convenient for those handloaders who mould their own bullets. This Ideal Bullet Metal No. 2 may be used as a basis for making softer alloys according to the following table.

```
1 tin to 10 lead equivalent to No. 2 Metal
1 tin to 15 lead equivalent to 2 parts No. 2 Metal to 1 part  lead
1 tin to 20 lead equivalent to 1 part  No. 2 Metal to 1 part  lead
1 tin to 25 lead equivalent to 2 parts No. 2 Metal to 3 parts lead
1 tin to 30 lead equivalent to 1 part  No. 2 Metal to 1 parts lead
1 tin to 40 lead equivalent to 1 part  No. 2 Metal to 1 parts lead
```

Bullets for revolvers should not be softer than 1 part of tin to 40 parts of lead, and alloys as hard as 1 to 10 may be used. Often quite a little experimenting is necessary with alloys in preparing revolver bullets to get just the right alloy for an individual revolver that gives fine accuracy but does not lead the bore. But with smokeless powders and the rifles of today the 1 to 10 tin and lead alloy or the Ideal Bullet Metal No. 2 seems to work excellently in almost all powder loads that are proper for lead bullets. The reason for using antimony is that it has a higher melting point than tin, and accordingly alloys with antimony are not so liable to suffer from powder gases melting the bases of bullets, and consequently slightly larger powder charges can be used with this alloy.

When for economy cable sheathing, storage battery plates, plumber solder, and type metal is used for lead it is almost impossible to accurately determine the hardness of the alloy unless one has a lead tester such as made by the Potter Engineering Company that tests the hardness of a slab or ingot of lead by forcing a small steel ball into the lead in much the same manner as Brinnell hardness is measured. Then if the metal is not of the required hardness other kinds of metal can be added to make it right.

114. **Leading.**   Lead bullets deposit lead in the bore of a weapon for many reasons—too soft an alloy, too little lubrication, too small or too large a bullet, too high a velocity, too hot a powder charge, or a rough bore. Lead deposited in the bore means inaccuracy. Generally in rifles it appears as smears or occasionally as lumps of metal which look darker than the bore metal. It is generally distributed through the bore, although in some cases the lead may be deposited in the bullet seat. In revolvers it is usually found in the cone at the rear end of the bore, or smeared through the barrel.

Leading can be prevented by attending to one or all of the causes listed above, all except one. A rough bore will always lead with lead alloy bullets because the rough surface tears lead particles from the bullet as would sandpaper or a file. In a rough barrel use only metal cased bullets.

Leading can almost always be removed with a brass wire bristle brush. In aggravated cases roughen up the surface of the lead deposit in the bore with the brass brush. Put a small amount of mercury within and cork both ends of the barrel. Tilt the barrel end for end for a few minutes, pour out the mercury which will have amalgamated the lead, use the brass brush, then clean with a powder solvent. In a very bad case this treatment may have to be repeated several times.

115. **Typical lead bullets and their use.**   We have no space to illustrate and describe all of the many hundreds of lead bullets for which various reloading tool makers can provide moulds. For these please see the handbooks and cata-

logs of the manufacturers. In the following photographs we illustrate certain typical lead bullets and give briefly the cartridges to which they seem best adapted, and in general the type of loads that have seemed best with them. Lead bullets are a little more temperamental than metal cased bullets. For the best results in any individual rifle it may be desirable to slightly modify the exact diameter, temper of the bullet, and powder charge. We believe that no attempt should be made to obtain extremely high velocity with lead alloy bullets. Rather we should work for fine accuracy and to meet our requirements for game bullets. Handloading and experimenting with them is a very interesting pastime, and very profitable. If you get unusually good results, or poor results, we believe that you should report them to the Technical Staff, National Rifle Association. The Technical Staff wants to know about such matters so they will be in a better position to fully inform the members of the N.R.A. who write to them for information.

Bond
A-224525

Bond
B-257693

Bond
F-257730

Ideal
257361

Bond
B-280780

116. Modern Bond Bullet No. A-224525.   50 grains, gas check. One of the best lead alloy bullets for the .22 Hornet and .218 Bee cartridges. Cast bullets 1 to 10 alloy, and size to .224", seating them to just touch the lands. Best powder charges known are 7 to 9 grains of Hercules No. 2400 powder.

117. Modern Bond Bullet No. B-257693.   86 grains, plain base. Cast 1 to 10 alloy. Size to .258". For .25-20 cartridges use 8 to 9 grains of Hercules No. 2400, or 8 to 9 grains of du Pont No. 4759 powder. For .25-35 cartridges use 9 to 11 grains of du Pont No. 4759 powder.

118. Modern Bond Bullet No. F-257730. 89 grains, gas check. Cast 1 to 10 alloy and size to .258". For .250-3000 Savage and .257 Roberts use 12 to 14 grains du Pont No. 4759 powder. Very accurate.

119. Lyman Ideal Bullet No. 257361. 82 grains, plain base. A squirrel bullet. Cast of 1 to 10 alloy. Size .258". For .25-20 use 8 grains Hercules 2400. For .25-35 use 8 to 9 grains du Pont 4759 with Winchester 115 or Remington 2½ primers. For .250-3000 Savage or .257 Roberts try 4.9 grains Hercules Bullseye. All 50 yard loads that won't spoil meat.

120. Modern Bond Bullet No. B-280780. 109 grains, gas check. For .270 W.C.F. Cast 1 to 10 alloy and size to .280". 14 to 16 grains du Pont No. 4759. Seat bullets to touch lands. A very accurate small game or target load. Sighted for 50 yards, bullet drops about 2½ inches at 100 yards.

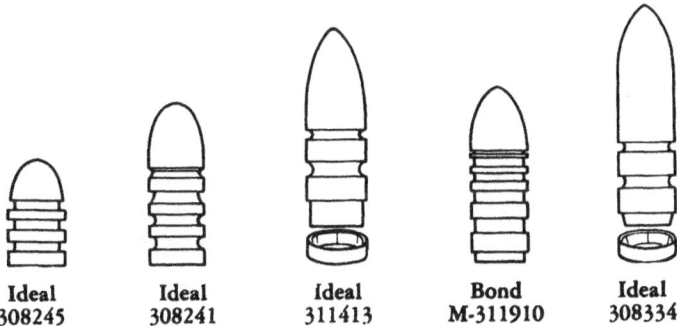

Ideal	Ideal	Ideal	Bond	Ideal
308245	308241	311413	M-311910	308334

121. Lyman Ideal Bullet No. 308245. 87 grains, plain base. For light gallery loads in .30 cal. rifles. Cast 1 to 10 alloy and size to .311". Use 3½ grains Hercules Bullseye powder.

122. Lyman Ideal Bullet No. 308241. 154 grains, plain base. Cast 1 to 10 alloy and size to .311". For .30-30,

.30-40 and .30-06 use 10 to 12 grains du Pont 4759 powder. An extremely satisfactory bullet that has been used very extensively for 40 years for 100 to 200 yard target shooting and small game.

123. Lyman Ideal Bullet No. 311413. 160 grains, gas check. The Squib bullet. Cast 1 to 10 alloy. Size to .311″. For the .30-40 cartridge use 14 to 16 grains of du Pont No. 4759, or 21 grains of Hercules Lightning powder. For the .30-06 cartridge use 16 to 18 grains du Pont No. 4759 or 23 grains Hercules Lightning powder. A very fine bullet for hunters. With the lighter charges will not spoil meat on grouse, and with the charges of Lightning powder it is fine for woodchucks to about 150 yards.

124. Modern Bond Bullet No. M-311910. 154 grains, gas check. Cast 1 to 10 alloy and size to .311″. Very fine in the .30-06 cartridge. When cast with a hollow point it is extremely accurate with 18 grains of du Pont No. 4759 powder, and is fine for woodchucks to 150 yards.

125. Lyman Ideal Bullet No. 308344. 194 grains, gas check. Cast 1 to 10 alloy and size to .311″. Seat bullet so that the front bearing portion extends into and just touches the lands. Used single loading in the .30-06 cartridge, with 23 grains of Hercules Lightning powder it is an exceedingly satisfactory bullet for target practice up to 600 yards, and has been used very extensively by the National Guard for target practice in years past.

126. Belding & Mull Bullet No. 322169. 188 grains, gas check. Cast 1 to 10 alloy. Size to .323″ or leave unsized. For 8mm (7.9mm) German Mauser Military rifles. Use 22 grains Hercules Lightning powder, and seat bullet out of the case sufficiently to contact the lands, single loading if necessary.

127. Lyman Ideal Bullet No. 321232. 170 grains, plain base. Cast 1 to 16 alloy, and size to .321″. Very fine and

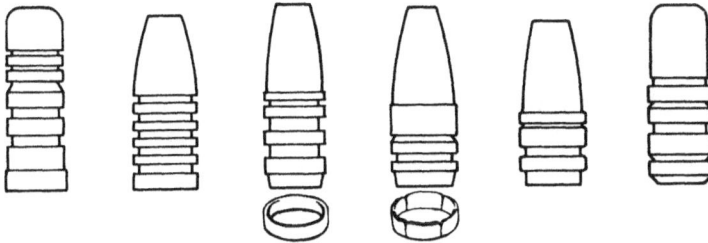

B & M	Ideal	Ideal	Ideal	Cramer	B & M
322169	321232	321297	338320	9-D	359220

accurate in .32-40 single shot rifles with 12 to 14 grains of du Pont No. 4759 powder and Winchester 115 or Remington 2½ primer, bullet seated to touch lands. In a Winchester single shot barrel measuring .3205-inch groove diameter this bullet with the above load gave the best lead bullet accuracy the writer ever obtained with bullet seated in the case.

128. Lyman Ideal Bullet No. 321297. 181 grains, gas check. Size to .321" and cast 1 to 10 alloy. For .32 Winchester Special cartridge. Load with 20 to 21 grains Hercules Lightning powder and Winchester 115 primer. Crimp bullet in the upper cannelure. Same charge for .32-40 repeating rifles. This flat pointed bullet should be O.K. for deer. When the writer was a boy he remembers a long discussion as to whether the .32-40 or the .45-90 cartridge was best for deer; black powder and low velocity of course. While neither side proved its point, there was ample evidence that the .32-40 low power cartridge (165 grain flat point lead bullet at a M.V. of 1440 f.s.) had ample killing power for deer, and this heavier bullet at a higher velocity should be at least equally as suitable.

129. Lyman Ideal Bullet No. 338320. 195 grains, gas check. Cast 1 to 10 alloy. Size to .340". For .33 W.C.F. cartridge. Use 28 grains Hercules Lightning powder and crimp bullet in top cannelure. Good for game including deer.

130. Cramer Bullet No. 9-D. 190 grains, gas check. Cast 1 to 10 alloy and size bullet to .350". For .348 Winchester. Use 31 grains du Pont 4198 or 28 grains Hercules Lightning powder and crimp bullet. Good for deer.

131. Belding & Mull Bullet No. 359220. 225 grains, gas check. Size to .359" and cast 1 to 10 alloy. For .35 Remington cartridge with 26 grains of Hercules HiVel powder. Crimp bullet in top cannelure just below the dirt scraping groove. Good for deer, but may not surely operate autoloading rifle mechanisms.

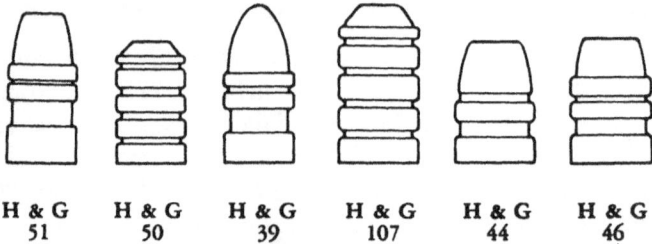

| H & G 51 | H & G 50 | H & G 39 | H & G 107 | H & G 44 | H & G 46 |

132. Hensley & Gibbs Bullet No. 51. 160 grains, plain base. Cast 1 to 16 alloy. Size to .358". For .38 S & W Special cartridge. Powder charges: 3.5 grains of Hercules Bullseye or 5.0 grains du Pont P-5066 powder will give a M.V. of about 900 f.s., or 5.6 grains Hercules Unique powder will give a M.V. of about 1010 f.s. Crimp bullet in upper crimping cannelure. A good stopper because of its flat point.

133. Hensley & Gibbs Bullet No. 50. 146 grains, plain base. Wad cutter bullet. Cast 1 to 16 alloy. Size to .358". For .38 S & W Special cartridge. Use 3.5 grains of Hercules Bullseye, or 5.0 grains du Pont P-5066 powder. M.V. about 960 f.s. Crimp in front crimping cannelure. This is the most popular bullet made for target shooting in .38 Special revolvers as it cuts a clean, full sized round hole in the paper target thus giving the shooter the full count for his shot, because it is extremely accurate to 50 yards, and because of its light recoil. More of these bullets have been cast and handloaded in the past fifteen years than any other caliber or type of lead alloy bullet, police departments and clubs using literally thousands and thousands of them. Bullet rather liable to keyhole beyond 50 yards.

134. Hensley & Gibbs Bullet No. 39. 158 grains, plain base. Cast 1 to 16 alloy and size to .358". Similar to standard factory bullet. For .38 S & W Special cartridge. Use 3.5 grains Hercules Bullseye or 5.0 grains du Pont P-5066 powder, crimping in top cannelure.

135. Hensley & Gibbs Bullet No. 107. 245 grains, plain base. Cast 1 to 16 alloy and size to .428". For .44 S & W Special cartridge. Use 4.0 grains Hercules Bullseye or 5.6 grains du Pont No. P-5066 powder. Crimp in top cannelure. A wad cutter bullet fine for target shooting to 50 yards.

136. Hensley & Gibbs Bullet No. 44. 240 grains, plain base. Cast 1 to 16 alloy and size to .428". For best stopping power in .44 S & W Special cartridge. Use 4.5 grains Hercules Bullseye or 6.8 grains du Pont P-5066 powder. Crimp in top cannelure.

137. Hensley & Gibbs Bullet No. 46. 240 grains, plain base. Cast 1 to 16 alloy and size to .452". For .45 Colt revolver cartridge. Use 5.0 grains Hercules Bullseye or 7.0 grains du Pont P-5066 powder to give a M.V. of about 785 f.s., or for maximum killing power use 10 grains Hercules Unique powder to give a M.V. of about 1,000 f.s. Crimp in top cannelure.

138. Lyman Ideal Bullet No. 375296. 280 grains, gas check. Cast 1 to 10 alloy and size to .380" for .38-55 rifles, and to .376" for .375 H & H Magnum rifles. Ideal Bullet No. 375449 may be better for .375 Magnum as it sizes better to .376".

For .38-55 rifles use 29 grains Hercules Hi-Vel No. 2 powder giving a M.V. of about 1650 f.s. Seat bullet to touch lands in single shot rifles, or crimp in top groove for repeating rifles. A quite powerful and good deer load.

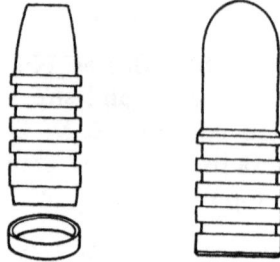

Ideal
375296

Ideal
457125

For .375 H & H Magnum rifles size bullet to .278", and use 25 grains of Hercules Lightning or 32 grains Hercules Hi-Vel No. 2 powder with Winchester No. 120 primer. Seat bullet to just touch lands. A very fine load for deer that does not destroy much meat or give anything like the recoil of the factory loads.

139. Lyman Ideal Bullet No. 457125.   500 grains, plain base. Cast 1 to 16 alloy and size to .458". The old reliable 500 grain service bullet for the .45-70 Springfield rifle, and the one that always gave the best accuracy and killing power. Use 70 grains Fg black powder only. A fine target and big game load superior to all lighter bullets.

139.1. Gas Check Revolver Bullets. When we use heavy powder charges in modern, heavy frame revolvers for the .38 Special, .38-44, and .357 Magnum cartridges we frequently have trouble from the hot gases melting the base of the lead bullet, and from leading. To enable heavier powder charges, within the pressure limitation of the weapon, to be used, and thus obtain higher velocities, Mr. Ray C. Thompson, Box 216, Grand Marais, Minn., can furnish moulds for gas check bullets of these calibers, weighing about 146, 153, and 161 grains. These bullets have hollow points, and loaded to permissible velocities in these revolvers, they probably give greater stopping power than other hand cast bullets. See Tables of Charges.

139.2. New Gas Check Bullets. The Lyman Gun Sight Corporation announce the availability of Ideal bullet moulds for the following new gas check bullets designed by H. Guy Loverin. I am indebted to Paul G. Mansfield, New Boston, N. H., for suggestions as to some suitable powder charges for them. In general these bullets should be cast of an alloy 10 to 1, lead and tin, or Ideal Bullet Metal No. 2, and should be lubricated and sized to the particular groove diameter of the rifle, or not more than .001″ to .003″ over groove diameter. They should be seated in the case so that the ogive or forward grooves of the bullet just contact the lands.

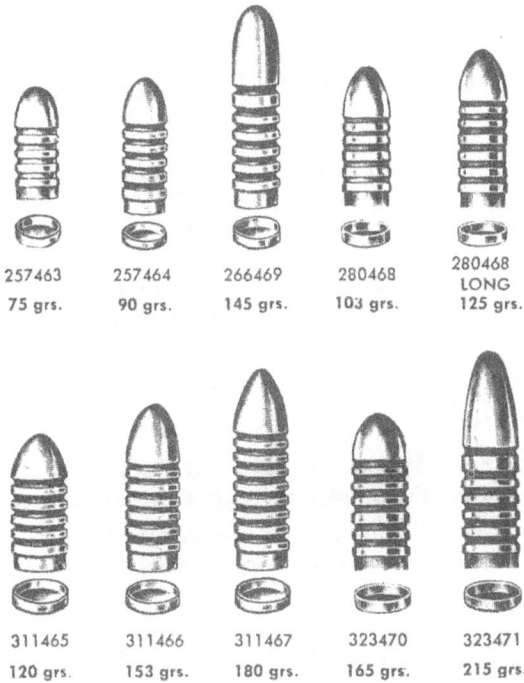

257463	257464	266469	280468	280468 LONG
75 grs.	90 grs.	145 grs.	103 grs.	125 grs.

311465	311466	311467	323470	323471
120 grs.	153 grs.	180 grs.	165 grs.	215 grs.

257463 — 75 grains. A short range bullet for .25 caliber high power rifles. Suggested charge for .250-3000 Savage: 15.5 grains 4198. For .257 Roberts: 16 grains 4198.

257464 — 90 grains. A heavier and slightly longer ranged bullet for .25 caliber high power rifles. Use 19 to 22 grains 4198 depending on size of case.

Either of the above bullets are fine for practice firing, or for small game and varmints when it is not desired to spoil meat or pelts. Fine wild turkey bullets.

266469 — 145 grains. A nice bullet for use in 6.5mm Mauser, Mannlicher or Japanese rifles. 20 grains of 4198 powder burns clean and usually gives good accuracy.

280468 — 103 grains, and 280468 Long — 125 grains. These are fine bullets for .270 rifles, together with the 280780 Loverin bullet (see original text). Usually bullets sized to about .2805 give best results. For 103 grain bullet use 16 grains 4198 or 16 grains 4759. For 125 grain bullet use 24.5 grains 3031.

311465 — 120 grains. The best light bullet for .30 caliber rifles. For .30-30 use 15 grains 4759. For .30-40 or .300 Savage use 18 grains 4759. For .30-06 use 20 grains 4759.

311466 — 133 grains. A fine medium range bullet for all .30 caliber rifles, and for practice shooting. For .30-30 use 14 grains 4759 or 20 grains 2400. For .300 Savage use 18 grains 4759. For .30-40 use 18 grains 4759, 16 grains 2400, or 18 grains 4227.

311467 — 180 grains. Fine for long range, up to 500 yards in .30-06. For moderate ranges use 20 grains 4759 or 25 grains 4198. For long range 30 grains of Hi-Vel No. 2 or 35 grains 3031. Shoot long range loads slowly so as not to heat barrel up too much.

323470 — 165 grains. The best bullet for .32-40 and 8mm rifles. In .32-40 use 16 grains 4759. In 8mm, 20 grains 4759.

323471 — 215 grains. A good heavy bullet for 8mm rifles. Use 28 grains 4198, 30 grains Hi-Vel No. 2, or 36 grains 3031.

Recent Gas-check Bullet Technique. Mr. Eric M. Farr, a careful experimental rifleman, has further developed methods of loading gas-check bullets to obtain very excellent accuracy. His work has been confined to a match rifle chambered for the .30-40 Krag cartridge having a Pfeiffer barrel with .308 to .3082-inch groove diameter, 12 inch twist, and outside dimensions 27¼ x 1¼ x 1 inch. He used Modern Bond Bullet No. 311890 and Ideal Bullet No. 311466 with gas checks, which were cast in an electric furnace with bottom spout to eliminate porous bases. Bullets were lubricated by the pan method with automobile water pump grease as described in the latter portion of par. 149. Then to obtain the greatest concentricity these lubricated bullets were sized point first to .311-inch in the special die shown in the cut. Bullets were seated in case necks carefully expanded to .311-inch so the ogive just touched the lands when loaded in the rifle. The powder charge in all cases was 20 grains of 4198 powder which gave about M.V. 1800 f.s. Both Western 8½ and Winchester 120 primers were used.

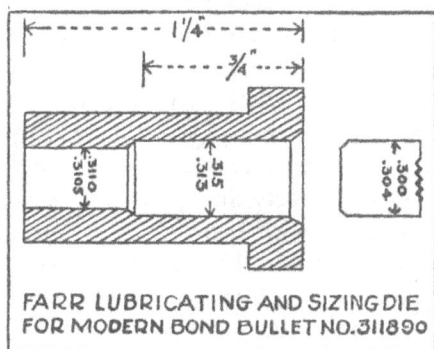

FARR LUBRICATING AND SIZING DIE
FOR MODERN BOND BULLET NO. 311890

The rifle was fired at 100 yards from bench rest. Best accuracy was obtained at temperatures around 60° F, and groups ran from .37-inch to .98-inch for five consecutive shots. Mr. Farr suggests close attention to all the above details including the selection of a case that will use 4198 powder to give M.V. 1800 f.s. or slightly less, in order to obtain the finest accuracy. Note that Mr. Farr's groups are equal to the finest accuracy that has been obtained with jacketed bullets in .30 caliber barrels. Probably we will soon be shooting bench rest matches for rifles using cast lead bullets.

140. Bullet weight in revolvers. A revolver barrel rises in recoil as soon as the bullet starts to move forward from the cylinder-chamber. The bullet velocity is relatively low and the barrel time is long so that before the bullet has left the muzzle the muzzle has risen an appreciable amount. Accordingly revolvers have front sights that stand higher above the axis of the bore than do the rear sight, and when aimed the bore points slightly below the bullseye. When the bullet leaves the bore the muzzle has recoiled upward so that then the bore points at a spot just slightly above the bullseye to allow for the drop of the bullet.

In a revolver a heavy bullet at a relatively low velocity will have a longer barrel time, the muzzle will rise more in recoil before the bullet leaves it, and consequently it will strike higher on the target than will a light bullet at higher velocity. The more we lighten the bullet, and the greater the velocity we give it, the quicker it gets out the muzzle, and the lower it strikes on the target. All this is precisely the opposite of what might be expected from experience with rifles.

The above does not necessarily hold with automatic pistols because here the barrel alone recoils at first against the recoil spring, and the upward movement of the frame and the whole pistol is delayed until after the bullet has left the muzzle.

CASTING LEAD ALLOY BULLETS

141. Tools required. The following tools and accessories will be required for casting bullets:

Bullet mould.	Blanket or cushion.
Lead melting pot.	Cloth to cover blanket.
Special dipper or ladle.	Old tin pan.
Lubricant.	Cotton gloves.
Furnace.	Chair.
Wooden mallet.	Bench or boxes.

The cast iron melting pot, procurable from reloading tool

THE DUNBAR RELOADING PRESS

Because this new tool carries instantly available both the resizing and
bullet seating dies, and has ample strength for forming metal cased bullets,
it is becoming very popular.

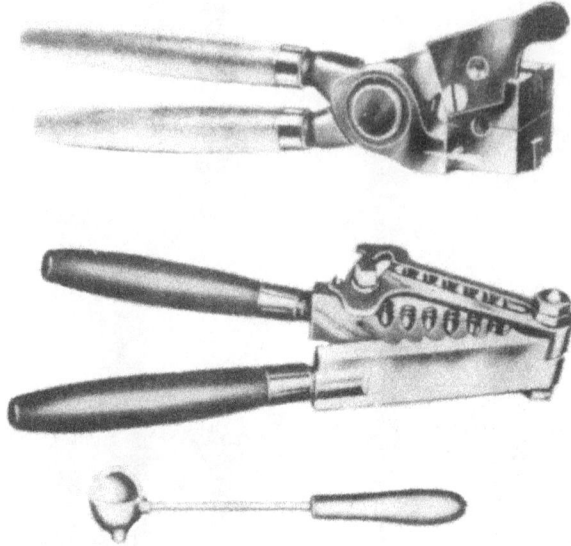

Single cavity and multiple cavity bullet moulds, and the dipper
used with them

makers, should hold not less than three pounds or better, about
10 pounds, for quantity casting. Most electric furnaces have a
greater capacity. A large quantity of molten lead holds its temperature more evenly, and you cast better bullets from it.

The original and most-used melting pot for home handloaders has been the small Ideal (Lyman) pot. If your home
has gas, then an ordinary Bunsen burner is most convenient as
a furnace for it. Also, one of the larger single-burner stoves
like the Coleman, burning gasoline, may be used. An Ideal
Dipper, which has a spout that fits the pouring hole of the
mold, is very necessary to dip the lead from the pot and pour

it into the mold. It works much better than the ordinary plumber's lead ladle, although the plumber's ladle is necessary with a mold having more than two bullet cavities, because the Ideal Dipper does not hold enough metal.

Many handloaders, particularly those molding bullets in quantity, are now using small modern electric furnaces, which have a spout with valve at the bottom of the kettle. The mold is connected with the spout and lead poured into it; thus a·dipper is not needed.

Bullet casting is time-consuming, and a rather hot job at that. You will hardly spend less than two hours in casting a lot of bullets, so it pays to adopt a method and arrangement of the needed equipment so you will be comfortable, to expedite the proceedings, and to do it in the best manner. The arrangement of materials to achieve these ends, and the method of using them in casting, is a little different if you use the old-fashioned Ideal pot and dipper, from that which is best with an electric furnace. Therefore these arrangements and methods of casting will be described separately.

142. **Arrangement of materials.** With the Ideal melting pot, casting will be much easier and less tiring if you can rest your elbows on your knees as you work. Therefore, have a sturdy kitchen chair to sit on, and perhaps a cushion on it. Arrange the Ideal pot on a level sturdy box or low bench so that the top of the melting pot comes on a level with your knees. Cover your lap, knees and lower legs with a heavy apron or piece of canvas to keep off any possible lead spatter. To the left of the pot, and at the same level, have another box on top of which you place a folded blanket on which to drop the cast bullets from the mold. Also have a third bench or box to the

(U.) BULLET SEATING

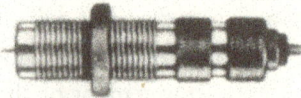

(W.) RIFLE RESIZING
DECAPPING, NECK EXPANDING

(Y.) PISTOL RESIZING

(Z.) PISTOL DECAPPING
& NECK RESIZING

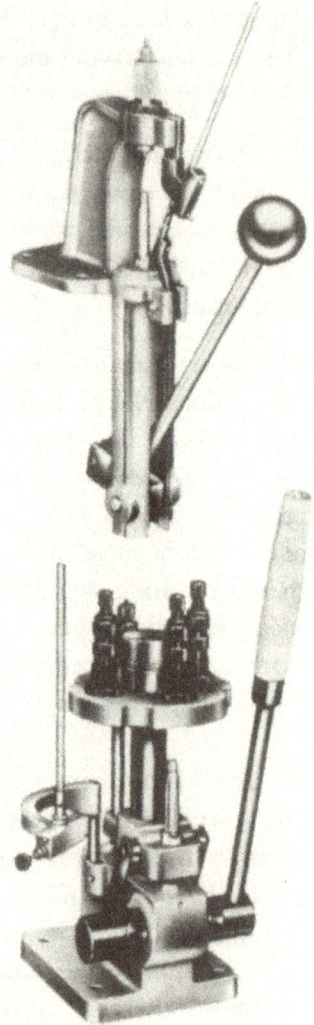

Lyman New Comet Loading Press (above) and Lyman New Turret Loading Press. Also Lyman New 7/8" X 14 Dies.

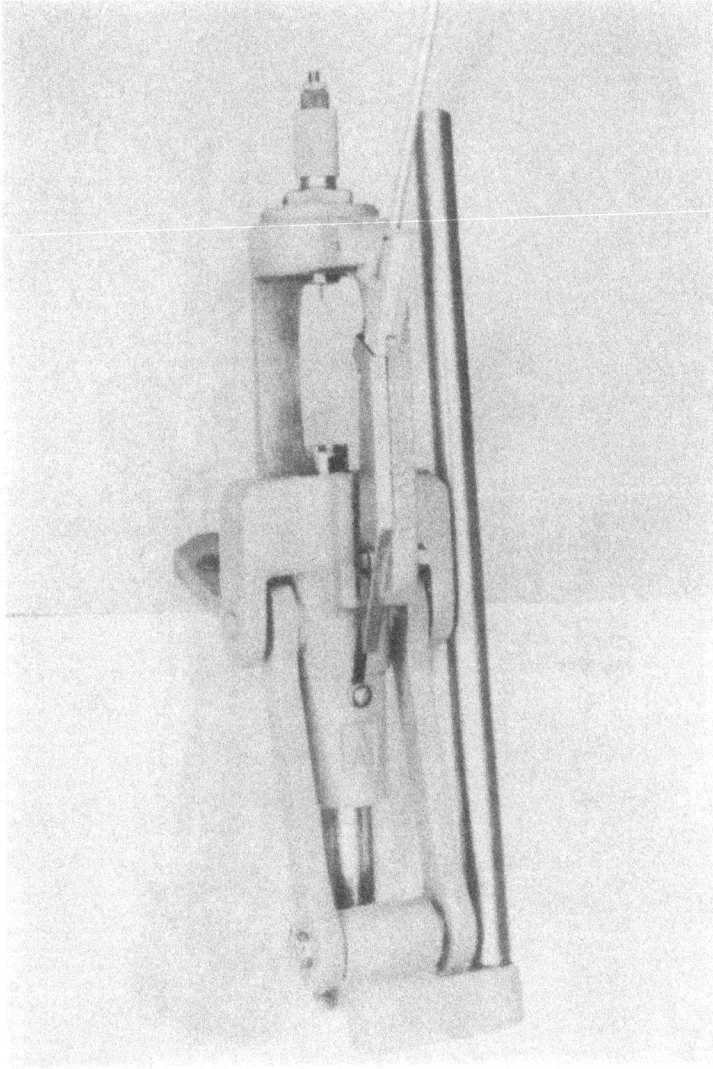

The R.C.B.S. Model A Loading Press is especially designed for extra-heavy work. It eases forming cases and bullet making, and it will resize a .30-06 case with as little difficulty as any other press would a Hornet case. It has a frame designed to resist spring, and leverage that has several times the ratio of other presses.

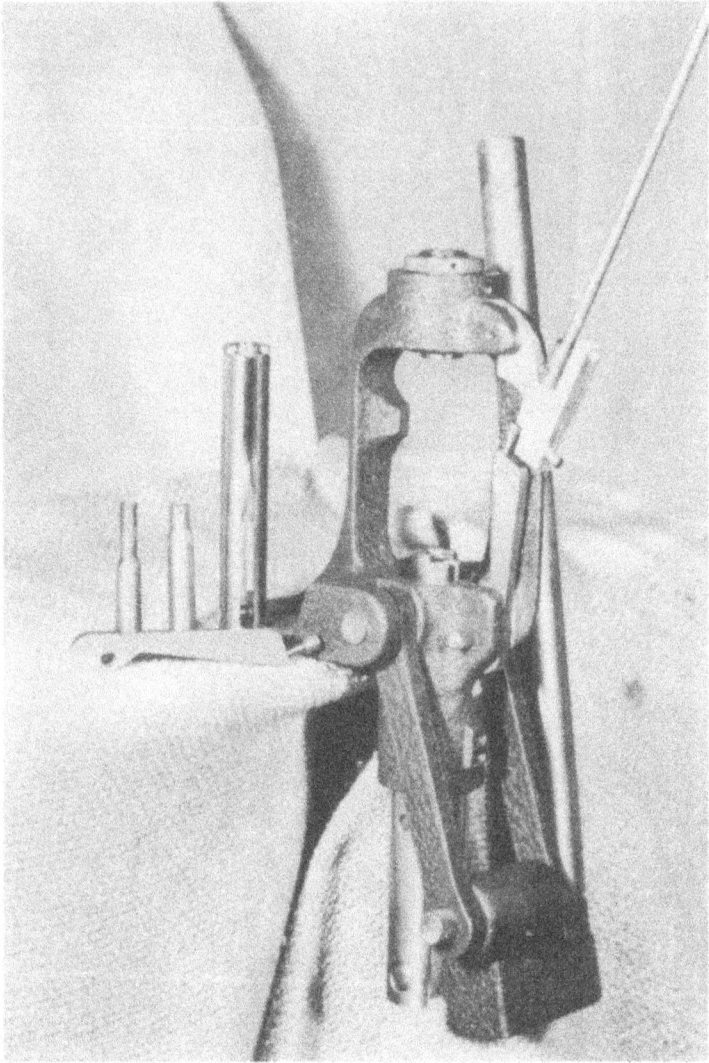

The R.C.B.S. Model B Loading Press is exceptionally fine in amount of leverage and power for so small a tool. The illustration shows it necking down a .30-06 case to .250 Savage. Both it and the Model A use ⅞" X 14 dies, and can be had with quickly interchangeable case holders.

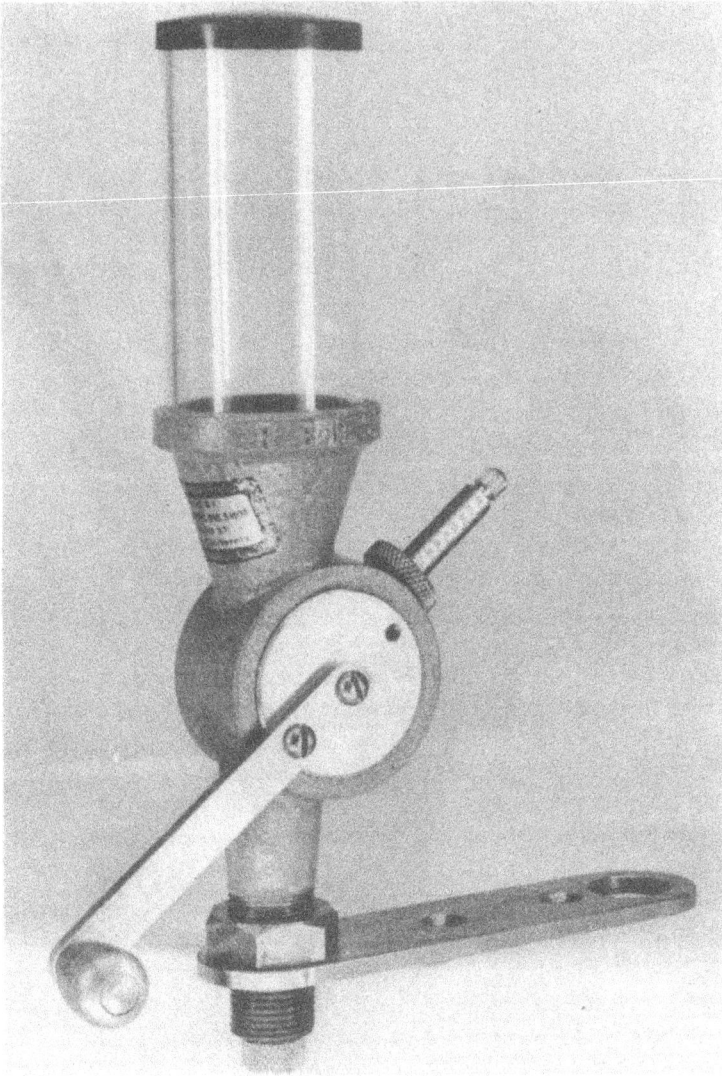

The R.C.B.S. Uniflow Powder Measure will adjust to throw changes from 2 grains of Bullseye to 110 grains of 4350 powder.

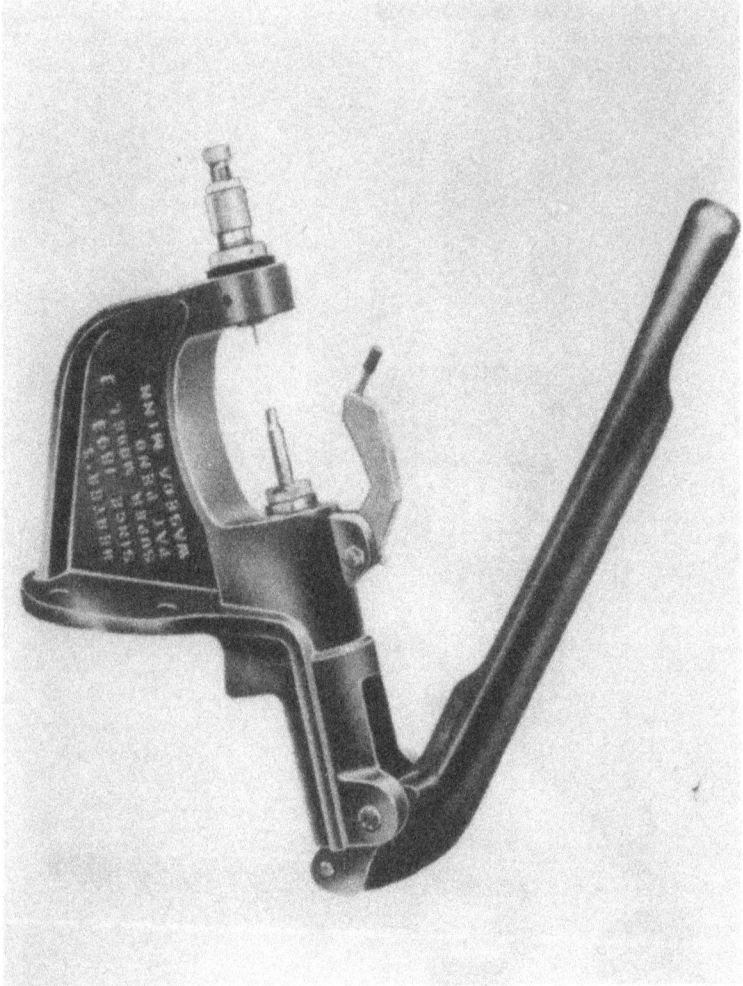

Herter's Model 3 Loading Press is the least expensive of all heavy bench presses, and an excellent one too. It operates on the down stroke of the lever, and case holders can be interchanged in a few seconds. Uses ⅞" X 14 dies.

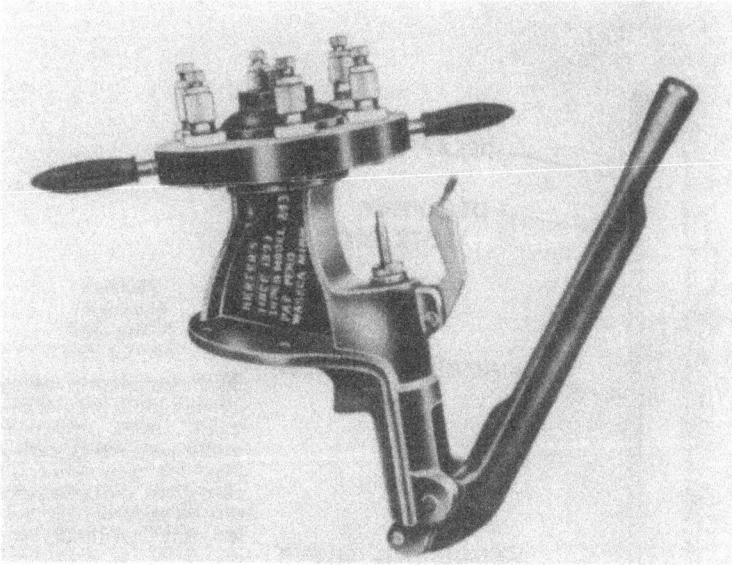

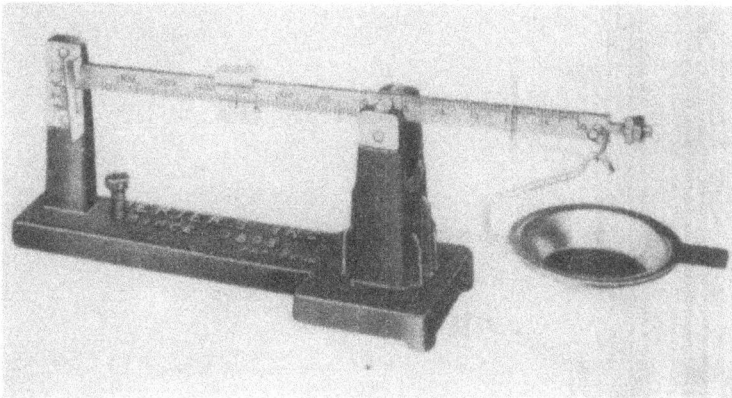

Top: Herter's Model 243 Turret Loading Press holding 6 different dies.
Bottom: Herter's Powder and Bullet Scales will weigh up to 350 grains
by 1/10th grain.

DECAPPING ROD

DECAPPING ROD
LOCK RING

ADJUSTING SLEEVE

ADJUSTING SLEEVE
LOCK RING

DIE BODY

SIZING HEAD

DIE LOCK RING

EXPANDER NIPPLE

DECAPPING PIN

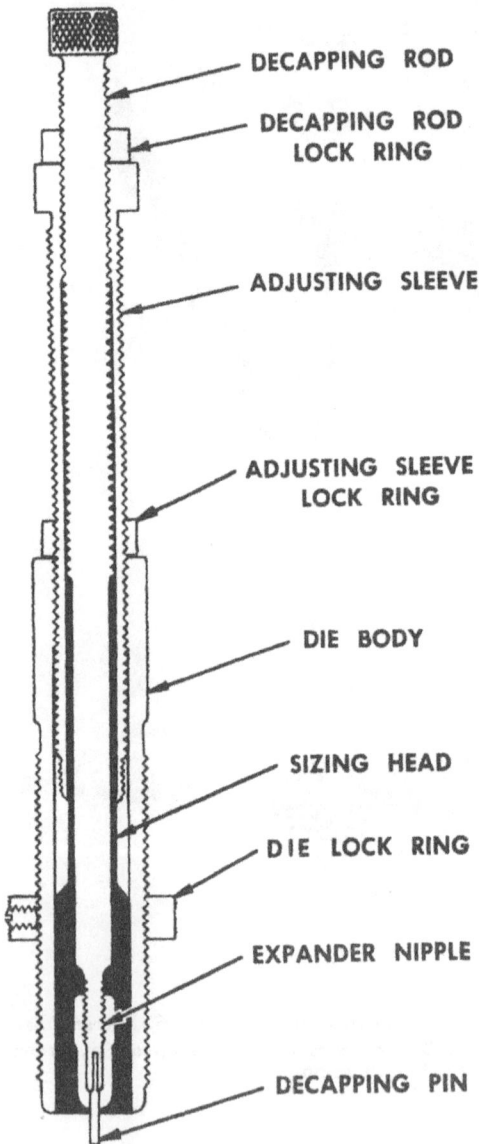

**Herter's
Universal
Sizing and
Seating Die**

With this one die and by obtaining the inexpensive sizing head, expander nipple, and bullet-seating head for each caliber of case, many different cases can be resized, and bullets seated without buying expensive sizing and seating dies for each cartridge one wishes to load.

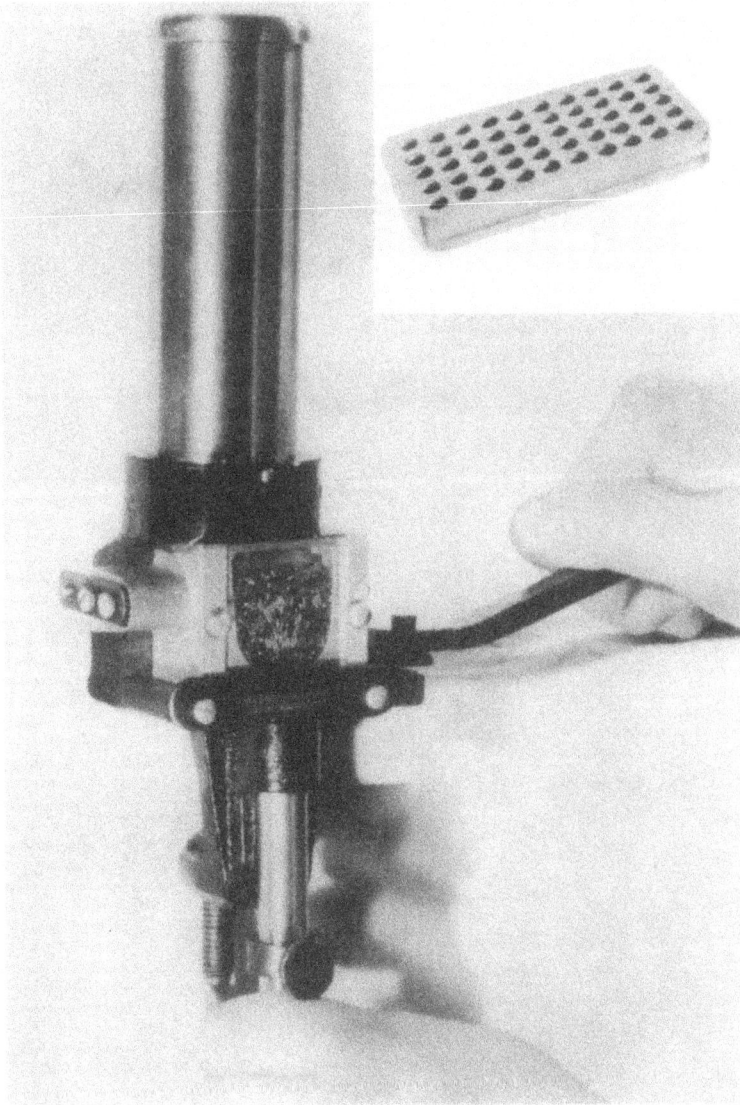

Belding & Mull Powder Measure and Loading Block.

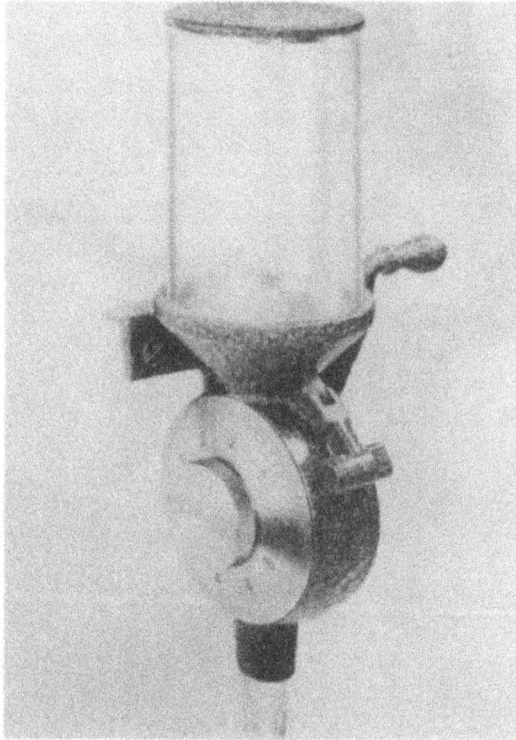

Redding Powder Scale weighs up to 325 grains by 1/10th grain.
Redding Powder Measure is easily set with graduations from 0 to 100.

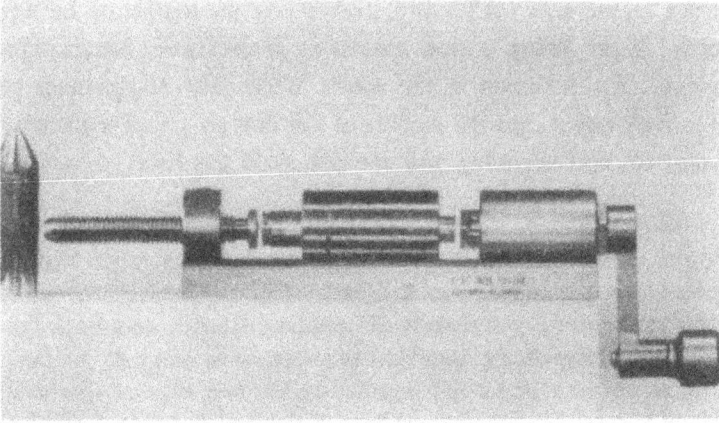

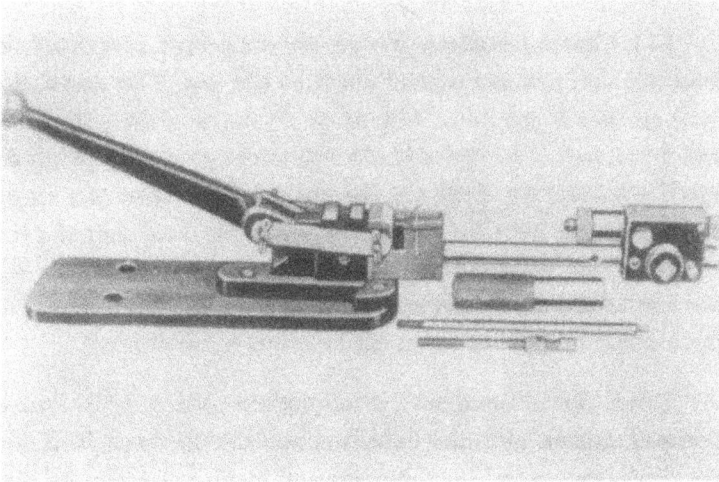

Upper: L. E. Wilson Case Trimmer. A holder is necessary for each different case, except those having the same body. To the left is the Wilson chamfering reamer.

Lower: The Belding & Mull Reloading Tool with resizing die in place and seating die below.

right of the pot for the tin pan on which to drop the dross, for extra metal, wax for fluxing, and to rest the mallet on between casts. Wear cheap cotton gloves to protect your hands. Have plenty of ventilation in the room. With this arrangement you can look down into the surface of the molten metal from which you cast, and see what you are doing all the time.

If you use an electric furnace, however, you must be able to see under the furnace where you connect the mold with the pouring spout. Therefore it is best to place the furnace on top of a carpenter's workbench of standard height, and back from the front edge of the bench so you can sit in front of the bench and rest your elbows or forearms on the top edge of the bench. Have the folded blanket on top of the bench to the left of the furnace, and the tin pan for dross on the right.

143. **Casting bullets.** Weigh out the proper proportions of lead, tin and antimony, and place in the pot. The metal will melt quicker if you place only several pounds in the pot at first, and when that is melted add the remainder gradually. With the small pot keep the dipper in the molten lead constantly except when pouring into the mold, and keep the lead stirred every minute or so, in order that the lighter tin and antimony will not rise to the top of the mass and give an uneven alloy. With the electric furnace have an old iron spoon for stirring.

When the alloyed lead is all melted, add a 3/4″ ball of beeswax, tallow, or bullet lubricant, and stir the metal well with the dipper or spoon. The lubricant will begin to smoke and then ignite; if it does not ignite, touch it off with a match. This fluxing helps to mix the metals of the alloy together, and causes any impurities or dross to rise to the surface, when it should be skimmed off and dumped on the tin plate, leaving the surface of the metal bright and mirror-like, as it always must be while casting bullets. Fluxing, thorough stirring and skimming off the dross may be necessary every fifteen minutes or so while casting, but never skim off dross without first fluxing with the wax.

The mold must be very hot—almost as hot as the lead— to cast good bullets. Therefore, to save time, prop the mold up with its cavity block touching the outside of the pot so it will receive some of the heat that comes up around the pot while the lead is melting.

Now, assuming you are using the small Ideal pot, fill the dipper about two thirds full of metal. Hold the mold, its top to the right, over the pot; connect the nozzle of the dipper with the pouring hole in the mold, then turn the mold and dipper upright. The lead will then flow from the dipper into the mold, and the weight of the lead in the dipper will cause it to completely fill the cavity in the mold. Keeping the mold upright, turn the dipper over in such a way that you leave a little puddle of melted lead above the pouring hole of the mold, and return the dipper to the metal in the pot. The temperature of the lead and mold should be such that it takes four or five seconds for the sprue (the puddle of lead in the pouring hole) to solidify.

With the electric furnace, you connect the pouring hole of the mold, holding the mold upright, with the nozzle of the spout under the pot, and operate the valve so that the metal pours into the mold, and you quickly learn the knack of operating the mold and valve so as to leave the little puddle of melted lead in the sprue hole of the mold, and not spill any lead, as you disconnect the mold and release the valve.

Then take the mallet in the right hand and cut off the sprue by striking the sprue cutter on the mould sharply so that the little piece of sprue falls into the melting pot. Hold the mould over the blanket, open it and let the bullet drop out on to the blanket. If the bullet does not drop from the mould of its own accord tap the mould with the mallet at the mould hinge to jar it out. Never strike the mould with anything metal.

A new mould will not cast good bullets until it has become oxidized, nor will any mould cast well until it has become very hot. Practically always you will have to cast ten to thirty bullets before the mould comes to the right temperature to cast good bullets that completely fill the mould with all their grooves, bases and points perfectly formed. The bullets should be perfect, bright, and shiny. If they have a frosted appearance it indicates that the metal and mould are too hot. Turn down the gas or current slightly on the furnace. The mould ·may also be cooled by dipping it for a few seconds into hot water, but only when its cavity is filled with a bullet. With a lead and tin alloy the metal should be at about 600 degrees F., but with an alloy containing antimony the temperature should be higher, about 750 degrees F.

When three or four imperfect bullets have accumulated on the blanket, pick them up with your gloved hand and drop them back in the pot again. Never drop imperfect bullets from the mould into the pot because lead might splash up onto the inside surface of the mould, and adhering there keep the mould from closing completely. If this happens lift the flake off carefully with a sharp knife.

Never dip from the surface of the metal. Insert the dipper down into the bottom of the pot, turn its cavity up and bring it to the surface. This stirs the metal at each dip and keeps the alloy properly mixed (the lighter metal—tin and antimony— tends to rise to the top of the molten mass).

Finally you are beginning to cast good bullets, and aside from occasionally fluxing and skimming off the dross you should be able to cast good bullets right along. As they begin to accumulate on the blanket push them to one side so you will always have a free spot for the bullets to fall on, and thus no bullet will strike another as it falls.

When you are through casting turn off the furnace and let the bullets on the blanket cool a bit. Then carefully pick each bullet up in turn and set it base down in a pasteboard box to be conveyed to the loading bench for sizing and lubricating. Never tumble bullets or pour them into a box, or handle them in any way that might dent or damage them, particularly that might dull the edges of their bases, as all such injuries will make them inaccurate.

When the mould has cooled so that it can be handled wipe it off with an oily rag and pack it away. When about to use that mould again wipe it off inside and out with gasoline, and then wipe all the gasoline off with a dry rag. When the metal remaining in the pot has solidified and cooled, scratch the alloy on its surface so you can identify it afterwards and dump the remaining ingot out of the pot.

144. Quantity casting.   The above technique will work with bullet moulds having one or two cavities. For casting in large quantities an armory or multiple cavity mould that casts four to ten bullets at a time is used. These moulds are heavy and tiresome, require considerable skill in their use, and do not pay for themselves unless thousands of bullets have to be cast for police or club use. When using them a large electric furnace with a large lead capacity is desirable. The sprue cutter on these multiple cavity moulds has a deep channel connecting the pouring holes of each cavity. An open ladle is used and the lead is run into the channel until all the cavities have filled, taking care to hold the mould level. Proper lubrication of the joint of the mould is necessary. Probably the best lubricant to stand the heat is Alemite Pyro Lubricant which may be ordered through any Alemite dealer.

145. Antimony alloys.   There is no difficulty in alloying lead and tin. Just keep the mixture stirred by always dipping from the bottom of the pot. Antimony has a higher melting point than lead. To alloy it with lead weigh out the proper quantity of the antimony and break it up very fine by pounding with a hammer. Melt the lead and raise it to a red heat, then add the antimony and cover the surface of the metal in the pot with powdered charcoal. Let the metal remain at this heat for a few minutes. Stir occasionally and when the antimony is completely melted flux with lubricant and skim off the charcoal and dross, then lower the heat slightly to bring the metal to proper casting temperature. With a mixture high in antimony keep the metal hotter and stir more often, and never skim without fluxing and stirring, because the light antimony has a decided tendency to float on top of the lead.

146. **Other suggestions.**   After casting for some time the mould may become too hot, and the bullet may not have set even though the metal in the sprue hole has solidified. Long and heavy bullets require more time to solidify and set than lighter ones. Also if the mould is too hot the bullets may not have time to shrink much and they may stick and not drop from the mould so readily. The cure for all this is simply to give more time after pouring before you open the mould. Also stop when the mould gets too hot and dip it in warm water, taking care however that there are bullets in the cavities. Do not tighten the cut-off plate screws on the mould so that they bind. The cut-off plate must be left free to swing with its own weight. Use great care never to injure or scratch the cavities, or to dull their edges. Never use a metal brush on a mould cavity or face. If a new mould refuses to close completely it may be that the dowel pins bind a little. Close the mould, gripping the handles tightly, and strike the mould a smart tap on the side with the wooden mallet which practically always overcomes this difficulty.

Question: How in thunder did our ancestors ever cast good bullets over a campfire? *Answer:* They cast only round balls, and they trued them up afterwards with a jack-knife!

LUBRICATING AND SIZING BULLETS

147. For best results bullets should be the same size as the groove diameter of the barrel, or possibly two or three thousandths of an inch larger than groove diameter (P 110). Also read the first page in this book—FIT.   Therefore very generally bullet moulds are made to cast bullets slightly larger

than these diameters, it being intended that they shall be afterwards sized to the exact diameter required. Good results usually cannot be obtained when using cast bullets the size that they come from the mould.

All lead alloy bullets must be lubricated, that is their grooves must be filled with lubricant. This is to prevent the lead scraping off the bullet and leading the bore. Therefore after bullets have been cast they must be sized and lubricated. These two operations are more or less combined in one.

The simplest method of lubricating and sizing is to first stand the cast bullets on their bases in a shallow pan, each bullet being at least an eighth of an inch from any other bullet. Then pour melted lubricant in the pan until it rises above the top lubricating groove of the bullets. Let the

Ideal Kake Kutter.

lubricant cool hard. Then take a "Cake Cutter" (procurable from tool makers) which is merely a cartridge case with the neck enlarged inside just slightly larger than the diameter of the cast bullet, and with the head drilled entirely out of it. Press this cake cutter down over each bullet in turn, thus cutting it out of the cake of lubricant. After pressing down over about three bullets the bullets will begin to come out of the top of the cake cutter. Place these bullets to one side. Finally you have all the bullets cut out of the cake and with their grooves filled with the lubricant, and probably a thin coating of lubricant all over their sides.

Now these lubricated bullets are forced base first through a bullet sizer such as the Belding and Mull bullet sizer or the bullet sizer provided for the Ideal tong tool. This sizer is simply a slightly funnel-shaped die with a plunger. As the bullets are pressed through it they are sized to the exact diameter required, the lubricant is pressed tightly into the grooves, and any excess lubricant on the sides of the bullet is scraped off. Be careful not to let the bullets fall or otherwise get deformed in the operation. Then finally it will probably be necessary to wipe the bases of the bullets free from lubricant that still more or less adheres there. The bullets are then ready for loading in the cartridges.

If the bullets are gas check bullets, before placing in the pan to lubricate them, put the gas checks on the bases. Simply place the gas check, cup up, on the loading bench and press the base of the bullet down on it, thus pressing the copper cup firmly onto the base of the bullet.

148. Bullet Lubricators and Sizers. These tools do a much better job of lubricating and sizing, they work easier and quicker, and usually the bullets done in them give better accuracy. All operate on the same principle as shown in the illustration. The dies and punches are interchangeable so that one machine will serve for all calibers and types of bullets, the proper dies and punches being provided for each. The die which sizes the bullet and which holds it while the lubricant is being forced into its grooves, has perforations around its diameter through which the lubricant enters into the grooves of the bullet. The bottom punch rides inside the die, and has its top surface flat for square, plain base bullets, or slightly concave for gas check bullets so that it fits the bullet base closely and prevents lubricant being forced in below the base of the bullet. This punch is adjusted so that it will go down in the die just far enough so that the top groove of the bullet stops in the die where the top hole in the die feeds lubricant to the bullet. The top punch is an exact fit for the point of the bullet. Extra top punches can be had for bullets of varying points. Dies are regularly made to the standard and most frequently used diameters, but can be had to order for any desired diameter.

The lubricant is contained in the cylindrical reservoir. The handle on the top of the reservoir forces the lubricant to flow through the die into the bullet holes. The lubricant

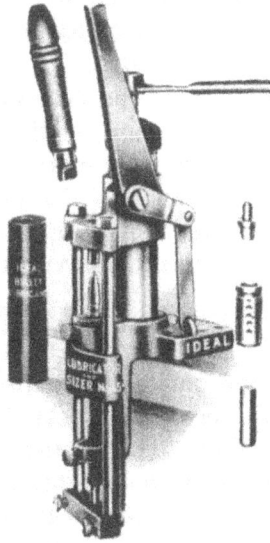

Ideal lubricator and sizer.

is usually in the form of a cylinder or stick which fits the reservoir, but melted lubricant may be poured into the reservoir, allowing it to cool therein before use.

To operate: with the handle of the tool raised, the bullet is placed base down in the mouth of the die, its base resting on the top of the bottom punch, which is raised even with the top of the die when the operating handle is raised.   Then the handle is brought down.   The top punch presses on the top of the bullet, and forces both bullet and bottom punch down into the die, thus sizing the bullet.   As the bullet enters the die the lubricant under pressure flows through the holes in the die into the grooves in the bullet, thus packing the lubricant in the grooves.   Keep the handle down for perhaps a second to give the lubricant time to fully flow into all the bullet grooves. Then raise the handle. The bottom punch also rises and forces the lubricated and sized bullet up out of the die. The bullet is then completely sized and lubricated, ready for loading in the cartridge.

From time to time give the handle at the top of the reservoir a turn to keep pressure on the lubricant and cause it to flow. Bullets can thus be lubricated and sized at the rate of about fifteen per minute. The machine is not costly, and is a great help to those who wish to make good, accurate bullets. It is also a great time saver over the simpler pan method.

149. Lubricants. The Lyman Gun Sight Corporation furnish their Ideal Lubricant for lubricating bullets. It is furnished in cylindrical perforated sticks for insertion in the Ideal Lubricator and Sizer. This lubricant is made on an old formula developed by Mr. E. A. Leopold and has been used for over fifty years in all temperatures with perfect results. Other makers of lubricating and sizing tools likewise furnish lubricant in sticks. All of these bullet lubricants can be melted if desired, but when so melted should be continuously stirred while cooling to prevent the ingredients from separating.

Bullet lubricant must not only lubricate at rather high temperatures, but it must remain in condition for years of storage, and must not melt enough to flow under temperatures that might occur when cartridges are exposed to hot tropical sun. Melted lubricant coming in contact with powder or primer will ruin them. A very satisfactory bullet lubricant is Japan (Carnauba) wax, either pure or with a small quantity of cylinder oil to soften it slightly. It usually needs to be softened a little to flow readily through tool dies. If cartridges are to be fired soon after loading, then the lubricant should be slightly softer for winter use than in summer.

Another very satisfactory lubricant consists of equal parts of Japan wax and beeswax with a small amount of cylinder oil to soften it. Very finely powdered graphite may also be added, stirring the wax while cooling to keep the graphite from gravitating to the bottom of the mass. Animal fats such as tallow are very unsatisfactory as they melt and flow at high temperatures, and soon turn rancid and deterioriate.

As described previously, Mr. Eric M. Farr has recently been obtaining very superior accuracy with lead bullets lubricated with Automobile Water Pump Grease instead of the other usual bullet lubricants described above. He suggests a test as follows:

"Take a barrel that has been shot 30 to 40 rounds with lead bullets lubricated with ordinary wax lubricant, such as has generally been used to date, and attempt to push a tight, dry patch through it. You would have one heck of a time. The patch would have to be wet. A bore in this condition will deform lead bullets as they pass through it. Make a similar test, but after firing bullets lubricated with Automobile Water Pump Grease. There will be no difficulty in pushing the dry patch through. The bore in this condition will not deform the lead bullets."

Mr. Farr refers to the water pump greases of the sodium soap filled oil type. He has used both the Automobile Water Pump Grease made by TEXACO, and marketed under the trade name "Marfak," and also that supplied by Sears Roebuck and called simply "Water Pump Grease." He states that his further experiments seem to indicate that this lubricant is best at comparatively low velocities — 1800 f.s. and under, and that it does not seem to be so good at higher velocities. Also that when loaded in cartridges for some time, particularly in summer, it tends to "migrate," that is seep out and into the powder. (Therefore the desirability of storing cartridges bullet down. T.W.) He also suggests further experiments with this type of lubricant to perfect it.

This automobile water pump grease has recently been tried on the writer's range in a genuine Pope rifle, seating the bullets from the muzzle, and has produced the typical fine Pope type of accuracy.

All the above applies to lubricants for lead alloy bullets only.

In lubricating bullets the writer has always thought there should be a little grease ahead of the first band so grease will strike the bore ahead of lead, but not too much.

150. Lubricating wads have been used to some extent in an effort to lubricate the bore, reduce leading or metal fouling, and increase barrel life. In black powder days a wax wad with a card wad under it was sometimes used between the powder and the base of the bullet to keep the black powder fouling moist and permit more rounds to be fired before the powder fouling began to cake and interfere with accuracy. I have seen black powder fouling accumulate and cake so hard in the bore in dry weather that after fifteen rounds or so you literally could not see through the bore. The bullet seemed to always get through the bore somehow, but it seldom hit the bullseye. Truly we have something to be thankful for in our fine modern smokeless powders.

In recent years some experimenting has been done with lubricating wads when loading high power cartridges with metal cased bullets. Some slight degree of success has frequently attended their use. The wads are about .03″ to .05″ thick and are made on several formulas, a common one being 4 ounces of beeswax, 4 ounces of Japan wax, 2 ounces of petrolatum. and 2 ounces of fine colloided graphite. The Industrial Products Company, Box 14, Wakefield, Mass., put out such a wad known as the IPCO wad. It is furnished in small sheets. After the case has been filled with powder the sheet is placed over its mouth and pressed down with the thumb. The case mouth acts as a wad cutter, the wad remaining in the mouth of the case. Then the bullet is seated, pressing the wad down. The wad remains against the base of the bullet and adhering to the walls of the case neck, remains in that position. The case neck inside must be cylindrical and the same diameter as the base of the bullet. With a bottle neck case and bullets seated with their bases below the lower end of the case neck, the wad would not stay in position and would fall down on top of the powder. The heat of the powder gas is supposed to melt the wad and lubricate the bore for the passage of the next bullet. Also it is thought that gas does not so readily pass a lubricating wad which thus to some small extent prevents erosion of the bore.

These wads have produced varying success and only a thorough trial and careful observation in any particular rifle and cartridge will determine if they are an advantage, give negative results, or are positively detrimental. They are used today almost exclusively with metal cased bullets. Apparently they are of no advantage with lubricated lead bullets, possibly because such bullets already have sufficient lubrication in their grooves.

In some particular loads, in certain cartridges and in some individual rifles they seem to slightly increase the accuracy, but in other instances they have decreased the accuracy. In some loads they also seem to definitely increase the breech pressure, and in other instances it seems as though the heat of the powder gases quickly reduced the wad to carbon which is an abrasive and not a lubricant.

We have carefully scanned all reports where it was stated that their use decreased barrel wear, but often other factors involved prevented a positive determination as to whether or not they decreased wear. If loaded cartridges are stored for several years, does the wad dry out and drop down in the powder charge? I believe that it has not yet been definitely proved that these lubricating wads pay for themselves.

METAL CASED BULLETS

151. As already explained, if lead alloy bullets with plain bases are fired in a rifle with a powder charge sufficient to give over about 1,700 f.s., the heat of the powder gases will melt the base of the bullet and good accuracy will not be obtained. Likewise with gas check bullets, powder charges necessary to give above about 2,000 to 2,200 f.s., produce

hot gases under considerable pressure which often cut past the gas check and melt streaks up the sides of the bullet, similarly preventing good accuracy. At high velocities lead bullets may strip and fail to take and follow the rifling. Therefore quite generally all bullets used in high power or high intensity rifles have a thin envelope or jacket covering the lead core of the bullet to keep the lead from melting and to cause the bullet to follow the grooves of the rifling. Such bullets are termed "metal cased" or "jacketed."

Today practically all metal cased bullets made in America have jackets made of an alloy called "gilding metal," composed of 90% copper and 10% zinc, or for pistol bullets, 95% copper and 5% zinc. To the 90-10 mixture the Western Cartridge Company add a small amount of tin and call the alloy "Lubaloy," tin having a small lubricating value. Pure copper is usually too soft and causes copper fouling in the bore.

Formerly bullet jackets were made of many materials. At first our military bullet jackets were made of cupro-nickel (60% copper and 40% nickel) and some few were made of mild steel plated lightly with tin to prevent the steel rusting. For sporting bullets our manufacturers have practically always used gilding metal for the jackets, which, until about 1915 was usually given a thin plating or wash of tin. Bullets jacketed with mild steel have been used very extensively in Europe, particularly in Germany. During war time English military bullets have frequently been jacketed with gilding metal containing a small percentage of tin, such alloy being called "Nobeloy."

Metal cased bullets are practically always used without any lubrication, and have a smooth surface except possibly for a crimping cannelure. Generally speaking no successful lubricant has yet been devised for metal cased bullets except a thin cadmium plate on gilding metal.

Cupro-nickel performed well as a jacket metal so long as the muzzle velocity was not over about 2,200 f.s. Above that velocity (due to heat and pressure) cupro-nickel caused metal fouling in the bore, sometimes as much as three or four thousandths of an inch thick. The steel surface of the bore under the fouling often rusted unless the fouling was removed promptly. This was a rather complicated process, requiring a strong solution of ammonia to dissolve the cupro-nickel.

This fault of cupro-nickel led about 1920 to the substitution of gilding metal for our military bullet jackets. Gilding metal does not deposit any thick, lumpy, or streaky metal fouling except at very ultra high velocities, and even at these very high velocities (over 4,000 f.s.) it can usually be prevented by thinly plating the jackets with cadmium. Gilding metal or Lubaloy jackets do very slightly plate or wash the bore with copper. By viewing the bore carefully from the muzzle the slight copper color can usually be seen. Apparently this copper wash never accumulates to a measurable thickness and does no harm. It need not be removed and can be disregarded in almost all cases.

Despite the fact that metal cased bullets are used without any lubrication, they cause practically no wear in the bore— not even those jacketed with mild steel. The bore of the rifle practically always wears out, and becomes inaccurate, because of the throat and breech erosion caused by hot powder gases before any detrimental amount of frictional wear from the bullet is discernible.

The jacket is stamped and formed in dies from sheet metal into the form of an elongated cup; then the lead core is inserted in this cup and the assembled bullet is swaged under heavy pressure into its final form and exact dimensions and weight in dies. In general there are two forms of jacketed bullets.

The full jacketed bullet is generally used for military and target shooting purposes. The point is formed at the closed end of the jacket, and the open end of the jacket is closed in over the core and base of the bullet. Thus the jacket completely covers the point of the bullet, but on the base of the bullet there is a small circular place in the center where the jacket does not cover the lead core.

With the *soft point* or *expanding bullet* used for hunting purposes the closed end of the jacket cup forms the base of the bullet and is formed flat and square in the final die. The open end of the cup is not completely closed in over the core, some of the core is left exposed without jacket covering to make a soft point, or the core may have an open, hollow point, or there may be a very thin, small, easily crushed jacket covering the point.

Bullet jackets are usually from .015″ to .030″ thick. The thinner jackets are used for pistol and small bullets and the thicker for larger and heavier rifle bullets. Also the higher the velocity at which a bullet is designed to be driven, the thicker its jacket. Some hunting bullets have portions of the jacket made much thicker so as to delay or localize expansion to give a more ideal effect on game.

The bullet cores are usually made from lead wire of the required diameter, the wire passing through a machine that cuts it to the required length and swages it into the right shape and weight to fit in the jacket cup.

152. Obtaining common metal cased bullets. The metal cased bullets with which American handloaders are almost exclusively concerned are jacketed with gilding metal, and most of them have soft points, hollow points, or are otherwise made to expand. Some few full jacketed bullets are used with light charges of powder for small game shooting, and of course any handloader may find it desirable to load full jacketed bullets for mid and long range target practice. Metal cased bullets were generally not made by the handloader (P 156) but were produced in quantity with heavy machinery by the large ammunition companies and by a number of smaller custom bullet makers (see list given in the Appendix), and are retailed to handloaders by dealers in ammunition components. Since about 1946, however, convenient hand tools for making these bullets have been available and many handloaders are now making excellent metal cased bullets (P 158). Members of the National Rifle Association have the privilege of purchasing Government full jacketed .30 and .45 caliber bullets from the Director of Civilian Marksmanship, Department of the Army. Generally speaking the price of metal cased bullets of various calibers and types runs from $1.50 to $6.00 per one hundred bullets, depending on weight, diameter and type.

153. Weights and types of bullets. Many weights and types of bullets are produced, and are available to handloaders. For example, many different .30 caliber rifles are made, all the way from the common .30-30 to the .300 Weatherby Magnum. All have a groove diameter of bore from .308″ to .309″, but with varying twists of rifling. There are also a great variety of .30 caliber metal-cased bullets available for handloaders, all having a diameter of .308″ to .3085″, and all suitable, so far as diameter goes, for use in all these .30 caliber rifles. These bullets are made in weights varying all the way from 110 grains to 250 grains, and with various kinds of points, and some expanding, others full-jacketed. But, for example, a 220-grain .30 caliber bullet would not be suitable for a rifle taking the .30-30 cartridge because a powder charge that would be safe in this small case would not give a muzzle velocity sufficient to spin this long bullet in the .30-30 twist of rifling of one turn in 12 inches, and also because if we seated this 220-grain bullet in a .30-30 case so the assembled cartridge will work through the magazine, the base of the bullet would extend way down below the neck and crowd into the powder space. Also, it is not safe to use sharp-pointed bullets in rifles with tubular magazines. Lastly, for use in rifles where the bullets require crimping, the bullet should have a crimping cannelure at the proper point. So the proper bullet for a certain cartridge must be selected, bearing all this in mind. But among the proper bullets of .30 caliber you will find many of various weights, some one of which is quite sure to meet your needs and produce good results. This applies to all other calibers as well as to .30 caliber.

Let us continue with examples of suitable bullets. A very common bullet of .25 caliber is one weighing 117 grains. The .250-3000 Savage rifle barrel has a twist of one turn in 14 inches, and this twist will not spin a 117-

grain bullet fast enough to keep it travelling point to the front. On the other hand this 117 grain bullet is entirely satisfactory in .257 Roberts rifles of standard make which have a 10 inch twist. The velocity must also be considered. Probably a 117 grain bullet would be stabilized in a 14 inch twist if we could give the bullet about M.V. 3,200 f.s. or more, but such a velocity is impossible in any standard .25 caliber rifle within safe pressure limits.

In selecting metal cased bullets for any particular cartridge give particular attention to their length, and also to the location of the crimping cannelure if they are to be used in tubular magazine rifles. For example, a .25 caliber bullet that weighs 125 grains is very long. It can be stabilized all right in the 10 inch twist of the .257 Roberts rifle. But if we seat the bullet in the .257 Roberts case with the standard overall cartridge length of 2.75″ so the cartridge will operate through the magazine, the base of the bullet will extend way down below the neck of the case into the powder chamber which is very undesirable. And if we seat that bullet projecting far enough out of the case so that the base of the bullet is not below the case neck and then load it into the standard .257 Roberts chamber, single loading, the throat or bullet seat of the chamber will promptly push the bullet back into the case so that we are just where we were in the first place. We could, of course, have this barrel throated with a longer lead so that it would accept the 125 grain bullet when loaded to an overall length of 3.05″ which would bring the base of the bullet above the lower end of the neck of the case. This longer cartridge could be loaded single loading. With the Winchester Model 70 rifle in .257 Roberts caliber we could even alter the action of the rifle to take this much longer cartridge in the magazine by removing the filler plate in the magazine and substituting a .30-06 floor plate, magazine spring and bolt stop. There is still another matter to watch in a case like this. The Remington Model 722 rifle in .257 Roberts caliber has a short breech action. We could load a cartridge with an overall length of 3.05″ into it all right (if it were throated for such a bullet) but we could not eject and extract that loaded cartridge from the action without taking out the bolt as it would not eject through the loading port.

Just a little study and measurement on these lines will tell you if you can use a specific bullet satisfactorily in a certain rifle.

154. Accuracy of metal cased bullets. We find that in some rifles certain makes and types of bullets shoot more accurately than others. This does not always depend on the weight of the bullet, but rather on the perfection with which the bullet is made, on how well it fits the individual rifle and its lead, and on how well the twist of rifling stabilizes it. (We are considering a rifle so constructed that it is basically accurate and dependable.) Where bullet weights are equal, one make of bullet may shoot more accurately than another, one weight of bullet may shoot more accurately in a given rifle than another weight, and one weight or make of bullet may shoot more accurately in a given rifle at a certain velocity than at a lower or higher velocity. We also find fairly frequently that a given bullet may shoot more accurately with one kind of powder than another, both powders being of satisfactory type for that cartridge, and both in charges giving the same velocity. Thus the handloader has a most interesting and instructive pastime in developing a load for a particular bullet and powder to give the best results in his rifle.

Even in any one particular instance we cannot say in advance of a test what accuracy a given load will give in a given rifle. Shooters often recommend a certain load based on what it has done in their rifle. This is not safe for there are too many variables in individual rifles. But if a certain load (bullet, powder, and primer) gives excellent results in ten different rifles of that caliber then we can pass that information on with reliance that another handloader will be likely to get at least fairly good results. In Part IV of this work, under each cartridge heading, we have endeavored to indicate the bullets and powder charges that have been most generally successful, not only from the standpoint of accuracy but for various purposes —gallery shooting, mid and long range target shooting, small game shooting, varmint shooting, and big game shooting. But we cannot guarantee that these loads will be entirely satisfactory in all rifles of that caliber because there are too many variables among individual rifles.

155. Safety.   In Part IV of this work we give the range of loads that will be safe in a given caliber of rifle, provided (and this is important) that the rifle is a standard rifle of that caliber in good condition, that the bullet is of a type, diameter and weight suitable for that cartridge, and that it is seated to a certain depth in the case, that the proper primer is used, as well of course as the proper powder charge.

Following the suggestions in Part IV we believe that the handloader can work up a load for his rifle that will be perfectly safe and satisfactory. In many loads that are particularly recommended the handloader using care can produce remarkably satisfactory and accurate handloaded ammunition. Indeed in most cases we think he will hit the nail on the head the first time.

156. Effect on game.   Here there are so many variables that we cannot state positively that any one bullet or load will be superior to another on any species of game, although we do mention certain loads that have made a reputation for being generally successful on certain game. Animals do not always react in the same way when struck in the same place with the same bullet at the same remaining velocity. A certain bullet may have a reputation for making around ninety per cent quick kills when it enters the chest cavity of deer within a range of 200 yards. But a certain hunter on his initial experience may shoot two deer where the bullet fails to kill promptly and thus lose all faith in that bullet, whereas those two bullets may be included in the ten per cent that failed in assigning a ninety per cent good killing average to this bullet. A bullet that gives around ninety per cent fairly quick kills when well placed is a whale of a good bullet on that species of game. May I give two interesting examples. I once shot a woodchuck right through the eye at 75 yards, using a 100 grain open point,

.25 caliber bullet at a M.V. of 2,600 f.s. The bullet failed to come out of the head. In another case I shot a full grown otter squarely in the open mouth as it faced me at 20 feet, using a 172 grain soft point .30 caliber bullet at a M.V. of 2,700 f.s., and no particle of the bullet came out of the otter anywhere. The first cartridge was an entirely satisfactory varmint cartridge, the second entirely satisfactory for big game, both so proved a hundred times.

157. **Failures.**   There are so many variables in arms and ammunition that no one, even the manufacturer, can guarantee performance, particularly performance in accuracy. This is true of standard weapons and standard factory ammunition. One weapon and one cartridge may give excellent results. Shift to another exactly similar weapon and another lot of the same cartridge and the results may be good, bad, or indifferent. So it is with handloaded ammunition. Certain components in a given weapon may give mediocre results. But the handloader has this great advantage: He can experiment. If certain components or certain loads do not give good results he can try others. With experience he can gradually fit his ammunition to his weapon, and soon he gets the results he hoped for. He can experiment with new arms, new components. He may have failures, and on the other hand he may have ideal results. He can chase the rainbow. This is the most interesting feature of handloading. The sky is always the limit, but in endeavoring to reach it there are bound to be failures.

Anyone can buy a set of loading tools and with them, following the manufacturer's instructions, he can load cartridges. What kind of cartridges will they be? We rather think that most of them will be failures. That is why this book has been written: To give certain instructions and lay down certain principles which if followed will go a long way towards eliminating failures.

Why all this in the portion of this work dealing with bullets? Because it has been my experience that with present day manufacture of weapons, cases, primers, and powders the greatest variable lies in the bullet. To reach the top the bullet is the most important component of the weapon and ammunition.

MAKING METAL CASED BULLETS

158. It is now becoming possible for handloaders to make their own metal cased bullets. They can save money and strive for better results than they can obtain with factory bullets. Hand making these bullets started during World War II when handloaders were unable to purchase any metal cased bullets, or any factory loaded cartridges either for that matter. Certain mechanically minded riflemen developed methods, dies and swages with which they made their own bullets. The results were rather crude at first, but the tools and technique have now progressed to the point where handloaders can equal and in many cases excel the factory bullets in accuracy. In fact such hand made bullets now hold the world's accuracy records at 100 and 200 yards.

The hand making of metal cased bullets may now be said to have passed the development stage. Many efficient swages and other tools are available, the precise technique of using them has been determined, and for several years many handloaders have been making superior bullets with these tools. For the brief description of the best ways of using these tools I am indebted to Mr. Samuel Clark, Jr., and Mr. Ray Biehler. Readers are particularly referred to their exhaustive treatise of the subject contained in *The Ultimate in Rifle Precision, 1951.**

159. **Tools needed and expense.** The tools, dies, swages, etc., necessary for making metal cased bullets are rather-expensive, costing from seventy five to one hundred dollars. But factory made metal cased bullets now cost from $2\frac{1}{2}$ to 6 cents each, and the components for hand making (jacket cups and lead) cost only about one cent per bullet. Therefore the handloader does not have to make many thousand bullets before he has written off the cost of his tools. A set of tools will supply not only the handloader himself, but his friends, with very excellent bullets at extremely low cost.

* Now out of print.

The tools required are:

Lead wire cutters for cutting the lead wire used for bullet cores to correct length and weight.

Uniform Weight Core Forming Die (the Biehler is recommended) for forming the lead core into exact shape and weight for insertion into the jacket cups.

Core Seater to insert the lead core truly to the bottom of the jacket cup. Usually procured from the swage maker or from Biehler.

Bullet Swages or Dies for forming the assembled jacket and core into the finished bullet of size, shape and weight desired. These are made by Biehler & Astles, the R.C.B.S Gun & Die Shop, the Hollywood Gun Shop, and others. They are generally made to operate in the R.C.B.S. Press, the Hollywood Reloading Tool, the Super Pacific Reloading Tool, or other very strong tool or press as ordered. To date swages and dies have been made for .22, .25, .270 and .30 caliber bullets.

The following components are also required:

Copper Jacket Cups obtainable from the makers of swages and dies. In the various calibers they should be ordered of the proper length for making the weight of bullet desired.

Lead wire of the proper diameter for bullet cores, obtainable from the makers of swages and dies, or from Rochester Lead Works. The wire is usually supplied in 5, 10 or 25 pound spools.

The addresses of the above dealers will be found in the Directory at the end of this book.

160. Lead Wire Cutter. The first operation is to cut the extruded lead wire into short lengths for the cores, so that the combined weight of the jacket cup and core will be several grains more than the weight of the bullet desired. Afterwards the grain or two extra weight will be extruded when shaping the core in the Uniform Weight Core Forming Die. The wire as it comes from the spool or coil is slightly curved, and it is best to cut it into about 12-inch lengths and roll it between two flat surfaces to straighten it before cutting into core lengths.

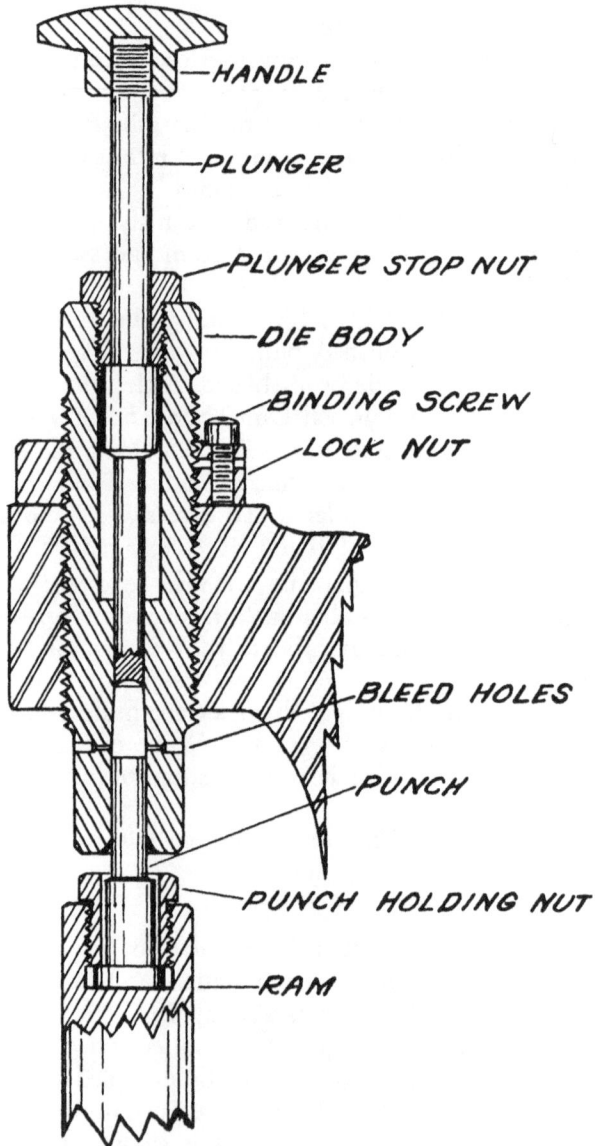

HANDLE

PLUNGER

PLUNGER STOP NUT

DIE BODY

BINDING SCREW

LOCK NUT

BLEED HOLES

PUNCH

PUNCH HOLDING NUT

RAM

A cross-section, showing construction of the Biehler die and ram.

The uniform weight core-forming die with ram and punch.

161. Uniform Weight Core Forming Die. This is a most valuable and essential tool. It eliminates not only the tedious and time consuming operation of weighing and filling each individual bullet core until it exactly matches the weight of all others to be used, but also accurately eliminates any air that may be trapped between the lead core and the jacket. In use the die is screwed into the loading press. When the handle of the tool is brought up the cut core is forced into the die so that the excess lead is extruded through two fine holes in the side of the die. A light blow with the palm of the hand on the plunger expels the finished core which so closely matches all others in weight that any additional weighing is needless.

162. Core seater. The purpose of this tool is to seat the core in the bullet jacket and expand it just sufficiently so that it entirely fills out the sides of the jacket. The core pre-swaged in the Biehler die is tapered and inserted in the jacket tapered end first. Since it will naturally expand at its weakest point first while being seated in the jacket, the lead in the base of the jacket expands first to fill out the sides, and continuing to expand progressively towards the mouth of the jacket expels all air that might become entrapped. Such air would cause the bullet to become unbalanced and inaccurate. Lifting the handle of the press tool forces the core into the jacket and properly expands it, and a downward movement expels it from the die. Like all other tools mentioned here it is adjustable within the range of bullet weights in common use.

163. Weight, Length and Point. From most swage and die makers you can obtain dies to make bullets with several shapes of point of the caliber you desire—sharp or round point. Such dies can be adjusted to form bullets of any weight (length) desired within reasonable limits by altering the depth that the base pouch enters the cylindrical portion of the die. If you wish a long, heavy bullet then you should order long jacket cups. If you wish considerable of a soft point extending beyond the front end of the jacket then your jacket cups should be shorter, or your cores should be cut to a greater length. Hollow point bullets can be made by using a short core and long jacket cups so that when the point is formed the core falls short of protruding from the jacket. Many competitive bench rest shooters when making bullets have found that they obtain better accuracy if the core falls about 1/16 inch short of the point of the jacket leaving a slight hollow point. This form of point also contributes to soft swaging (P 165). Such hollow point bullets usually give good killing effect on varmints. Your die maker can advise you as to the length of jacket cups you should order for the weight and type of bullet you desire, and then a little experimenting with the length you cut your cores will solve this problem.

164. Bullet Swages. All swages or bullet forming dies for hand operation are made on much the same principle. There are two portions to the die; the ogive or point forming portion, and the body or cylindrical portion. These two parts are joined together by screw threads or a push fit socket so they can be easily separated. The precise fit and alinement of the cavities in each portion are extremely important.

The assembled jacket cup and core is inserted in the cylindrical portion of the die, the jacket being very slightly smaller in diameter than the die so such insertion is easy. The two portions of the die are then joined together, and the base punch (operated by the handle of the loading tool) is brought up through the cylindrical portion of the die, pushing the jacket cup and core up into the die, and by the pressure expanding the entire bullet to the diameter and shape of the die and forming the point. The pressure or pull on the tool handle is relatively light to form .22 caliber bullets with hollow points, and heavier for soft points and bullets larger than .22 caliber. The ordinary loading tool is not strong enough for the pressure required to swage large caliber soft point bullets, these requiring the strong R.C.B.S. press, the new Hollywood or Super Pacific tools, or an arbor press.

The bullet having thus been formed by pressure, the handle is lowered and the point portion of the die separated from the cylindrical portion, when the bullet will be seen with its point projecting out of the latter portion. The base punch is then raised again, and the completely formed bullet is pressed up and out of the cylindrical die. With some dies a small ring may then be in evidence on the jacket between the body and ogive sections where the two dies came together, and the makers furnish a third die through which the bullets are pushed to eliminate this projecting rim or fin.

165. Soft Swaging. Bullets that are soft swaged, that is, with the minimum pressure on the tool handle to give them perfect form, usually shoot more accurately than if hard swaged with more pressure. There are three reasons for this. In the first place when hard swaging a metal cased bullet it is compressed in a die with great pressure and the entire die surrounding the bullet swells out quite materially. Then when the pressure is relieved it assumes its original size, compressing the jacketed bullet. When the bullet is then ejected from the die, the jacket, having more spring than the lead core actually springs outward from the core, leaving a slight space between the core and the jacket and causing the bullet to become unbalanced, or causing a variation between bullets as the outward spring of the jacket varies.

In the second place, soft swaging tends to eliminate the inaccuracy which is the result of the bullet point not being exactly concentric with the bullet body. If the point is not concentric and is filled with lead the bullet is thrown considerably out of balance. If, on the other hand, the point is not concentric but contains little lead as in soft swaging the bullet may not be thrown out of balance enough to effect its accuracy.

In the third place, when a bullet is hard swaged so as to expose a material amount of lead at the point, and is shot at a velocity of around 4,000 f.s., the unsupported lead point that projects beyond the jacket may set back so that its shape is altered from a sharp point to more or less of a mushroom. This exposed lead may be still further deformed by melting from the heat generated by friction with the air, all of which would certainly make for a loss in accuracy.

166. Lubrication. It is essential that the jacket cups be slightly lubricated before they are placed in the cylindrical die prior to swaging; otherwise the swaged bullet would stick in the die and it would not be possible to force it out without destructive force. But the lubrication must be both thin and slight otherwise the jackets will wrinkle from the trapped oil.

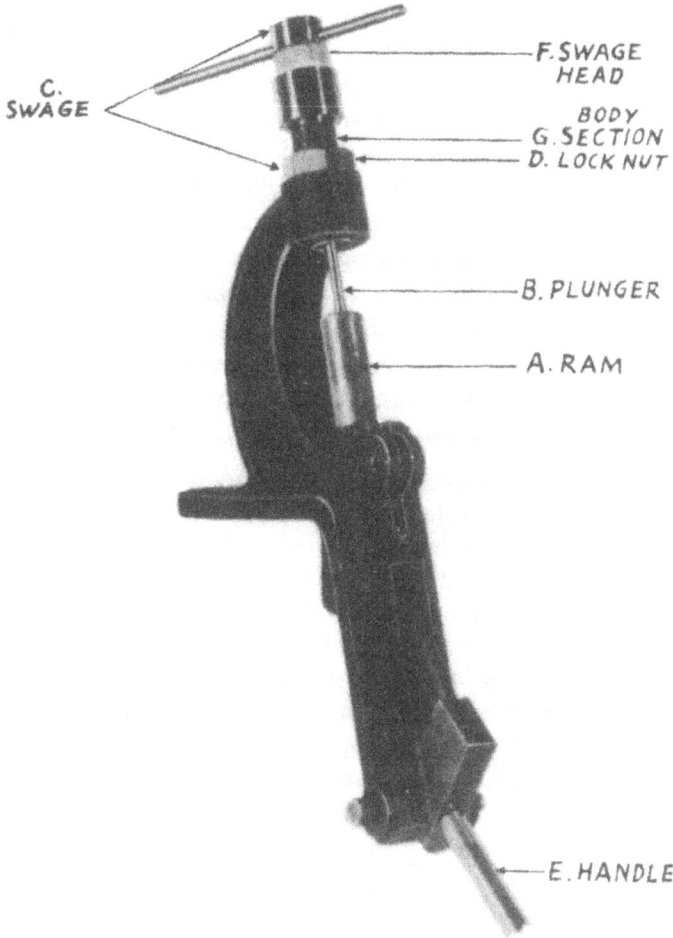

C.
SWAGE

F. SWAGE
HEAD

BODY
G. SECTION
D. LOCK NUT

B. PLUNGER

A. RAM

E. HANDLE

Super Pacific tool with RCBS die in place.

One of the best methods is to lightly moisten the finger tips of the left hand with Hoppe's Powder Solvent No. 9, and work it in by rubbing the fingers together. Then as you pick up the jacket and core assembly preparatory to placing it in either the core seater or the bullet swage, the jacket will receive sufficient lubrication from the fingers.

The R.C.B.S. die lubricant is also very effective. It is about the color and consistency of liquid honey. Follow the instructions carefully. Only the very slightest amount is necessary. Using a piece of flannel cloth about a foot square, apply not over one drop to seven or eight places over the surface of the cloth. Then rub the cloth together vigorously until the lubricant is well worked in. Set the cloth aside exposed to the air for a couple of days before use. A small handful of bullet jackets can then be rubbed between the cloth before seating the cores, or before swaging the bullets.

167. **Progressive expanding principle.** At this point a matter should be explained which should receive the very careful attention of the handloader who plans to hand swage his own bullets. This is the size relationship of each of the above tools to the others in the set. We have theorized that a progressive expanding principle between each operation in the process of making bullets is the correct one to follow. In other words the diameter of the core seater should be slightly greater, not over .0005", than the diameter of the bullet jacket as received. Similarly the diameter of the bullet swage should be slightly greater, not over .0005", than the diameter of the jacket received from the core seater. The reason for this is that when a bullet jacket containing its lead core is compressed by being forced through a die smaller than the jacket itself, the jacket, upon being ejected, is free to expand or spring out, which it does, leaving a space between the jacket and the core, because lead does not expand after it has been compressed.

If, on the other hand, the work is expanded each time rather than reduced in diameter in the die, it does not expand materially after being ejected from the die, the jacket does not expand away from the lead core, and the finished bullet will give greater accuracy.

IV

SPECIFIC CARTRIDGE DATA
AND LOADS

Be sure to read this chapter carefully before selecting components, choosing the load for your cartridge from the tables, and starting to load.

168. The following tables give the loads which, in my experience, have proved to be the best and most useful for any specific purpose, and for the more popular rifle and pistol cartridges of today. The greatest care has been taken to list only those loads within the allowable breech pressure of standard rifles of the particular caliber, that will be entirely safe in standard arms, and with bullets of close to standard diameter, bearing, and hardness, under all conditions in the field and on the target range. *However, I cannot assume any responsibility.*

In general, the heaviest loads given in each table are maximum loads, giving the heaviest breech pressure permissible in rifles adapted to that particular cartridge. THESE LOADS SHOULD NEVER BE EXCEEDED. In almost all cases it is far better to reduce the powder charge one to three grains, thus obtaining better accuracy, longer barrel life, less recoil, and an absence of extraction difficulties that may interfere with rapid fire. It is also best to work up to these maximum loads by degrees, loading several cartridges with one to three grains less of powder, firing them, and watching for any indication of excessive pressure. This is particularly advisable for any loads to be used in the tropics or hot desert countries.

In fact there is no sense in striving for the utmost in power and flat trajectory from any particular cartridge. If they are desired, one must go to a rifle and cartridge that will give them permissible and sane breech pressure.

169. **Pressures.** The limiting factor with any load is the permissible breech pressure for that rifle and cartridge, established by standard American ballistic practice. The heaviest charges of a particular type of powder given for any weight

of bullet must be regarded as the maximum load that should never be exceeded. When loading for any individual weapon it is extremely important that the handloader ascertain that his weapon is normal, standard, and in good, serviceable condition, and that the bullet he is to load falls within the standard for that caliber. Variations from the standard in chamber and groove diameter, and in bullet diameter, may cause a dangerous raise in pressure. Particularly, headspace and groove diameter of barrel should be measured (See Pars. 30 to 35 and 91.) And the diameter of the bullet should be measured. To a certain extent these dimensions may be taken for granted in the case of new standard arms by the large American manufacturers, but inspectors are human, and it is always safest to ascertain these dimensions, and this is particularly indicated in the cast of custom weapons or those of foreign manufacture.

170. **Other important details:** *Powder charges* are given in grains weight (not in grains bulk nor in readings on powder measures). The powder charges may be weighed on accurate scales or thrown from a standard powder measure. In the latter case the charge thrown should be checked on a scale. The tables take into consideration that all measures may occasionally throw a charge a half grain greater or less than that for which they are set.

Cases and Primers. The charges given are for use only with standard American cases and primers as made since about World War II. There are very slight differences in the capacity of cases and the strength of these American primers, but they are so slight as not to exceed the safe pressure limits, or the muzzle velocity. However, it is best to use the same make of case and primer. When using cases or primers of foreign manufacture maximum charges must be approached with extreme caution.

Seating depth: The maximum length of loaded cartridge that will feed through the magazines of standard American repeating rifles is given under each cartridge. When not otherwise stated the bullet should be seated in the case to give this standard overall length. However, the bullet seats of individual barrels may differ slightly, and so may the ogives of various makes and kinds of bullets of the same weight. Irrespective of standard overall length a bullet should not be seated so far out of the case that, on forcing it into the chamber, its ogive is jammed up into the rifling so that the ogive is engraved by the lands. Such loading usually causes an excessive raise in breech pressure, and if such a cartridge be extracted without firing, the bullet is likely to pull out of the case and remain in the barrel. The bullet seating plunger of the loading die should be backed out so the bullet just does not touch the lands when loaded into the rifle. However, many short, light bullets must be seated to a much shorter overall length in order that enough of the base of the bullet may remain within the case for security; generally speaking, all bullets should be seated at least their diameter within the case neck.

Velocities: Muzzle velocities of the various charges are given in even multiples of 25 feet per second, and for barrels of standard length. It is futile to quote velocities closer, because they may vary 20 foot seconds or more for individual rifles and individual bullets of the same weight.

171. **Working up a safe charge.** Whenever there is the slightest doubt about the weapon or the bullet being within the standards, or whenever the variation from standard is very slight, maximum charges should never be loaded to start with. Instead, load several cartridges with two to three grains less powder than the maximum, and try them in the rifle. If there is any indication of high pressure, that charge should not be increased, but rather decreased. Indications of high pressure are: cartridge cases that stick slightly in the chamber and are difficult to extract; gas leaks around the edges of the primer pockets; and blown primers. Flattened primers are not necessarily an indication of a dangerous pressure. Considerable extrusion of the primer around the firing pin indentation also is more likely to be due to the shape of the striker point or the firing-pin hole in the bolt face rather than to excessive pressure. If no sign of excess pressure is noted, then test cartridges containing a grain more may be tried, and finally the

maximum pressure as given in the tables may be worked up to. But when any sign of pressure appears the charge should be reduced at least a grain, and under no circumstances should the maximum loads given be exceeded. Remember that cartridges heated in the sun, or left in a very hot rifle give much higher pressure, but such excessive heat as might occur in a desert or in the tropics in normal field use has been taken into consideration in establishing the maximum charges given in the tables.

172. **Exceeding maximum charges.** Today the popular demand is for more velocity and more power. We frequently hear or read of shooters using or recommending much heavier charges than those given in the tables. Apparently they are getting away with it, but there is always a reason. They may be using a bore or chamber larger than standard (usually meaning poor accuracy), or they may be using these heavy charges in relatively low temperatures. They are flirting with danger. They may be getting 75 or even 150 feet higher muzzle velocity, and hence they think they have a load of flatter trajectory or more power. But slight increases in muzzle velocity amount to an infinitesimal small increase at 200 yards and beyond, and a drop of the bullet so much less as to be insignificant. And always there is the danger of a sticking cartridge case that will preclude a second quick shot, often an undesirable increase in recoil, or indeed a pressure that may wreck the weapon or seriously injure the shooter. If you want flatter trajectory and more power, go to another cartridge that will give it.

173. **Wildcat cartridges.** Charges for only a few of the wildcat cartridges are given here, the ones that have become most popular, for which many rifles have been built, and which have been more or less standardized. Most other wildcat cartridges have not been so standardized. There are no standards of groove diameter of barrel, chamber dimensions, and case shape and dimensions. Custom-rifle makers build these rifles largely to their own ideas. The handloader should obtain from the custom gunsmith the charges and other details for handloading cartridges for these rifles.

Weatherby rifles and Weatherby Magnum cartridges are no longer in the wildcat class, both having been thoroughly standardized, and factory-loaded ammunition is available. Hand-loaders should be governed by the tables of charges given in the folder which accompanies the rifle.

Abbreviations

B	For bolt action rifles only
G	Lead bullet with gas check
I	Lyman Ideal bullet
J	Metal-jacketed bullet
L	Plain lead bullet
OL	Overall length of cartridge
P	Breech pressure—lbs. per sq. in.
R	Remington-Peters
W	Winchester-Western

.22 HORNET

Standard case length..1.40"
Standard cartridge length.................................1.72"
Groove diameter of barrels.............2225"to .224"

The Hornet is perhaps the most desirable of all cartridges for small varmint shooting in settled and farming country because of its light report and small cost. It is entirely adequate for woodchuck, prairie dog, rabbit, fox and crow up to a distance of about 175 yards, or to 200 yards on still days. Also it is not too destructive of meat for wild turkey. Good reloads with selected bullets should group in about 1¼ minutes. The loads given are for new cases made since World War II, which are slightly thicker than older cases, with less powder capacity, hence charges must be slightly lower than with older cases to keep within pressure limits. Many rifles, particularly the excellent Winchester Model 70, have rather small bores. If the groove diameter of the barrel is .223″ or smaller, use .223″ bullets. For larger groove diameters use .224″ bullets. There is little difference between the killing effect of soft-point and hollow-point bullets. The cartridge is at its best with bullets of 45 or 50 grains weight.

.22 HORNET

No.	Bullet Grains	Bullet Type	Powder Grains	Powder Type	Velocity f.p.s.	Remarks
1	35	J	11.6	2400	3020	Highest velocity.
2	35	J	10.0	4227	2750	
3	40	J	7.7	2400	1825	Full jacketed for squirrels.
4	40	J	11.2	2400	2850	
5	43	G	10.2	2400	2400	I-225438. Reduce powder for best accuracy.
6	43	G	10.3	4227	2275	I-225438. Reduce powder for best accuracy.
7	45	J	8.8	4227	2045	Full jacketed for squirrels.
8	45	J	10.8	4227	2410	Turkey load.
9	45	J	10.0	2400	2600	Duplicates factory load.
10	50	J	11.5	4227	2575	Max. Caution.
11	50	J	9.8	2400	2500	Max. Caution.

.218 BEE

Standard case length................................1.345″

Standard cartridge length........................1.68″

Groove diameter of barrel........................ .224″

The Bee has a slightly greater powder capacity than the Hornet. Slightly larger powder charges may be used, giving slightly greater velocity. It is slightly easier to handload than the Hornet, and cases can be reloaded more times. Bullets should measure .224″, but if using a custom-built barrel be sure that the bullet does not exceed the groove diameter by more than .0005″. Loads are based on new cases made since World War II which have smaller capacity than prewar cases. The Bee is rather sensitive to any increase in powder charges, and those given should not be exceeded. The attainable accuracy is about the same as for the Hornet cartridge, and the report just slightly louder.

.218 BEE

No.	BULLET Grains	Type	POWDER Grains	Type	VELOCITY f.p.s.	REMARKS
1	40	J	14.0	4198	2700	Powder fills case.
2	40	J	13.0	2400	3100	
3	40	J	14.0	4227	3100	
4	43	G	8.7	2400	2400	I-225438. Reduce charge for accuracy.
5	43	G	9.8	4227	2400	I-225438. Reduce charge for accuracy.
6	45	J	12.3	2400	2800	
7	45	J	12.8	4227	2800	
8	50	J	12.0	2400	2775	
9	50	J	12.5	4227	2700	
10	50	J	13.5	4198	2600	Powder fills case.

.22-3000 LOVELL 2R

Case length .... 1.635″
Cartridge length .... 2.09″ Approx.
Groove diameter .... .223″ to .224″

This wildcat cartridge is made by necking down the old .25-20 Single Shot case to hold .223″ or .224″ bullets and then fire-forming it in the rifle to a slightly greater diameter below the shoulder, with more of a shoulder. Griffin & Howe have also supplied ready-formed cases in this caliber. Before the introduction of the .222 Remington cartridge this one was very popular among well-informed riflemen for light varmint shooting. It is as accurate as any .22 caliber cartridge, and is good for sure hits on woodchuck to about 275 yards. If the groove diameter is under .2235″ use .223″ bullets. Barrels have been made with both 14 and 16 inch twists. The 16 inch twist will not stabilize 55 grain bullets. To get 17 grains of 4198 powder in the case the powder must be sifted in slowly. I have found no difference in the accuracy and trajectory of loads 7 and 8, but 4227 powder measures more accurately than 4198 and is much easier to load. These two loads are the lightest that can be recommended for coyote. Seat bullets to just barely touch lands.

.22-3000 LOVELL 2R

No.	BULLET Grains	Type	POWDER Grains	Type	VELOCITY f.p.s.	REMARKS
1	43	G	8.0	4227	1750	I-225438. Squirrel and Grouse.
2	43	G	8.0	2400	1750	I-225438. Squirrel and Grouse.
3	43	G	8.0	4759	1750	I-225438. Squirrel and Grouse.
4	40	J	17.0	4198	3300	Powder compressed.
5	45	J	17.0	4198	3100	Powder compressed.
6	45	J	16.0	4227	3250	
7	50	J	15.5	4227	3050	Best varmint load.
8	50	J	16.5	4198	3050	Powder compressed.
9	50	J	11.0	4227	2300	Turkey load.
10	50	J	9.0	4227	1875	Full jacketed. Squirrel and grouse.
11	55	J	15.0	4227	2850	
12	55	J	16.0	4198	2850	Compressed powder.

.222 REMINGTON

Standard case length..1.692"

Standard cartridge length................................2.15"

Groove diameter of barrel................................ .224"

Since its introduction the .222 Remington has become the most popular of all high-speed .22 caliber cartridges. It is just about right in power for all American varmint shooting, its report and recoil are light, its trajectory is ample, the barrel life is long, and it is easy to handload. It is also superior in accuracy, up to 300 yards at least, to any other cartridge, and recently many world records have been made with it at 100 and 200 yards in heavy bench rest rifles. In fact, it seems to be the one best all-around cartridge for everything short of big-game shooting. It is usually at its best when handloaded with 4198 powder and 50 or 55 grain bullets. Bullets should be seated in the case (if magazine length permits) so as to just not touch the lands.

.222 REMINGTON

No.	Bullet Grains	Type	Powder Grains	Type	Velocity f.p.s.	Remarks
1	40	J	22.0	4198	3375	
2	40	J	23.0	3031	3100	
3	43	G	9.0	2400	1850	I-225438. Small game.
4	43	G	9.0	4227	1750	I-225438. Small game.
5	43	G	10.6	4198	2000	I-225438. Small game.
6	45	J	22.0	4198	3400	
7	45	J	23.0	3031	3100	
8	50	J	26.0	4320	3050	
9	50	J	23.0	3031	3000	
10	50	J	21.5	4198	3150	
11	50	J	20.5	4198	3100	Very accurate.
12	50	J	19.5	4198	2800	Full jacketed bullet. Small game.
13	55	J	25.0	4320	2925	
14	55	J	23.0	3031	3000	
15	55	J	20.0	4198	2875	
16	55	J	21.0	4198	3175	

.219 DONALDSON WASP

Case length..1.73″ Approx.

Cartridge length ....2.18″ Approx.

Groove diameter of barrel................................ .224″

This wildcat cartridge has been the most popular of all for competitive bench rest shooting at 100 and 200 yards. It has repeatedly held most of the world records. The case is made from the .219 Winchester Zipper case, which is formed in a .219 Wasp forming die, then the long neck is cut off to the length (about 1.73″) of the chamber of the custom-built rifle. Afterward the case is fire-formed in the chamber of the rifle, and finally the neck is sized correctly to hold .224″ bullets friction-tight. Many custom-rifle makers furnish cases ready-formed.

The cartridge, being of the rimmed type, has also been very popular for varmint shooting in single-shot rifles.

The heavier charges given should not be exceeded because the pressure is very high.

.219 DONALDSON WASP

No.	Bullet Grains	Type	Powder Grains	Type	Velocity f.p.s.	Remarks
1	40	J	31.0	3031	3925	
2	43	G	10.0	2400	2100	I-225488. Small game.
3	43	G	10.0	4227	2000	I-225488. Small game.
4	43	G	10.0	4198	1800	I-225488. Small game.
5	45	J	29.0	3031	3700	
6	50	J	28.0	3031	3600	
7	50	J	27.0	3031	3550	Varmint load.
8	55	J	26.0	3031	3450	Bench rest load.
9	55	J	28.0	3031	3525	Varmint load.

.22-250 VARMINTER

Case length .... 1.91″
Cartridge length .... 2.40″ approx.
Groove diameter of barrel .... .224″

This is the most popular of all wildcat cartridges. Thousands of custom-built rifles have been made for it. It is very popular for varmint shooting, even to extreme ranges, and has been much used by bench rest shooters. Its accuracy capabilities are fully the equal of any other .22 caliber cartridge. The case is made easily by simply running the .250-3000 Savage case into a varminter resizing die and sizing the neck down to hold .224″ bullets friction-tight. Cases may also be formed from .30-06 brass, but have smaller capacity, and the heavier charges in the table give very excessive pressures. Best accuracy is usually attained with 50 and 55 grain bullets and charges of 31 to 33 grains of 3031 powder.

.22-250 VARMINTER

No.	Bullet Grains	Type	Powder Grains	Type	Velocity f.p.s.	Remarks
1	43	G	10.5	2400	1900	I-225488. Small game.
2	43	G	8.5	4227	1800	I-225488. Small game.
3	43	G	12.0	4198	1650	I-225488. Small game.
4	45	J	33.0	4320	3450	
5	50	J	35.0	3031	3925	
6	50	J	35.0	4320	3625	
7	50	J	38.0	4320	3975	
8	50	J	15.0	4759	2550	Full jacketed bullet. Small game.
9	55	J	31.0	3031	3475	
10	55	J	32.0	3031	3575	
11	55	J	25.0	4198	3200	
12	55	J	34.0	4320	3550	
13	55	J	36.0	4320	3600	

.220 SWIFT

Standard case length..2.20"

Standard cartridge length...2.68"

Groove diameter of barrel...224"

The .220 Swift has the highest muzzle velocity of any American factory cartridge. It is wise, however, to handload slightly under these velocities to get more moderate pressure, and longer case and barrel life. Cases should be watched for length, and when they have stretched to 2.22" they should be trimmed back to 2.20". In many cases greater accuracy will be attained by reducing the charges here given by one to two grains. The effect on remaining velocity and drop of the bullet at 200 yards with these moderate charges is very slight.

.220 SWIFT

No.	BULLET Grains	Type	POWDER Grains	Type	VELOCITY f.p.s.	REMARKS
1	45	J	41.0	4320	3900	
2	45	J	41.0	4064	4000	
3	45	J	38.0	3031	3900	
4	50	J	37.0	3031	3800	
5	50	J	39.5	4064	3800	
6	50	J	39.0	4320	3700	
7	55	J	43.0	4350	3650	
8	55	J	38.0	4064	3700	
9	55	J	38.0	4320	3600	
10	55	J	36.5	3031	3650	

.243 WINCHESTER

Standard case length..2.04"

Standard cartridge length...2.71"

Groove diameter of barrel...243"

This new cartridge is proving excellent, not only for varmints, but also for deer, sheep, and antelope. The twist of rifling, one turn in ten inches, will handle all weights of bullets from 70 to 105 grains with excellent accuracy. The lighter bullets, 70 to 87 grains, all of which are constructed to expand easily, should be used for varmints. The heavier bullets, 90 to 105 grains, are of heavier construction, and should be used only for larger game. With the 100 and 105 grain Spitzer bullets the wind deflection up to at least 300 yards is probably less than with any other standard cartridge, and this rather indicates the undesirability of round-nose bullets in this caliber.

Slow-burning powders seem to be much the best. Either 4064 or 4350 for the lighter bullets, and 4350 to 4831 for the heavier. The velocities given in the table are for a rifle with 26-inch barrel. For 22-inch barrels deduct about 100 foot seconds. For low pressure, long accuracy life, and general all around use I would suggest 43.5 grains of 4350 powder with 80 or 85 grain bullets, and 39.5 grains of the same powder with 100 or 105 grain bullets.

.243 WINCHESTER

No.	Bullet Grains	Bullet Type	Powder Grains	Powder Type	Velocity f.p.s.	Remarks
1	70	J	40.0	4064	3450	Hornady bullet.
2	70	J	47.0	4350	3500	Hornady bullet.
3	75	J	40.0	4064	3400	Speer bullet.
4	75	J	46.0	4350	3400	Speer bullet.
5	80	J	46.0	4350	3400	Winchester bullet.
6	85	J	38.0	4064	3150	Sierra bullet.
7	85	J	45.0	4350	3225	Sierra bullet.
8	87	J	38.0	4064	3125	Hornady bullet.
9	87	J	44.0	4350	3200	Hornady bullet.
10	100	J	41.0	4350	3000	Winchester and Sierra bullets.
11	100	J	44.0	4831	2925	Winchester and Sierra bullets.
12	105	J	40.0	4350	2900	Speer bullet.
13	105	J	44.0	4831	2875	Speer bullet.

.244 REMINGTON

Standard case length................................. 2.23″

Standard cartridge length........................ 2.75″

Groove diameter of barrel...................... .243″

The cartridge case is practically that of the .257 Roberts necked down to hold .243″ bullets friction tight. The cartridge is very similar to the .243 Winchester except that the case has slightly greater powder capacity, and the twist of rifling is one turn in 12 inches. Rifles shoot excellently with the lighter-weight bullets, but will seldom stabilize those of 100 and 105 grains. Loads are generally the same as for the .243 Winchester, except that about one grain more powder may be used in the .244 to give the same velocity as the .243.

.25-20 W.C.F.

Standard case length .... 1.35"
Standard cartridge length .... 1.60"
Groove diameter of barrel .... .257"

Rifles are no longer made for this cartridge, but many are still in use, and are very excellent for varmints and small game up to about 125 yards. The 60-grain loads give much the flatter trajectory, but the 86-grain bullets are usually slightly more accurate. Bullets for lever-action rifles should have flat points, and should be crimped in the case, with an overall cartridge length (for magazine rifles) of not over 1.60". Load No. 7 is for strong single-shot rifles only, the sharp-pointed 87-grain bullet being seated out of the case enough to contact the lands. It has shown fine accuracy.

.25-20 W.C.F.

No.	BULLET Grains	Type	POWDER Grains	Type	VELOCITY f.p.s.	REMARKS
1	60	J	9.7	4227	1800	
2	60	J	12.7	4227	2200	
3	86	J	8.7	4227	1400	
4	86	J	10.7	4227	1750	
5	86	G	8.0	2400	1575	I-257312.
6	86	G	9.0	4759	1450	I-257312.
7	87	J	12.0	4227	1900	Sharp point. OL to touch lands.

.250-3000 SAVAGE

Standard case length .... 1.91"
Standard cartridge length .... 2.51"
Groove diameter of barrel .... .257"

This has been a very popular cartridge for a long time, and has been noted for its great accuracy both in Savage Model 99 lever-action, and in bolt-action rifles. With 87-grain bullets it has been a favorite varmint cartridge, and with 100-grain bullets it has proved quite satisfactory for deer, sheep, and antelope. The recoil is quite moderate. For lever-action rifles the case must be full-length resized each time because there is enough spring in such actions to cause the case to lengthen so it will not go into the chamber without prohibitive force. The heavier charges are for bolt-action rifles only. The standard 14-inch twist of rifling will not stabilize bullets weighing over 100 grains.

.250-3000 SAVAGE

No.	Bullet Grains	Type	Powder Grains	Type	Velocity f.p.s.	Remarks
1	60	J	35.0	3031	3250	
2	60	J	38.0	3031	3700	Bolt action only.
3	75	G	13.0	4759	1700	I-257463. Small game.
4	75	G	14.5	4198	1600	I-257463. Small game.
5	87	J	36.0	3031	3100	Bolt action only.
6	87	J	35.0	3031	3000	
7	87	J	38.0	4320	3050	Bolt action only.
8	87	J	37.0	4320	3000	
9	97	G	16.0	4198	1800	I-257464. Small game.
10	97	G	13.0	4759	1700	I-257464. Small game.
11	100	J	31.0	3031	2650	
12	100	J	32.0	3031	2800	Bolt action only.
13	100	J	36.5	4320	2875	
14	100	J	40.5	4350	2925	Bolt action only.

.257 ROBERTS

Standard case length..2.23"
Standard cartridge length...2.75"
Groove diameter of barrel...257"

I think this is one of the very best cartridges made, particularly for the handloader, who desires a cartridge heavy enough for deer, sheep, goat and antelope, and at the same time it is excellent for varmint shooting. It has been much handicapped in its factory loadings by round-nose bullets seated to standard cartridge length (2.75"). Using pointed bullets seated to almost touch the lands, which in most rifles will be an overall cartridge length of 2.95", superior accuracy and velocity may be obtained. Such loadings will not feed through standard factory rifles, but will through most custom-built arms. The excellent Winchester Model 70 rifle is easily altered for such long loading by removing the filler plate in the magazine, substituting a .30-06 follower, and cutting back the bolt stop. For heavier game the 117-grain bullets are a little better in killing power than those of 100 grains. Bullets of 87 grain are not quite so accurate as those of 100 grains, and their trajectory is not as flat beyond 200 yards, and there is little excuse for their use in this cartridge. The above is based on barrels having a twist of one turn in 10 inches.

.257 ROBERTS

| | BULLET | | POWDER | | VELOCITY | |
No.	Grains	Type	Grains	Type	f.p.s.	REMARKS
1	87	J	14.0	4759	1850	Small game and turkeys.
2	87	J	40.5	3031	3200	
3	87	J	43.0	4064	3200	
4	87	J	43.0	4320	3200	
5	97	G	14.0	4759	1850	I-257464. Small game.
6	100	J	38.5	3031	2925	
7	100	J	40.0	4064	3050	
8	100	J	40.0	4320	3050	
9	100	J	46.0	4350	3050	
10	100	J	48.0	4831	3100	
11	117	J	42.0	4350	2825	Sierra boat-tail.
12	117	J	44.0	4831	2850	Sierra boat-tail.

6.5mm MANNLICHER-SCHOENAUER

Standard case length..2.11″

Standard cartridge length with 160 gr.
   bullet ....3.03″

Groove diameter of barrel..................264″ to .268″

This has been the Britisher's favorite cartridge for medium game from about 1895 almost to today. It has been for him what the .30-06 cartridge has been for the American sportsman. However, his rifles almost always had a 26-inch barrel, and he used the cartridge loaded with the 160-grain bullet, which in that barrel length gave about 2,300 f.p.s. muzzle velocity. Incidentally, one of these rifles barrelled by Jeffery of London was used exclusively by the late Charles Sheldon, whom most of us regard as the most experienced American big-game hunter who ever lived. With his rifle he shot about 500 head of American big game, including between 70 and 80 grizzly and Alaskan brown bear.

The only firm that has regularly made the 6.5mm Mann-licher-Schoenauer sporting rifle is Steyr-Werke of Austria (now Steyr-Daimler-Puch) and they have quite regularly furnished it with short barrels, usually 17¾ to 18 inches. These barrels give much lower velocity than the British 26-inch barrel, as will be seen from the tables which are for a rifle with 17¾ inch barrel. But even at these lower velocities the long bullets with their high sectional density give considerably more killing power than does, for example, our .30-30 cartridge.

This cartridge seems to be very sensitive to even a very small increase in the powder charge, *and the charges given in these tables should not be exceeded.* Lighter bullets than those given do not do well because of the 7½ inch twist of rifling, and the short overall length to which they must be seated does not feed well in the spool magazine of the Mannlicher-Schoenauer rifle. The cartridge is no longer made by our United States cartridge companies, but is furnished by Canadian Industries, Ltd. (Dominion Cartridge Co.) loaded with a 160-grain bullet, and their cases use our .210" primer.

6.5mm MANNLICHER SCHOENAUER

	BULLET		POWDER		VELOCITY	
No.	Grains	Type	Grains	Type	f.p.s.	REMARKS
1	140	J	33.5	3031	2200	Sierra Boat-tail.
2	140	J	31.0	HiVel 2	2125	Sierra Boat-tail.
3	140	J	35.0	4320	2200	Sierra boat-tail.
4	156	J	32.5	3031	2000	Norma S. P.
5	156	J	33.0	HiVel 2	2025	Norma S. P.
6	156	J	35.0	4320	2075	Norma S. P.
7	160	J	33.5	3031	2050	Dominion
8	160	J	34.0	HiVel 2	2025	Dominion
9	160	J	34.5	4320	2075	Dominion

.270 WINCHESTER

Standard case length..............................2.54"
Standard cartridge length.......................3.34"
Groove diameter of barrel...............277" to .278"

This cartridge, and the .30-06, are the two most popular cartridges for all American big game. It is a most excellent all-around cartridge where the hunter is seeking game larger than deer, sheep, and antelope. Its trajectory and accuracy are such that hunters can reliably hit large game at longer estimated distances than with any other rifle. Rifles hold their zero well, and usually shoot all the various 130 and 150 grain loads to approximately the same point of impact with the zero sight adjustment. The cartridge has the reputation of giving a larger percentage of instantaneous kill, on game the size of deer, than any other factory cartridge. In handloads for game larger than deer the 150-grain bullet is now being preferred, and particularly the 150-grain boattail bullet loaded to a muzzle velocity of 3,000 f.p.s., which gives a flatter trajectory and less bullet drop beyond 200 yards than the standard loadings with 130-grain bullet. This is the favorite cartridge of Mr. Jack O'Connor and the writer.

.270 WINCHESTER

No.	Bullet Grains	Type	Powder Grains	Type	Velocity f.p.s.	Remarks
1	100	J	48.5	3031	3375	
2	100	J	54.0	4320	3400	
3	103	G	16.0	4759	1750	I-230468-S. Small game.
4	103	G	19.0	4198	1750	I-230468-S. Small game.
5	110	J	46.0	3031	3150	Sierra bullet.
6	110	J	53.0	4320	3450	Sierra bullet.
7	110	J	58.0	4350	3400	Sierra bullet. Very accurate.
8	110	J	25.0	4198	2000	Sierra bullet. Small game.
9	130	J	43.0	3031	2900	
10	130	J	47.0	4320	3000	
11	130	J	47.0	4064	3000	
12	130	J	56.0	4350	3100	
13	130	J	58.0	4831	3100	
14	150	J	53.5	4350	2900	
15	150	J	56.0	4831	2950	
16	150	J	57.0	4831	3000	Sierra boat-tail bullet.

7mm MAUSER (7 X 57)

Standard case length..2.235"
Standard cartridge length................................3.065"
Groove diameter of barrel................................. .285"

This is one of the oldest high-power cartridges, having been developed for the Spanish Government in 1892. The original loading was with a 175-grain jacketed bullet at a muzzle velocity of 2,300 f.p.s. With this loading and full-jacketed bullets, W. D. M. Bell, a professional elephant hunter, killed over 800 elephants, mostly with brain shots. But don't forget that Bell was a most remarkable shot, knew the anatomy of the elephant perfectly, and hunted them in more or less open country.

With modern loadings the 7mm is an excellent cartridge for all American big game, and not too powerful for varmints with light bullets. It is characterized by light recoil, which makes it very desirable for ladies, or for those who object to kick. With the 145-grain bullet loaded to 2,700 f.s. it is the equal of the old .30-06 loading, and perhaps better because the bullet has greater sectional density—a fine deer load. For the largest game—moose, elk, and grizzly—the 175-grain bullet will be found superior in killing qualities. The 160-grain bullet is fine as all-around loading. Most jacketed bullets measure .284″ and the loads given are for such bullets.

7mm MAUSER (7x57)

No.	Bullet Grains	Type	Powder Grains	Type	Velocity f.p.s.	Remarks
1	120	J	42.5	3031	2900	
2	120	J	46.0	4064	2975	
3	120	J	44.0	4320	2800	
4	125	G	15.0	4759	1700	I-285448. Small game.
5	125	G	17.5	4198	1700	I-285448. Small game.
6	139	J	42.0	4320	2700	
7	139	J	37.5	3031	2600	
8	145	J	42.0	4320	2700	Equals old .30-06 load.
9	154	J	41.0	4064	2600	
10	154	J	47.0	4350	2600	
11	160	J	46.0	4350	2575	All-around load.
12	160	J	42.0	4064	2700	
13	160	J	42.0	4320	2700	
14	175	J	45.0	4350	2425	
15	175	J	47.0	4831	2500	
16	175	J	40.0	4064	2400	
17	175	J	40.0	4320	2400	
18	180	J	43.0	4350	2325	

7 X 61mm SHARPE AND HART

Standard case length...2.40″
Cartridge length for heavy bullets...3.26″ to 3.30″
Groove diameter of barrel.................284″ to .2854″

This new 7mm cartridge was designed by Philip B. Sharpe and Richard F. Hart after seven years of experimenting. The

case has a belted head similar to that of the .300 H&H
Magnum case. Empty unprimed cases for American .210
primers, and factory-loaded cartridges are supplied by Norma,
and are available from retailers in the United States. Re-forming
cases from .300 H&H Magnum brass is not recommended.
For light bullets only, 120 to 130 grains, for varmint shooting,
a twist of rifling of one turn in 14 to 16 inches is advised.
For all bullets including the heavier weights the twist should
be 12 inches. Heavier bullets should be seated to an overall
cartridge length of 3.26″ to 3.30″ so as to just not touch the
lands. The lighter bullets should be seated to a depth of at
least .125″, and .200″ is better. The H&M Tool Company are
the authorized chamber-reamer makers. Their reamer does not
include the bullet seat, and they furnish separate throating
reamers so the gunsmith can throat to seat any bullet desired.
The chambers on Schultz & Larson rifles are throated to handle
all bullets. No. 4350 has proved to be decidedly the best
powder. Nos. 4064 and 4320 powders will do fairly well with
the lighter bullets. This information is supplied through the
courtesy of Sharpe & Hart Associates, Inc., Emmitsburg, Mary-
land.

The overall length of the cartridge, being slightly shorter
than that of the .30-06, any strong bolt action for that cartridge
may be used, the bolt head and magazine being altered. Featherweight barrels are not advisable. Schultz & Larson rifles for
this cartridge, available through retailers in the United States,
have a very strong breech action, and will safely stand a mean
breech pressure of 60,000 pounds, although slightly lower
pressures are advised. But the writer thinks that with other
actions the mean pressure should not exceed 55,000 pounds,
and the suggested loads in the table are so given.

The trajectory is very flat, slightly flatter than that of the
.270 Winchester, considerably flatter with the 160-grain Sierra
boattail bullet. The killing power has proved superb on all
American big game with the possible exception of Alaskan
brown bear in thick cover. The accuracy life of chrome-moly

barrels has proved to be longer than expected, possibly 4,000 to 6,000 rounds.

Leading ballisticians have long thought that 7mm was the best caliber for a shoulder rifle, because it is the largest caliber from which a bullet with the highest ballistic coefficient can be fired at the highest velocity possible with existing powders, and not give recoil in a 9-pound rifle that would be detrimental to the best marksmanship of the average rifleman.

7 x 61mm SHARPE & HART

No.	Bullet Grains	Type	Powder Grains	Type	Velocity f.p.f.	Remarks
1	120	J	64.0	4350	3500	Sierra bullet.
2	130	J	64.0	4350	3400	Speer bullet.
3	140	J	64.0	4350	3375	Sierra bullet.
4	145	J	63.0	4350	3350	Speer bullet.
5	156	J	63.0	4350	3300	Norma boat-tail bullet.
6	160	J	63.0	4350	3300	Sierra boat-tail bullet.
7	175	J	60.0	4350	3200	Hornady bullet.

The capacity of this case is such that it is decidedly "over bore capacity" with any powder faster burning than 4350.

.30-30 WINCHESTER

Standard case length................................2.047" to 2.054"
Standard cartridge length..............................2.517"
Groove diameter of barrel............................ .308"

In the past this has been our most popular deer cartridge. It is a medium-range cartridge when used in the usual lever-action rifle with tubular magazine, for its accuracy with the best sighting equipment is not better than about 3-inch groups at 100 yards for the first three shots from a cold rifle. When these rifles warm up the groups open up considerably, which, however, is of little importance in a deer rifle.

In the past many charges heavier than those recommended in the accompanying table have been published, but it has been found that many of these, with modern primers and bullets measuring .308-inch, give very excessive pressures. The charges given should not be exceeded.

For tubular-magazine rifles only round or flat nosed bullets should be used, loaded to the standard overall cartridge length of 2.517 inches, and the bullets should be crimped in the cases. Also, cases that have been fired once with full charges should be full-length resized before loading again, and should be trimmed to standard length if necessary, for all lever actions have enough unavoidable back spring to the breech bolt, allowing the case to lengthen enough so that if not resized it cannot be gotten into the chamber without prohibitive force.

For all these reasons it hardly pays to reload full-charged cartridges, but loads 5, 6, 7, and 8, starting with new primed cases, or full-length resized cases, then neck resizing only, not crimping, and using single loading only (not through the magazine), usually shoot with great accuracy and make excellent small-game and general target loads. Way back in 1901 and 1902 I shot many mule deer, sheep, and goats with my .30-30, and very successfully up to about 150 yards, but I also subsisted largely on grouse, rabbit, ducks, porcupine, and beaver shot with reduced loads. The .30-30 is not to be despised as an all-around rifle.

.30-30 WINCHESTER

No.	Bullet Grains	Bullet Type	Powder Grains	Powder Type	Velocity f.p.s.	Remarks
1	110	J	35.0	3031	2500	
2	110	J	32.0	HiVel	2550	
3	150	J	31.0	3031	2300	
4	150	J	31.0	HiVel	2250	
5	154	L	10.0	4759	1300	I-308241. Small game.
6	154	L	18.0	4198	1675	I-308241. Small game.
7	165	G	14.0	4759	1500	I-308291. Small game.
8	165	G	24.0	4198	2000	I-308291. Small game.
9	170	J	31.5	3031	2250	
10	170	J	30.0	HiVel	2175	

.300 SAVAGE

Standard case length .... 1.87"
Standard cartridge length .... 2.60"
Groove diameter of barrel .... .308"

This is an excellent deer cartridge for use in Savage Model 99 lever-action rifles, giving much greater killing power than the .250-3000, .30-30, and .303 Savage cartridges. Before the advent of the .308 Winchester cartridge it was the nearest approach to the .30-06 cartridge that could be obtained in a lever-action rifle. Now, however, it seems destined to be largely replaced by the .308 Winchester cartridge, for which Savage Model 99 rifles can also be obtained.

Due to the slight spring in the breech block of lever-action rifles, cases fired with the full charge lengthen, and must be full-length resized before reloading. For Savage rifles, however, it is not necessary to crimp the bullet in the case, and pointed bullets also may be used.

.300 SAVAGE

| | Bullet | | Powder | | Velocity | |
No.	Grains	Type	Grains	Type	f.p.s.	Remarks
1	110	J	34.0	4198	2800	
2	110	J	43.0	3031	3050	
3	110	J	45.5	4064	2925	Powder compressed.
4	125	J	42.0	3031	2925	
5	150	J	39.5	3031	2650	
6	150	J	33.0	4198	2500	
7	150	J	42.0	4064	2625	
8	165	G	15.0	4759	1700	I-308291. Small game.
9	180	J	36.0	3031	2375	
10	200	J	35.5	3031	2250	

.30-40 KRAG

Standard case length.................................2.30″ to 2.31″
Standard cartridge length.........................3.09″
Groove diameter of barrel................308″ to .309″

I have a great admiration for this cartridge. I won the U.S. Army Rifle Competitions with the old .30-40 Krag rifle in 1903, and shot for three years on the Infantry Rifle Team with it. I have also shot a lot of both big and small game with it. The fact that the cartridge has a rimmed case gets us away from a lot of troubles associated with headspace with it. It is the most powerful cartridge not having a recoil in 8- and 9-pound rifles that is not at least a little annoying. The Krag rifle with its one locking lug was not well designed to stand high pressure, and for that reason breech pressures should never exceed 42,000 pounds. The loads given in the accompanying table do not exceed that pressure in standard rifles with .308″ diameter bullets.

Because most rifles are throated for the long 220-grain bullet, they do not give very great accuracy with jacketed bullets of less than 150 grains, and all bullets should be seated as far out of the case as possible, provided the cartridge does not exceed the standard overall length of 3.09 inches. Because of the target shooting and hunting I have done with it in the past, I believe it to be at its best with 220-grain bullets. It also gives exceptionally great accuracy with cast-lead bullets, both plain base and gas check, at moderate velocities. Cases fired with full loads in the Winchester Model 95 rifle should be full-length resized before reloading.

.30-40 KRAG

No.	Bullet		Powder		Velocity f.p.s.	Remarks
	Grains	Type	Grains	Type		
1	150	J	43.0	4320	2450	
2	150	J	43.0	4064	2500	
3	150	J	41.0	3031	2550	
4	154	L	12.0	4759	1325	I-308241. Gallery, small game.
5	154	L	18.0	4227	1600	I-308241. Gallery, small game.
6	180	J	40.0	4064	2325	
7	180	J	40.0	4820	2300	
8	180	J	46.0	4350	2400	
9	180	J	34.0	HiVel	2200	Target load.
10	180	J	48.0	4831	2200	
11	194	G	22.0	4759	1800	I-308334. Accurate to 500 yds.
12	194	G	28.0	HiVel	1800	I-308334. Accurate to 500 yds.
13	207	G	22.0	4759	1800	I-308284. Accurate to 500 yds.
14	207	G	28.0	HiVel	1800	I-308284. Accurate to 500 yds.
15	220	J	44.0	4350	2250	Max. for Krag.
16	220	J	46.0	4831	2000	Fine load.
17	220	J	38.0	4320	2100	
18	220	J	38.0	4064	2100	
19	220	J	36.0	3031	2100	

.308 WINCHESTER

Standard case length...............................2.015"
Standard cartridge length.........................2.75"
Groove diameter of barrel........................ .308"

This is basically the same as the new 7.62mm NATO military cartridge, and will interchange with it. Having less powder capacity than the .30-06, not quite such high velocities can be obtained with it, but it should shoot just as accurately, and kill game just as well as that cartridge, although it will not "buck the wind" quite as well. Like the .30-06, it is very versatile, and can be loaded with all weights of bullets from 110 to 200 grains, but not with the 220-grain bullet for which its usual 12-inch twist is not adequate. It will also use the same cast-lead bullets as the .30-06. The case is a very strong one, and should stand reloading many times. Do not seat the bullets farther out of the case than to the standard overall length (2.75"); that is, to just not touch the lands. The powder for the heavier charges should be reduced two grains for use in the Savage Model 99 rifle, and cases fired in that rifle may require full-length resizing each time they are reloaded.

.308 WINCHESTER

No.	Bullet Grains	Bullet Type	Powder Grains	Powder Type	Velocity f.p.s.	Remarks
1	110	J	48.0	3031	3175	*
2	110	J	51.0	4064	3100	*
3	125	J	46.0	3031	2800	*
4	125	J	48.0	4064	2800	*
5	125	J	48.0	4320	2800	*
6	150	J	45.0	3031	2800	*
7	150	J	47.0	4064	2700	*
8	150	J	47.0	4320	2700	*
9	154	L	13.0	4759	1300	I-308241. Small game.
10	154	G	18.0	4759	1600	I-311466. Small game.
11	169	G	18.0	4759	1550	I-311413. Small game.
12	169	G	24.0	4198	1800	I-311413. Small game.
13	180	J	40.0	3031	2450	*
14	180	J	44.0	4320	2500	*
15	180	J	51.5	4350	2625	*Best big game and long range.
16	180	J	36.0	HiVel 2	2300	300 meter load.
17	200	J	48.0	4350	2450	Speer bullet.

* Decrease powder two grains for Savage Model 99 Rifle.

.30-06 U.S.

Standard case length..2.494"
Standard cartridge length...............................3.34"
Groove diameter of barrel.............................. .308"

The standard U.S. Government (Army) cartridge since 1906, and one of the most versatile of all cartridges. Proved loads have been developed for it: for gallery and small game with light-cast bullets, for varmints and for 200- and 300-yard target with light recoil, with 150-grain jacketed bullets for service and for explosive effect on medium game, with 180-grain bullets for general big game, 300-meter target, and 1,000-yard target, and with 220-grain bullets for the largest American big game.

With the heavier loads it is a high-intensity cartridge that is at its best in rifles with heavy barrels weighing over 9 pounds, and these loads may prove to have excessive recoil for some in lighter arms. For featherweight rifles, the loads should be reduced two to four grains.

Load No. 14 gives light recoil, long barrel life, and is usually the most accurate load to 300 meters. It also has ample power for deer. Load No. 18 is the standard and one of the best loads for all big game. Load No. 20 gives maximum pressure, and should not be used in high-temperature countries. Many 220-grain bullets, intended for the largest game, do not expand well on deer. With none of these loads should the overall cartridge length of 3.34" be exceeded.

.30-06 U.S.

No.	BULLET Grains	Type	POWDER Grains	Type	VELOCITY f.p.s.	REMARKS
1	110	J	53.0	3031	3325	To 200 yds. only. No ricochets.
2	110	J	58.0	4320	3325	To 200 yds. only. No ricochets.
3	125	J	52.0	3031	3150	200 & 300 yard target load.
4	125	J	56.0	4320	3200	200 & 300 yard target load.
5	150	J	18.0	4759	1500	Full jacketed bullet. Small game.
6	150	J	51.0	3031	3000	
7	150	J	53.5	4064	3000	
8	150	J	53.5	4320	3000	
9	153	G	18.0	4759	1600	I-311466. Small game.
10	153	G	23.0	4198	1750	I-311466. Small game.
11	154	L	12.0	4759	1100	I-308241. Small game.
12	169	G	18.0	4759	1600	I-311413. Small game.
13	169	G	23.0	4198	1700	I-311413. Small game.
14	180	J	36.5	HiVel 2	2250	300 meter load.
15	180	J	50.0	4064	2725	
16	180	J	50.0	4320	2725	
17	180	J	46.0	3031	2675	
18	180	J	56.0	4350	2725	Best for big game.
19	180	J	59.0	4831	2725	Best for big game.
20	180	J	57.0	4350	2750	Sierra boat-tail bullet, Wimbledon load.
21	200	J	53.0	4350	2575	Speer bullet.
22	200	J	56.0	4831	2500	Speer bullet.
23	220	J	53.0	4350	2550	
24	220	J	57.0	4831	2525	

.300 H&H MAGNUM

Standard case length...2.85"
Standard cartridge length.......................................3.65"
Groove diameter of barrel.....................................308"

Introduced by Holland & Holland, British rifle makers, it has since been adapted to Winchester Model 70, Remington Model 721, and many imported and custom-built rifles. Higher velocities can be obtained with it than with the .30-06, but it is not so well adapted to light loads. It is decidedly at its best in heavy rifles, and in the Winchester Model 70 Bull Gun has given better results at 1,000 yards than any other cartridge. In rifles weighing less than 9 pounds the recoil is rather severe for many shooters, and accuracy not so good. With the 180-grain bullet at maximum velocity it is generally conceded to give better killing power at extremely long range (350 yards and over) than any other load that can be shot with the required accuracy at these long game ranges. It has become a very popular cartridge in northwestern America for heavy game, but it is thought that many hunters are over-gunned with it, particularly in light rifles.

.300 H & H MAGNUM

No.	BULLET Grains	Type	POWDER Grains	Type	VELOCITY f.p.s.	REMARKS
1	125	J	65.0	3031	3475	
2	150	J	77.0	4350	3350	
3	180	J	68.0	4350	2950	Long range target.
4	180	J	67.0	4064	2850	
5	200	J	65.0	4350	2775	Speer bullet.
6	220	J	64.5	4350	2675	
7	250	J	63.0	4350	2500	Barnes bullet.

.32 WINCHESTER SPECIAL

Standard case length...2.05"
Standard cartridge length.......................................2.55"
Groove diameter of barrel.....................................321"

This cartridge is adapted now only to the old Winchester Model 1894 rifle and carbine, and to the new Winchester

Model 65 rifle, all lever actions. It is very similar in its characteristics, both accuracy and killing power, to the .30-30 cartridge. For use in tubular-magazine rifles, select a bullet with crimping cannelure and crimp the bullet in the case. But with lead-alloy bullets you will get greater accuracy by seating the bullet friction-tight, and using the cartridge single-loading only. The twist of rifling is one turn in 16 inches.

.32 WINCHESTER SPECIAL

| | BULLET | | POWDER | | VELOCITY | |
No.	Grains	Type	Grains	Type	f.p.s.	REMARKS
1	170	L	15.0	4759	1600	I-321232
2	170	J	28.0	3031	1900	Reduced recoil.
3	170	J	33.5	3031	2225	Maximum.
4	170	J	32.0	4320	1900	Reduced recoil.
5	170	J	36.5	4320	2200	Maximum.
6	181	G	17.0	4759	1725	I-321297

8 X 57mm MAUSER

Standard case length ....2.24″
Standard cartridge length ....3.17″
Groove diameter of barrel .... .323″ to .326″

Sometimes designated as 7.92mm. First of all, be sure your 8mm Mauser rifle barrel has a groove diameter of .323″ or slightly larger. Early Mauser rifles, Model 1888, and also the Model 1898 manufactured up until 1905, had a groove diameter of from .318″ to .3208″. Almost all present-day jacketed bullets measure about .323″, and if used in these older rifles will give very dangerous pressures, usually resulting in serious accidents. Most 8 X 57 Mauser rifles have a twist of rifling of one turn in 9.1 inches. There is also a rimmed variety of this cartridge, generally called the 8 X 57 RS, and using a Berdan primer, for use in three-barrel drillings, and double-barrel rifles. It should be loaded with two grains less powder than shown in the tables.

8 x 57mm MAUSER

No.	BULLET Grains	Type	POWDER Grains	Type	VELOCITY f.p.s.	REMARKS
1	125	J	50.0	3031	2900	
2	125	J	54.0	4320	2925	
3	150	J	49.0	3031	2875	
4	150	J	52.0	4320	2800	
5	150	J	51.0	4064	2750	
6	165	G	18.0	4759	1700	I-323470
7	165	G	22.0	4198	1750	I-323470
8	170	J	47.0	3031	2700	Good game load.
9	170	J	52.0	4320	2700	Good game load.
10	170	J	54.0	4350	2500	Powder compressed.

.348 WINCHESTER

Standard case length...2.25″
Standard cartridge length...2.75″
Groove diameter of barrel..348″

This is an excellent cartridge for deer, moose, elk, and bear in forested country and at moderate ranges. It is adapted only to the Winchester Model 71 lever-action rifle. Bullets should have a flat point and should be crimped in the case. Fired cases must be full-length resized before reloading. The charges given should not be exceeded, and may with benefit be dropped two grains to give less recoil without killing power or trajectory being reduced appreciably. Load No. 1 is suitable for deer, gives light recoil and long barrel life, and usually cases loaded with it do not need to be full-length resized. Load No. 3 often will shoot the first three shots from a cold rifle into 3 inches at 100 yards. Before loading cartridges into the rifle they should be wiped free of grease or oil on the outside, or the back thrust on the breech block will be increased greatly.

.348 WINCHESTER

No.	BULLET Grains	Type	POWDER Grains	Type	VELOCITY f.p.s.	REMARKS
1	190	G	23.0	4759	1550	I-350447
2	200	J	52.0	4320	2400	
3	200	J	53.5	4064	2475	
4	200	J	59.0	4350	2350	
5	250	J	51.0	4064	2250	
6	250	J	51.0	4320	2175	
7	250	J	57.0	4350	2250	

.35 REMINGTON

Standard case length..1.92"
Standard cartridge length..................................2.525"
Groove diameter of barrel............................. .359"

This is a very popular cartridge for deer and similar game at moderate ranges up to about 200 yards, giving good killing power and very fair accuracy. For use in rifles having tubular magazines the case should be crimped on the bullet. Cases once fired with full loads will probably require full-length resizing before being reloaded. The reduced loads with plain lead and gas-check bullets will probably not operate the action of semiautomatic rifles, and should be used single-loading. Most jacketed bullets measure about .358-inch.

.35 REMINGTON

No.	Bullet Grains	Type	Powder Grains	Type	Velocity f.p.s.	Remarks
1	156	L	15.0	4759	1600	I-358250
2	180	J	37.0	3031	2175	
3	180	J	41.0	4320	2100	
4	200	G	20.0	4759	1750	I-358315
5	200	G	24.0	4198	1700	I-358315
6	200	J	37.0	3031	2125	Best full load.
7	200	J	40.0	4064	2100	
8	220	J	34.0	3031	1900	
9	220	J	36.0	4064	1800	

.358 WINCHESTER

Standard case length...2.015"
Standard cartridge length...................................2.75"
Groove diameter of barrel............................. .358"

This new cartridge is developed from the .308 Winchester, the case being that of the latter cartridge with neck expanded to .358 inch. It is adapted so far to the Winchester Model 88 lever-action rifle, and has ample power for any American big game, the 250-grain bullet being advised for game larger than deer, sheep, and antelope.

The charges given in the table were developed by the Speer Products Company for use with their bullets, the velocities being for a 22-inch barrel. It is suggested that the lighter charges of each kind of powder given be used for deer as giving ample killing power, not destroying so much meat, and giving more moderate recoil. It is also suggested that the handloader start with the lighter charge, watching for signs of pressure, before proceeding to the heavier one.

.358 WINCHESTER

No.	Bullet Grains	Bullet Type	Powder Grains	Powder Type	Velocity f.p.s.	Remarks
1	200	G	17.5	4759	1400	I-358314
2	220	J	51.0	4064	2550	Speer bullet.
3	220	J	47.0	4064	2400	Speer bullet.
4	220	J	53.0	4320	2550	Speer bullet.
5	220	J	49.0	4320	2400	Speer bullet.
6	220	J	49.0	3031	2550	Speer bullet.
7	220	J	45.0	3031	2400	Speer bullet.
9	220	J	41.0	4198	2500	Speer bullet.
10	220	J	37.0	4198	2225	Speer bullet.
11	220	J	49.0	HiVel 2	2500	Speer bullet.
12	220	J	47.0	HiVel 2	2425	Speer bullet.
13	250	J	48.0	4064	2450	Speer bullet.
14	250	J	44.0	4064	2300	Speer bullet.
15	250	J	49.0	4320	2400	Speer bullet.
16	250	J	45.0	4320	2250	Speer bullet.
17	250	J	46.0	3031	2450	Speer bullet.
18	250	J	42.0	3031	2250	Speer bullet.
19	250	J	37.0	4198	2250	Speer bullet.
20	250	J	33.0	4198	2000	Speer bullet.
21	250	J	48.0	HiVel 2	2500	Speer bullet.
22	250	J	44.0	HiVel 2	2350	Speer bullet.
23	250	J	48.0	4350	2075	Speer bullet.
24	250	J	44.0	4350	1900	Speer bullet.

.35 WHELEN

Standard case length.................................2.49"
Standard cartridge length........................3.35"
Groove diameter of barrel.......................359"

This cartridge was developed by James V. Howe in 1922, and was named for the writer, the idea being a cartridge, more powerful than the .30-06, that could be used in any bolt action suitable for the latter cartridge without alteration. It has been quite extensively used in custom-built rifles, has proved quite accurate and with ample killing power (with the heavier bullets) for any American and most African game. It is almost as powerful as the .375 H&H Magnum cartridge, with much more moderate recoil. Barrels should be at least 24 inches long, and preferably 26 inches. The twist of rifling should be one turn in 14 inches. The case is simply the .30-06 case with neck expanded to hold .358″ or .359″ bullets friction-tight—very easy to prepare. R.C.B.S. makes an excellent expanding die for the necks.

The writer advises Load No. 6 in the table for all-around heavy game. With scope sight adjusted to strike point of aim at 200 yards with this load, the height of trajectory at 100 yards is 2.5 inches, and the drop of the bullet below aim at 300 yards is 11 inches.

.35 WHELEN

No.	Bullet Grains	Type	Powder Grains	Type	Velocity f.p.s.	Remarks
1	200	G	18.0	4759	1400	I-358315
2	200	J	56.0	3031	2625	
3	200	J	60.0	4064	2800	Deer load.
4	250	J	57.0	4064	2600	
5	275	J	53.0	4064	2400	Hornady bullet.
6	275	J	61.0	4350	2375	Hornady bullet.
7	300	J	60.0	4350	2350	Barnes bullet.

.375 H&H MAGNUM

Standard case length................................2.85″
Standard cartridge length.........................3.65″
Groove diameter of barrel.........................375″

This cartridge is adapted to Holland & Holland British rifles, to our Winchester Model 70 rifle, and to many foreign and custom-built rifles. It is decidedly a cartridge for the heaviest game—moose, elk, and grizzly and brown bear. It is also the lightest cartridge that is legal in Kenya Colony, Africa, for lion, buffalo, rhino, and elephant, although much on the light side for the last-named animal. It is a remarkably accurate cartridge, being about on a par with sporting .30-06 rifles when used in the Winchester Model 70. The average sportsman is decidedly over-gunned with a rifle taking this cartridge because his dread of the rather heavy recoil precludes the shooting necessary to place his shots in vital parts on game. Also, as with all other big-bore rifles, one of the heavier bullets, 270 or 300 grains, should always be used to assure the necessary penetration on hindquarter and quartering shots. The difference in trajectory between the heavy and the light bullet loads is so small that there seems to be no sense in the latter loads. Loads No. 5 and 6, however, are fine for deer, killing well, usually leaving a good blood trail, and they have light recoil.

.375 H & H MAGNUM

No.	Bullet Grains	Type	Powder Grains	Type	Velocity f.p.s.	Remarks
1	235	J	74.0	4064	2800	
2	235	J	80.0	4350	2700	
3	270	J	69.0	4064	2600	
4	270	J	82.0	4350	2650	
5	270	J	84.0	4831	2600	
6	278	G	30.0	4759	1650	I-375449. Deer load.
7	278	G	32.0	4198	1650	I-375449. Deer load.
8	300	J	64.0	4064	2400	
9	300	J	78.0	4350	2475	
10	300	J	80.0	4831	2350	

.45-70 U.S. GOVERNMENT

Standard case length..2.10"
Cartridge length, 500 gr. bullet......................2.70"
Groove diameter of barrel..................456" to .459"

This old cartridge was the standard U.S. Army service cartridge from 1873 to 1894. As such it was loaded with 70 grains of F.G. black powder and a 500-grain lubricated lead bullet for use in the Springfield Model 1873 rifle with 32.6-inch barrel, and with the same powder charge and a 405-grain bullet for use in the Springfield carbine with 22-inch barrel. It was also more or less the standard cartridge for Western big-game shooting in Winchester and other rifles until the advent of high-velocity smokeless cartridges of .30 caliber. It still retains a fair popularity for big game because of the knock-down blow its long, heavy bullet delivers, and its ability to penetrate brush with little deflection. But for big game it is decidedly limited to a range of not more than 150 yards because of its very curved trajectory.

It is thought that decidedly the best loads are the first five in the table, loaded with 70 grains of F.G. black powder and plain lead-lubricated bullets. Excellent accuracy has often been obtained by sizing the bullets to exact groove diameter of the barrel, and seating bullets without crimp. However, for use in tubular-magazine rifles the case should be crimped on the bullet. When using black powder loads it is very necessary to clean the bore after every five shots to maintain good accuracy. Cases fired with black powder must be thoroughly washed and dried before reloading. Loads Nos. 6 and 8 are for Winchester Model 1886 rifles in good condition only; dangerous in the Springfield rifle.

.45–70 US GOVERNMENT

No.	BULLET Grains	Type	POWDER Grains	Type	VELOCITY f.p.s.	REMARKS
1	330	L	70	FG	1338	I-456122. Hollow point, deer load.
2	405	L	70	FG	1286	I-457124. In 26″ barrel.
3	405	L	70	FG	1150	I-457124. In 22″ carbine barrel.
4	500	L	70	FG	1179	I-457125. In 26″ barrel.
5	500	L	70	FG	1315	I-457125. In 32.6″ Springfield barrel.
6	300	J	48	3031	1675	
7	300	J	42	HiVel 2	1500	
8	405	J	53	3031	1827	For Winchester M/1886 only.
9	405	J	36	4198	1400	

REVOLVER AND PISTOL CARTRIDGES

174. With all revolver cartridges, the length of the loaded cartridge and the seating depth of the bullet are more or less governed by the crimping cannelure of the bullet used. Of course, the total length of the loaded cartridge should not exceed the length of the cylinder.

With all revolver cartridges the case must be firmly and uniformly crimped in the cannelure of the bullet. This is ncessary both to cause the powder to burn properly, and to prevent the bullets from jumping forward in the case from the recoil and jamming the revolver. (See Par. 90.) For a uniform crimp it is necessary that the cases be frequently trimmed to standard length. Lead bullets for revolvers should always have a crimping cannelure which preferably should be slightly beveled on the side toward the base of the bullet so it will open up the crimp evenly when fired. Wide bands between the lubricating grooves are also desirable.

Full-length resizing of the case is necessary to hold the bullet friction-tight, and to keep it in its proper place while the crimp is being formed. Three loading dies are necessary to reload revolver cartridges with straight cases. The first die resizes the case expanded by previous firing. The second re-sizing die expels the old primer, expands the inside of the neck to hold the bullet friction-tight, and "bell muzzles" the mouth of the case just slightly. The expanding plug of this die should be set so that it just bell muzzles the mouth of the case slightly; enough so that it can be just barely felt when running the fingers over the outside of the case. The third die seats the bullet, and crimps the case on it.

The .45 Colt Auto Pistol cartridge is a law unto itself. It headspaces on the mouth of the case, which must be square, with no crimp, and must be continually inspected and trimmed when necessary to maintain standard length. The case must be resized at each loading so that it holds the bullet firmly friction-tight in position, and the overall length of the loaded cartridge should be standard so as to feed properly through the magazine. Lead bullets should be cast of rather hard alloy, say 1 part of tin to 16 parts of lead, so they will slide smoothly up the ramp.

Leading of the barrel, sometimes encountered, is caused by too hot or heavy powder charges, by over- or under-sized bullets, or bullets cast of too soft alloy. Bullets should be sized to groove diameter of the barrel—not more than .001″ over or under this size.

In loading all cartridges care must be taken not to get two charges of powder in the same case. The powder charges are very small, and occupy little space in the case. Always use pistol primers, never rifle primers.

.38 S&W SPECIAL

Groove diameter of barrel...............354" to .357"

This is the most accurate of all revolver cartridges, and holds all records. Loads Nos. 1 and 2 are used by ninety percent of all our best shots for target shooting at 25 and 50 yards, the wad-cutter bullet punching clean holes in the target and giving full count. The recoil is light, and thus favors rapid fire. These loads, however, are not accurate beyond about 50 yards. Loads Nos. 3 to 6 are with bullets designed by Elmer Keith, and are used when more killing power and longer range is desired, or for police use. They will kill small game well. The factory bullet with its round nose is not a good killer or stopper, even on small game. Even on grouse and jack rabbits it penetrates too cleanly, making only a very small hole.

The heavy loads in the second table, Nos. 7 to 9, are to be used only when exceptional stopping power is desired, and should be confined exclusively to heavy-frame revolvers manufactured of steel with high tensile strength since World War II. They will give dangerous pressures for older and lighter revolvers chambered for this cartridge, and their recoil in such light revolvers is excessive.

.38 S&W SPECIAL

Standard Target and Light Loads.

No.	BULLET Grains	Type	POWDER Grains	Type	VELOCITY f.p.s.	REMARKS
1	148	L	2.8	Bullseye	775	I-358395 and Hensley No. 50.
2	148	L	3.2	5066	775	I-358395 and Hensley No. 50.
3	160	L	3.0	Bullseye	840	I-358431 or I-358439.
4	160	L	5.0	5066	950	I-358431 or I-358439.
5	173	L	3.5	Bullseye	890	I-358429.
6	173	L	5.0	5066	890	I-358429.

Heavy Loads for Heavy Frame Revolvers Only.

No.	BULLET Grains	Type	POWDER Grains	Type	VELOCITY f.p.s.	REMARKS
7	150	G	6.4	Unique	1150	Thompson H. P. Gas Check.
8	150	G	13.0	2400	1175	Thompson H. P. Gas Check.
9	160	L	12.0	2400	1225	I-358431 or I-358439.

.357 MAGNUM

Groove diameter of barrel..357″

The .357 Magnum case is about .10″ longer than the .38 S&W Special case, made so intentionally to prevent the use of .357 Magnum cartridges in revolvers chambered for the .38 S&W Special cartridge. However, the .38 S&W Special cartridge and its handloads can be used in .357 Magnum revolvers, and will usually give excellent results. In fact more .38 S&W Special cartridges are used in .357 Magnum revolvers than are the .357 loads, because the former give much less recoil, and are pleasanter to shoot. However, the moderate loads, Nos. 1, 2, and 3 in the accompanying table (in .357 cases), give excellent results and moderate recoil.

The heavier loads, Nos. 4 to 7, give much heavier recoil and higher pressure, and these loads should never be exceeded. Their use should be confined to occasions where greater penetration and stopping power are required. These loads will usually kill deer fairly well at short ranges provided the bullet is properly placed in a vital area. Bullseye and No. 5066 powders are not adapted to loads heavier than shown, giving high pressure, and tending to lead the bore.

.357 MAGNUM

No.	BULLET Grains	Type	POWDER Grains	Type	VELOCITY f.p.s.	REMARKS
1	146	L	3.0	Bullseye	890	I-358395 and Hensley No. 50.
2	146	L	4.0	5066	1000	I-358395 and Hensley No. 50.
3	160	L	6.5	Unique	1290	I-358439
4	160	L	7.0	Unique	1350	I-358439
5	160	L	15.0	2400	1550	I-358439
6	160	G	8.0	Unique	1400	Thompson H. P. Gas check.
7	160	G	16.0	2400	1600	Thompson H. P. Gas check.

.44 S&W SPECIAL

Groove diameter of barrel................................427″ to .431″

This heavy cartridge is thought by many to be the best where killing and knockdown power is desired in a handgun for protection and for such game as deer, excelling even the

.357 Magnum. Of course, in this respect it is now excelled by the very new .44 Magnum cartridge, but it seems to lend itself, so far as known at present, to a variety of handloads better than this latter cartridge. Loads from those of moderate velocity, giving light recoil and accuracy almost equal to the .38 S&W Special, up to very high velocity loads giving maximum power, may be used. However, charges heavier than those shown in the table should never be exceeded, and these heavy charges should be confined to the latest Smith & Wesson heavy-duty revolvers, or to the new revolvers for the .44 Magnum cartridge. Incidentally, all these loads (in .44 S&W Magnum cases) can be used with good results in the new .44 Magnum revolvers made by Smith & Wesson and Ruger. Some old revolvers have a groove diameter of barrel as small as .427", and for such bullets should be sized to that diameter. Most modern revolvers perform well with bullets sized to .429-inch. All bullets should be heavily crimped in the cases.

.44 S&W SPECIAL

| | BULLET | | POWDER | | VELOCITY | |
No.	Grains	Type	Grains	Type	f.p.s.	REMARKS
1	158	G	9.0	Unique	1100	Harvey Prot-X-Bore
2	170	G	5.5	Bullseye	925	Harvey Prot-X-Bore
3	170	G	19.0	2400	1325	Harvey Prot-X-Bore.
4	184	L	4.5	Bullseye	829	Hensley 107-B.
5	184	L	6.0	Bullseye	1000	Hensley 107-B.
6	215	L	5.0	Bullseye	800	I-431215—Thompson.
7	220	G	7.5	Unique	872	Harvey Prot-X-Bore.
8	235	L	16.0	2400	1056	I-429422—Keith.
9	235	L	8.0	Unique	950	I-429422—Keith.
10	250	L	6.5	5066	900	I-429421—Keith.
11	250	L	7.5	Unique	925	I-429421—Keith.
12	250	L	5.0	Bullseye	825	I-429421—Keith.
13	254	G	6.5	5066	900	I-431244—Thompson.
14	254	G	17.5	2400	1150	I-431244—Thompson.

.44 MAGNUM REVOLVER

Standard case length...1.285"
Groove diameter of barrel....................429" to .431"

This newest and most powerful of all revolver cartridges was developed by the Remington Arms Company shortly before this book went to press, and few handloads have been developed for it so far. Probably most shooters will want a light load for target practice, and general shooting as the full loads give considerable and often rather unpleasant recoil. Ideal bullet No. 429421, weighing 250 grains, and designed by Elmer Keith, gives excellent results with a charge of 5.0 grains of Bullseye powder. The same bullet may also be used with 8.5 grains of Unique powder for higher velocity but occasional leading of the barrel has been reported.

The following heavy loads have been reported as giving good results, but the charges given should not be exceeded. The 170-grain Harvey Prot-X-Bore bullet with a charge of 19 grains of 2400 powder gives a velocity of 1,325 f.p.s., and up to 24.0 grains may be used for a very heavy load giving about 1,750 f.s. Ideal bullet No. 431244 with gas check, weighing 244 grains and designed by Ray Thompson, may also be used, 20.0 grains of 2400 powder giving about 1,000 f.p.s. and 23.0 grains about 1250 f.p.s.

.45 AUTO COLT PISTOL

Standard case length.. .90"
Standard cartridge length........................1.27"
Groove diameter of barrel.........................451"

All handloads should approximate the velocity and pressure of the standard U.S. Government cartridge (230-grain jacketed bullet, 800 f.p.s.) in order to function the slide properly in semiautomatic fire. Cases should be resized so as to hold the bullet firmly friction-tight, and should not be crimped. Remember that this cartridge headspaces on the mouth of the case, and it may be necessary to trim the cases rather often to maintain the standard length of .90 inch. When loading with lead bullets the mouth of the case should be very slightly chamfered to prevent the shaving of the bullet when seating. Lead bullets should be cast rather hard, about 1 tin to 16 lead, so as to slide smoothly up the ramp of the pistol. Commercial .45 A.C.P. cases use the .210" pistol primer, while those of

Frankford Arsenal make use the smaller .206″ primer of Frankford Arsenal make.

With some .45 auto pistols the parts are not very closely fitted, and there is considerable play in the action which is not conducive to the best accuracy. But with pistols precisioned by leading pistol gunsmiths very satisfactory accuracy should be obtained, particularly with loads 4 and 5.

.45 AUTO COLT PISTOL

No.	Bullet Grains	Type	Powder Grains	Type	Velocity f.p.s.	Remarks
1	200	L	4.7	Bullseye	900	I-452460
2	200	L	7.0	Unique	980	I-452460
3	207	L	4.0	Bullseye	900	Hensley S-68.
4	215	L	7.5	Unique	900	Hensley 78.
5	215	L	7.5	Unique	900	Hensley 118.
6	230	J	4.9	Bullseye	825	Government
7	230	J	6.0	5066	825	Government
8	230	J	7.7	Unique	875	Government

.45 COLT REVOLVER

Groove diameter of barrel..................452″ to .454″

The original U.S. Government cartridge, adapted to the .45 caliber Colt Single-Action Revolver, Model 1873, was loaded with a 250-grain lubricated lead bullet, and 40 grains of FFG black powder. With modern handloads the bullet should be sized to the groove diameter of the barrel, cases should be resized to hold that bullet friction-tight, and should be crimped on the bullet. The alloy should be rather hard, about 1 tin to 16 lead, or 1 tin to 20 lead.

.45 COLT REVOLVER

No.	Bullet Grains	Type	Powder Grains	Type	Velocity f.p.s.	Remarks
1	237	L	6.8	Bullseye	950	I-454309
2	237	L	9.0	5066	900	I-454309
3	237	L	10.7	Unique	1050	I-454309
4	250	L	7.7	Bullseye	900	I-454117—Keith.
5	250	L	8.5	5066	925	I-454117—Keith.
6	250	L	10.8	Unique	1030	I-454117—Keith.
7	250	L	40.0	FFG	1000	Black powder.

V

THE PROOF OF THE PUDDING

175. To learn how well you have succeeded in handloading it is desirable to test the accuracy and probably the trajectory of your product. Not every man has opportunity for the study and practice needed to develop into a fine rifle or pistol marksman, capable of determining the accuracy of ammunition by the usual shooting methods. But there is a way by which anyone can learn to shoot with extreme accuracy in perhaps an hour of practice, and practically eliminate the human error so that the accuracy and the characteristics of your weapon and its ammunition will be clearly demonstrated. This is by bench rest shooting. All that is needed is a safe range, a table roughly and solidly made according to directions, two small sandbags, paper targets, and of course the rifle and ammunition.

176. **Sights.** Our success in eliminating human error from shooting depends on the type of sights with which the rifle is equipped, but the errors in various sights are well known and can be allowed for. If you have fairly good eyesight with or without correcting spectacles, and you know how to aim, take great pains in doing so, and shoot in a good light, then your error of aim at 100 yards with various types of rifle sights will be approximately as follows:

Open rear sight.....................Unpredictable
Aperture rear, gold or ivory front........1½" to 2"
Aperture rear, black post front.................1"
Aperture rear, hooded aperture front......½" to ¾"
2½ power hunting scope..............¼" to ½"
6 power hunting scope................½" to ⅛"
10 power target scope................⅛" to 1/16"
20 power target scope............Practically none

With revolvers and pistols and Patridge sights smoked black the error is probably close to ½ to 1 inch at 25 yards, and 1 to 2 inches at 50 yards.

100 Yard Range

This is not a lucky group, but represents one of several hundred such groups that Mr. Samuel Clark, Jr. has obtained with his .219 Donaldson Wasp rifle at 100 yards. As Mr. Clark loaded his own ammunition, and even made his own metal cased bullets, this target indicates the degree of accuracy that can be obtained by handloading.

The above errors should be deducted from the size of the groups you obtain in shooting your rifle and ammunition for accuracy. For example, if you are shooting a typical big game rifle with an aperture receiver sight, front bead sight smoked black, aiming at an 8″ black bullseye at 100 yards, your error of aim will be approximately one inch, and if you make a 2½″ group then it would be perfectly proper for you to deduct your one inch aim error, and assume that the error of your rifle and ammunition is 1½″ at 100 yards, or 1½ minutes. But it is better to base your estimate of the accuracy of your weapon and ammunition on the average of five groups. One group really tells nothing for sure because it may be a lucky group —or an unlucky one.

177. **Distance.** The American shooter of today usually tests his rifle for accuracy at 100 yards and his pistol at 25 yards because these distances have proved most convenient for

J. Bushnell Smith
Chief Machinist's Mate
United States Navy
November 26, 1894—July 16, 1948
The greatest handloader of all times.

a number of reasons. As most modern records for accuracy are at these distances, one can compare his results with the records. If a rifle makes a certain size group at 100 yards it can usually be counted on to make just a trifle over double that size group at 200 yards provided that the ammunition is of a type that will be accurate at the longer distance. The group at 200 yards would probably be almost exactly double that at 100 yards if there was not usually a little dispersion from wind and because we do not see (aim) quite so clearly at the longer distance.

178. **Targets.** It is usually best to use the official National Rifle Association Small Bore Target or Pistol Target when using iron sights. With telescope sights place a round or square white paster in the center of the bullseye. Vary the size of the paster to get the clearest silhouette of the scope's reticule and therefore the clearest aim.

179. **Measurement.** Groups are measured from center to center of the bullet holes farthest apart—that is the extreme

spread. The number of shots in the group should be stated. It is common practice now to fire bolt action and single shot rifles in groups of five shots as more than that number are scarcely ever fired at one time in hunting. But a 10-shot group gives a better indication of the accuracy of a rifle to be used for competitive target shooting where scores usually include ten or twenty consecutive shots. Fire three shot groups with tubular magazine rifles and allow them to cool between groups as they often shoot off when heated.

180. **Holding steady.**   In the past, most shooters who were not well trained riflemen felt that they could not trust themselves to make an accuracy test because they could not hold the rifle or pistol steady enough. Until about 1947 the technique of bench rest shooting by which anyone can learn to hold absolutely steady in just a few minutes was practically unknown. Using this simple technique anyone can now elim- inate all the human errors of shooting except only the aim error of the sights (P 184).

BENCH REST SHOOTING

181. **The bench rest.**   This is simply a sturdy table, steady enough so it will not shake in the wind, and slightly cut out at the left rear side where the shooter's chest presses against it. It may have three or four legs, 4 x 4's or heavier, and it may stand on the ground and thus be portable, or the legs may be sunk a foot or two into the soil. The top of the table or bench had best be made of 2" planks, and should be level and stand about 32" above the ground. A sturdy stool or chair should be provided to sit on. The accompanying sketch shows the shape and dimensions of the bench top which is shaped so that it can be used by either a right or left hand shooter.

Two small sandbags of any durable material will be needed. Make one about 7" x 10", and the other about 6" x 8". Fill each almost full of sand and tie the mouth tightly. Don't pack the sand tightly in the bags, but rather loosely so that when the rifle is laid on them it will press a groove perhaps an inch deep. Also provide several small boards and planks, about

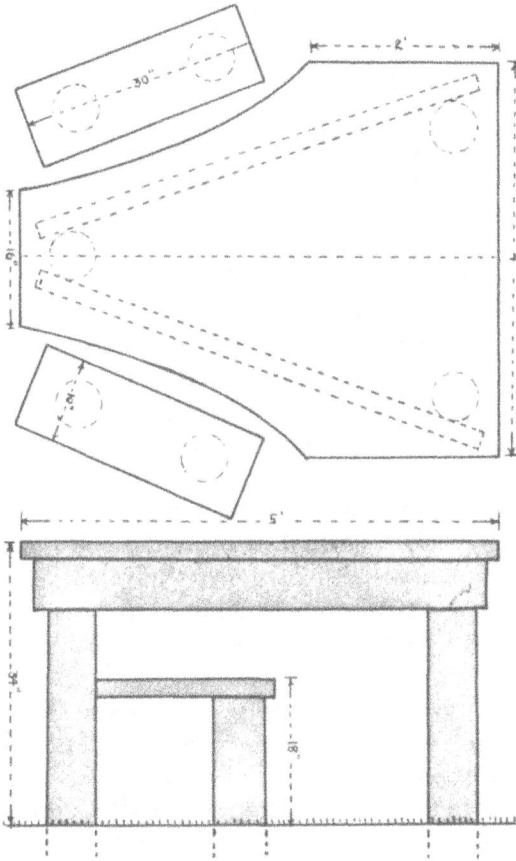

Diagram for making a bench rest.

6″ x 8″ to raise the bags to the required height above the bench top.

Rest the rifle on the sandbags as shown in the photograph. Adjust the height of the bags so the rifle can be aimed at the target with the toe of the butt-plate about one inch above the top of the bench as shown. The forearm of the rifle, several inches in rear of its tip, and always in the same place, rests on the front bag, and the under edge of the butt-stock, several inches in front of the toe of the butt-plate, rests on the rear bag. The rifle snuggles in slight grooves in the bags so it does not lean to the right or left.

182. Technique of bench rest shooting.   Sit on the stool. Chest rests only lightly against the curved or cut-out edge of the bench. Place your left arm under the rifle, left forearm resting on the bench and carried back so the left hand grasps the rear sandbag lightly. The right hand grasps the small of the stock, forefinger on the trigger, right elbow resting down steady and almost flat on the bench top. Butt-plate just barely touching your clothing over your right shoulder so that when the rifle is fired it will slide freely to the rear at least an inch before it encounters shoulder pressure. Lean your head down and aim the rifle, but do not rest your face heavily enough on the comb of the stock to transfer a heart pulsation to the rifle. Now with your left hand slightly move the rear sandbag right, left, forward or back until the aim at the target is absolutely correct. Take great pains about aiming. You will now notice that the rifle is aimed and stays absolutely steady on the target. There is no tremor at all.

Now with your right forefinger, assuming that the rifle is loaded, start to press the trigger. With just a little practice you will find that you can increase the pressure on the trigger gradually without causing the rifle to move at all. Continue increasing the pressure gradually until the rifle is discharged *unexpectedly*. The rifle must go off unexpectedly while it lies steady and aimed with perfect accuracy for each and every shot. Sounds hard until you try it, then in about a minute you will find that it is dead easy. That is all there is to it. You have mastered the art of shooting consecutively without error.

183. Recoil.   The recoil of ordinary rifles is not felt at all in bench rest shooting, and the above technique works up to about an eight pound .30-06 rifle. With heavier charged rifles the weapon is liable to jump too high off the sandbags when it recoils. Eliminate the rear bag, raise the front bag

Position of rifle on bench rest and sandbags.

slightly higher, rest both elbows on the table and use a tight gunsling. The head, arms, upper chest and sling are almost the same as when shooting in the standard prone position on the ground. The position is not absolutely steady, but nevertheless is quite satisfactory.

184. **With revolver or pistol.** Absolutely steady holding is not possible without a machine rest. Nevertheless by the following method you will find that you can, with just a little practice, hold and shoot steady enough to determine quite definitely the accuracy of the pistol and ammunition.

It is best to stand erect and hold the pistol at the same distance from your eye that it would be in regular target shooting. Have a step-ladder or some kind of a firm support about shoulder high to rest your forearm on. On top of this support have a folded blanket or hard cushion and rest the forearm and wrist on this. Do not rest the hand at all. It must be free and unsupported, with a very uniform grip from shot to shot. With a little practice in shooting from this ladder rest you will find that you can hold very steadily while you squeeze to get an unexpected discharge. Certainly if there is as much as an inch difference in the grouping of two loads you can determine it shooting in this manner.

The Potter Engineering Co., 10 Albany St., Cazenovia, N. Y., have developed a machine rest for target and police revolvers (but not auto pistols) which is proving very useful in accuracy testing.

Firing position at bench rest.

185. Uniformity. Just another word about accuracy. Everything must be done as uniformly as possible from shot to shot. If you stop shooting, get up from the bench, then sit down and start shooting again, your firing position will probably not be exactly the same as it was the first time you shot, and while your rifle may shoot groups just as good the second time as the first, they may not center on the target at exactly the same spot because there may be enough difference between the two firing positions and tension of holding to affect the vibration and jump of the rifle. This might introduce a serious error in a trajectory test.

186. A simple trajectory and bullet drop test. To determine the mid-range height of trajectory or the bullet drop, set up four targets, say 100 yards, 200 yards, 300 yards and 400 yards, so closely in line that one appears almost behind the other so you can fire on any one with the minimum change in your firing position. From the bench rest fire on the 200 yard target and if necessary adjust your sights until the shots are grouping right on the point of aim. Then with as little change in your firing position as possible, fire two shots on the 100, two on the 300, and two on the 400 yard targets. Then immediately go back on the 200 yard target to see if you are still striking very close to the point of aim. If you are, consider the two shots fired at each of the other targets as "record shots." Repeat the test until you have three or four series of two record shots on each target. Then measure the average height of your shots on the 100 yard target above your point of aim on that target. This will be the average practical trajectory height at 100 yards when shooting at 200 yards with this rifle.

To obtain the pure trajectory height from the axis of the bore to the center of the bullet hole in the target, add to this practical trajectory height half the distance from the axis of the bore to the line of aim of your rifle. Note that in the trajectory tables of the ammunition companies it is this pure trajectory figure that is given, and not the practical trajectory above the line of aim.

If you will compare the true trajectory of your hand loaded ammunition with that of the nearest corresponding factory ammunition given in the trajectory tables in the Appendix you can get a rough indication of the approximate muzzle velocity of your hand loads. That is if the true trajectory of your cartridge at 100 yards when shooting over 200 yards is 3", then its velocity is probably close to 2,700 f.s., or the same as the .30-06 Springfield with 180 grain bullet, which also has a trajectory height of 3".

On the 100, 300, and 400 yard targets measure the vertical distance from the point of aim on that target to each of the record bullet holes, and take the average, which will be the rise or drop of the bullet at that distance.

187. **Forming Wildcat Cases.** A "wildcat" cartridge is a non-standard one, using a special case which is altered and formed from existing factory cartridge case. Wildcat cartridges are adapted to custom built rifles which are bored and chambered for them. Usually the shooter must form his own cases and load them, for factory loaded ammunition is not available. However, many custom hand-loaders can furnish loaded ammunition for many of the more popular wildcats. Reloading tool makers can furnish dies for forming and loading most of the wildcat cases, or the custom riflemaker who builds the rifle can furnish dies.

Instructions for forming many of the more popular wildcat cases will be found in Part IV.

Probably the finest accuracy will not be obtained until cases have been fired once in the rifle in which it is intended to use them so as to expand them to fit the chamber of that rifle precisely. There is no absolutely standard chamber or case dimensions for any wildcat cartridge. Chambers by various custom makers may vary slightly in dimensions, but usually this will cause no trouble. But in firing the first load from a formed *rimless* case always seat the bullet far enough out from the mouth of the case so that its ogive contacts the lands hard when loaded in the rifle. This results in the base of the case being pushed tight against the face of the bolt, and when fired this case expands both in diameter and *length* so that it is formed with correct headspace length. *This applies to the first fire-forming of all rimless wildcat cases.*

In necking down a case neck to take a smaller bullet there will be no particular trouble when the reduction in neck diameter is small, as in necking a .25 caliber case to .22 caliber, or a .30 caliber case to .270 caliber. But if the reduction if considerable, as in necking a .30 caliber case to .22 caliber, it may be necessary to use two necking dies, one to reduce the neck to about .26 caliber, and the last to finally neck it down from about .26 to .22 caliber.

When we neck a case of large caliber down to hold a much smaller bullet we crowd a lot of brass into the neck which results in considerable thickening of the walls of the neck. Then to bring the neck wall to normal thickness so that the neck of the loaded cartridge will not be too great for the chamber of the rifle it will often be necessary to ream out the inside of the neck with a special reamer. This reamer is usually made to operate in a case trimmer. Consult your rifle maker as to the exact diameter of the reamer you should use. After reaming tap the neck of the case on the workbench to insure that no brass shavings remain inside the neck, then chamfer the mouth, and size and expand the neck in the regular resizing die to hold the bullet friction tight. With the .22 caliber wildcats that are formed by necking down .25 caliber factory cases it is almost universal practice to chamber the rifle correctly for the very slight increase in wall thickness of the neck caused by this operation, and usually no inside reaming of the neck is necessary or desirable. Of course, if you shorten as well as neck down a case, as when you form a .219 Donaldson Wasp from the .219 Winchester Zipper case, then you do crowd a lot of brass into the final neck, and reaming the inside of the neck becomes necessary.

In forming all wildcat cases see that both the neck and body of the case are evenly lubricated with anhydrous lanolin before forcing the factory case into the die. If there is considerable necking down or forcing back of the original shoulder to be done a fairly powerful loading press should be used, such as the Super Pacific, Dunbar, Hollywood, or R.C.B.S.

Of course the fire forming of, say 200, wildcat cases in one's rifle causes just that much wear on the bore. Many gunsmiths and custom hand-loaders can furnish wildcat cases which they have already fireformed in a barrel which they have for that purpose, and thus the shooter avoids much work and consequent wear on his own barrel. Good results will usually be had with the first firing of these formed cases in one's own rifle, and then excellent accuracy on the second firing when the cases are expanded exactly to fit the chamber.

In every case get advice from the workman who chambered the barrel to get exact chamber dimensions.

188. Obtaining the greatest accuracy. On testing your handload, should you not obtain the accuracy you think you should, then the following notes may help you.

When the rifle is a gilt-edge weapon, and everything pertaining to it is as it should be, the most important factor is the particular bullet you use. First, the bullet must be of the correct weight and diameter for the twist of rifling and the groove diameter of your barrel. For example, do not expect the finest accuracy from 86-grain bullets in a .25 caliber rifle having a twist or one turn in ten inches, nor that a bullet as heavy as 117 grains will be stabilized (travel point to the front) in a .25 caliber rifle with a 14-inch twist. If the groove diameter of your barrel is .257 inch, do not expect the finest accuracy with bullets that average under .256 inch, or over .2575 inch. Weigh ten bullets separately on your powder scales. Their weight should not vary more than one grain. Similarly measure their diameter with a micrometer caliper. This should not vary more than .0005 inch.

Different makes and weights of bullets will give quite different accuracy in the same rifle with proper powder charges adapted to that caliber and bullet. Some bullets will consistently give the finest accuracy, and others seemingly perfect will perform only in a mediocre manner. While certain bullets have made a reputation for accurate shooting, there is nothing positive about this. It seems as though many individual barrels preferred a certain make and weight of bullet to shoot with their finest accuracy. Try several other makes of bullets if one does not give the results you wish.

Lead-alloy bullets must be cast, lubricated, and sized well nigh perfectly to insure fine accuracy. Inspect such bullets as carefully as you would jacketed bullets, and reject all that seem faulty. Usually you will get best results from lead-alloy bullets when their diameter is the same as groove diameter of the barrel, or not over .001 inch to .003 inch larger than groove diameter. Within these limits groove diameter of lead-alloy bullets do not seem important, provided all bullets are the same diameter and weight. The alloy of lead bullets is important. Generally speaking, for modern high-velocity rifles the alloy should be quite hard, about 1 part by weight of tin to 10 parts of lead, or the Ideal Alloy.

Despite what has been said before, seating the bullet in the case so that the ogive of the bullet does not quite touch the lands when the cartridge is inserted in the chamber of the rifle, is not conducive to the very finest accuracy. Seating the bullet to just touch the lands—that is, so that when you place the cartridge in the chamber and then extract it, you will just barely see where the lands have slightly marked the ogive of the bullet—may give you slightly greater breech pressure, and a little greater variation in velocity from shot to shot, but bullets seated to such an overall length may also shoot noticeably more accurately than those seated so as to just not touch the lands. Bullets seated to such an overall length may not operate through the magazine of your rifle, the loaded cartridge being too long. On the other hand, when you are shooting for the finest accuracy you usually load single cartridges into the chamber and do not use the magazine.

When shooting for accuracy with a bolt-action rifle, do not insert the cartridge into the chamber and close the bolt on it. Loading in this way the extractor is pressed forcibly over the head of the case, and may force the cartridge farther into the chamber than is proper, making it as though you were shooting with a variable headspace. Instead, press the cartridge down into the magazine and let the extractor pick it up from there and carry it evenly into the chamber.

With a bolt-action rifle, when starting to shoot for accuracy see that the bore is wiped out clean and dry for the first shot, and fire one shot through that rifle before starting your record group. The first shot fired through a clean, slightly oily bore is likely to fly slightly wild, and so may a shot from a clean, dry bore, but not quite so much.

Despite the fact that your handload may be absolutely perfectly fitted to the bore and chamber of your rifle, and you may be using the particular weight and make of bullet that best agrees with that barrel, you may still get mediocre results due to defects in the rifle other than barrel.

The most common defect in a rifle that causes mediocre results, other than the barrel, is poor bedding of the rifle and its action in the stock. Poor bedding can easily account for the difference between a 3-inch group and a 1-inch group at 100 yards. If you have any reason to doubt the bedding of your rifle in its stock, take it to a competent gunsmith for inspection and rebedding if necessary. We often see the very finest machine-made rifles, and even the products of our best custom-rifle makers come to their purchasers with defects in the bedding. But at the start, always see that the two guard screws of a bolt-action rifle are kept screwed up very tight. Look to that first of all if you are getting poor results from what you think is a first-rate arm; and second, look to see that your telescope-sight mountings are not loose.

Do not expect the finest accuracy from a featherweight bolt-action rifle except for the first five shots from a cold barrel, or with a tubular-magazine rifle except for the first three shots from a cold rifle. A medium or heavy barrel bolt-action rifle in first-class condition, and using an accurate load, should shoot very consistently for at least ten or fifteen consecutive shots.

We hear lots of talk about certain rifles and cartridges shooting minute-of-angle groups; that is, all shots in a 1-inch circle at 100, or a 2-inch circle at 200 yards. Take these tall tales by inexperienced writers with a grain of salt. I have never seen any rifles that would average minute-of-angle groups except only very fine bench rest or varmint rifles with at least a medium heavy barrel, shooting a small caliber cartridge of proved accuracy, loaded with the best components—all bolt actions. If you have an 8 to 9-pound hunting rifle that averages one and a half minutes with a certain handload you have a jewel of a weapon and load.

Trajectory of a load makes little difference to the target shooter because he shoots at a known distance, and sets his sights correctly for the drop of the bullet at that distance. But it is very important to the hunter who shoots at estimated distances, except perhaps to the deer hunter who shoots only at short ranges in forested country.

Trajectory depends upon two factors: the muzzle velocity of the load, and the ballistic coefficient of the bullet. With two bullets of the same caliber and weight, fired at the same muzzle velocity, that bullet which has the highest ballistic coefficient will have the flattest trajectory at distances beyond about 200 yards. Below 200 yards the ballistic coefficient does not make any important difference in the trajectory. A sharp, Spitzer point bullet has a much higher ballistic coefficient than a round-nose bullet of the same weight, and at a given muzzle velocity will have a much flatter trajectory. For example, take the .30 caliber 180-grain bullet at a muzzle velocity of 2700 f.p.s. With the rifle sighted to strike point of aim at 200 yards, the sharp Spitzer or spire point bullet will drop about 9 inches below aim at 300 yards, while the typical round-nose bullet will drop about 12 inches. The difference at 400 yards will be greater still. Therefore, if you want flat trajectory for long-range game shooting, choose a heavy Spitzer or spire pointed bullet.

The tables of charges for various cartridges in Part IV give the maximum powder charges that are entirely safe to use to obtain the highest muzzle velocity with that weight of bullet. These charges should never be exceeded. It certainly does not pay to exceed them, for if you do you will be getting excessive —and perhaps dangerous—pressures. You will have trouble with sticking cases which delay rapid fire. A case may even stick in your chamber and you may have to rely on your gunsmith to get it out. The accuracy will almost always be poorer than with the advised charge, and hitting at long range depends not only on trajectory, but on accuracy as well.

Trajectory is not in proportion to muzzle velocity, because the air resistance, as the bullet is speeded up, increases out of all proportion to the increase in velocity. Thus, if you were, by using a greater and excessive powder charge, able to increase your muzzle velocity about 200 feet per second, you would in all likelihood only decrease the drop of the bullet about an inch at 300 yards. And what does that amount to when shooting at game? Nothing at all.

When I was a young officer there was a paragraph in the old Army Regulations which read something like this: "Quibbling over the minutiae of form is prohibited." This certainly applies when trying to figure out the last inch in trajectory, or in trying to read velocities closer than about 25 f.p.s. Two different rifles of the same caliber, by the same maker, with the same length of barrel, when fired with the same load, may and often do vary 25 f.p.s. and more in the velocity they record on the chronograph.

So far I have had little to say about the powder you select to use with a certain bullet. My own experience has been that, provided you use a suitable powder for that cartridge and bullet, as given in the table of charges, and use it in an amount that will give clean burning and safe and normal pressures, the selection of the type of powder is not much of a factor in obtaining the best accuracy. However, under the remarks on each cartridge I do give the type of powder for various weights of bullet that has in general given the best accuracy among target shooters. Thus, in striving for the best accuracy, instead of confining yourself to one bullet, and trying to find the best powder charge for it, start out with a recommended powder charge, and try to find the particular bullet which will give the best accuracy. Don't be too hide-bound in your selection of components. Try them all until you get one that suits you.

A few years ago I started to test a certain .22 Varminter rifle with a certain make and weight of bullet. I tried all safe amounts of all powders with this bullet, and with ten 10-shot groups with each charge, the average accuracy at 100 yards was just about 1.3 inches. Later, in this same rifle I switched to another bullet which, with all kinds of powders in normal loads, averaged close to .75 inch at 100 yards.

189. Records. Keep a complete, systematic record of all your handloading: Charges, components, methods, measurements and results. Have a special book for the purpose. Do not trust to memory or to notations on targets that might get lost. This is very important. You will not progress, neither will you be a reliable and safe handloader unless you keep such a record.

For instance, two years ago you developed a very accurate load for your .270 rifle, determined the drop of the bullet at all distances with it as well as the adjustment of the telescope sight to give those results. Today a friend asks you to go on an antelope or mountain sheep hunt with him. Do you have the record available that will enable you to load a fresh batch of cartridges and set your telescope sight correctly to make a clean kill on the first shot? Things like that are acid tests of well kept records. A rifleman should know his rifle like his ABC's. Trouble is that with more than one rifle and many different components and loads there is more than any man can remember. Faulty memory might lead to a serious accident, not only to you but perhaps to your best friend, your son, or your daughter. Don't trust to memory—keep a record.

APPENDIX

HORNADY JACKETED BULLETS

Obtainable from Hornady Manufacturing Co., 216 West Fourth Street, Grand Island, Nebraska, and from most dealers in reloading components. 1957 prices range from $2.80 to $8.00 per hundred.

22 CALIBER (.244)
  45 grain Hornet
  50 grain spire point
  55 grain spire point
  60 grain spire point

22 CALIBER (.2225)
  45 grain Hornet
  50 grain spire point

6MM CALIBER (.243)
  70 grain spire H.P.
  87 grain spire point
  100 grain round nose

25 CALIBER (.257)
  60 grain spire point
  75 grain spire H.P. (Dec. '56)
  87 grain spire point
  100 grain spire point
  117 grain round nose

6.5MM CALIBER (.263)
  100 grain spire point
  129 grain round nose*
  160 grain round nose*

270 CALIBER (.277)
  100 grain spire point
  130 grain spire point*
  150 grain round nose*

7MM CALIBER (.284)
  120 grain spire point
  139 grain spire point*
  154 grain round nose*
  175 grain round nose*

30 CALIBER (.308)
  110 grain spire point
  110 grain round nose
  130 grain spire point
  150 grain spire point*
  150 grain round nose*
  170 grain flat point (30-30)*
  180 grain spire point*
  180 grain round nose*
  220 grain round nose*
  220 grain, full jacket†

303 CAL. 7.7 JAP (.312)
  150 grain round nose*

32 SPECIAL (.321)
  170 grain flat point*

8MM CALIBER (.323)
  150 grain round nose*
  170 grain round nose*

348 CALIBER (.348)
  200 grain flat point*

35 CALIBER (.358)
  200 grain round nose*
  250 grain round nose*
  275 grain round nose*

375 CALIBER (.375)
  270 grain round nose
  300 grain round nose*
  300 grain, full jacket†

CRIMP-ON GAS CHECKS
  22 Caliber
  25 Caliber
  6.5MM Caliber
  270 Caliber
  30 Caliber
  35 Caliber
  44 Caliber

*Cannelured bullet.
†Full steel jacket for heavy African game.

(214)

BARNES JACKETED BULLETS

Obtainable from Fred M. Barnes, 318 Rosevale Road, Grand Junction, Colorado. Prices range from $4.00 to $20.00 per hundred.

.17 CALIBER
| | Jacket Thickness |
.172- 25 Gr. Spitzer Soft Point....030"

.22 CALIBER
.224- 50 Gr. Spitzer Soft Point....030"
.224- 60 Gr. Spitzer Soft Point....030"
.227- 70 Gr. Spitzer Soft Point....030"

6mm. CALIBER
.243- 75 Gr. Spitzer Soft Point....030"
.243- 90 Gr. Spitzer Soft Point....030"
.243-100 Gr. Spitzer Soft Point....030"
.243-110 Gr. Spitzer Soft Point....030"

.25 CALIBER
.257- 75 Gr. Spitzer Soft Point....032"
.257- 90 Gr. Spitzer Soft Point....032"
.257-125 Gr. Spitzer Soft Point....032"

256 (6.5mm.) CALIBER
.264-130 Gr. Spitzer Soft Point....032"
.264-150 Gr. Spitzer Soft Point....032"
.264-165 Gr. Spitzer Soft Point....032"

.270 WIN. CALIBER
.277-100 Gr. Spitzer Soft Point....Cup
.277-120 Gr. Spitzer Soft Point....032"
.277-130 Gr. Spitzer Soft Point....032"
.277-160 Gr. Spitzer Soft Point....032"
.277-180 Gr. Round Nose S. P.....032"

.276 (7mm.) CALIBER
.284-120 Gr. Spitzer Soft Point....032"
.284-140 Gr. Spitzer Soft Point....032"
.284-160 Gr. Spitzer Soft Point....032"
.284-180 Gr. Spitzer Soft Point....032"
.284-195 Gr. Spitzer S. P. & RN...032"

.280 CALIBER
.288-160 Gr. Spitzer Soft Point....032"
.288-180 Gr. Spitzer Soft Point....032"
.288-200 Gr. Spitzer Soft Point....032"

.30 CALIBER
.308-110 Gr. Carbine Round Nose..032"
.308-125 Gr. Spitzer Soft Point....032"
.308-150 Gr. Spitzer Soft Point....032"
.308-180 Gr. Spitzer Soft Point....032"
.308-200 Gr. Spitzer Soft Point....032"
.308-220 & 250 Gr. R. N. S. P.....032"
.308-250 & 250 Gr. R. N. Solid.....035"

7.7mm JAP & BRITISH
.313-150 Gr. Spitzer Soft Point....032"
.313-180 Gr. Spitzer Soft Point....032"

8mm. CALIBER
| | Jacket Thickness |
.323-150 Gr. Spitzer Soft Point....032"
.323-180 Gr. Spitzer Soft Point....032"
.323-200 Gr. Spitzer Soft Point....032"
.323-250 Gr. Spitzer Soft Point....032"
Sized to .318—50c extra

.333 O. K. H. CALIBER
.333-200 Gr. Spitzer Soft Point....032"
.333-250 Gr. Spitzer Soft Point....032"
.333-250 Gr. Spitzer Soft Point....049"
.333-300 Gr. Round Nose S. P.....032"
.333-300 Gr. Round Nose S. P.....049"

.35 CALIBER
.358-180 Gr. Spitzer Soft Point....032".
.358-220 Gr. Spitzer Soft Point....032"
.358-250 Gr. Spitzer Soft Point....032"
.358-250 Gr. Spitzer Soft Point....049"
.358-300 Gr. Round Nose S. P.....032"
.358-300 Gr. Round Nose S. P.....049"
.358-300 Gr. Round Nose Solid....049"

.375 MAG. CALIBER
.375-250 Gr. Spitzer Soft Point....032"
.375-250 Gr. Spitzer Soft Point....049"
.375-300 Gr. Round Nose S. P.....032"
.375-300 Gr. Round Nose S. P.....049"
.375-300 Gr. Round Nose Solid....049"
.375-350 Gr. Round Nose S. P.....032"
.375-350 Gr. Round Nose Solid....049"

.401 WINCHESTER S. L.
.406-250 Gr. R. N. S. P. only.....032"

.404 (.411) CALIBER (.405 WIN.)
.411-250 Gr. Semi-Spitzer S. P.....032"
.411-300 Gr. Semi-Spitzer S. P.....032"
.411-400 Gr. Semi-Spitzer S. P.....032"
.411-400 Gr. Round Nose S. P.....032"
.411-400 Gr. Round Nose S. P.....049"
.411-400 Gr. Round Nose Solid....049"

.45-70 CALIBER
.458-300 Gr. Round Nose S. P.....032"
.458-400 Gr. Round Nose S. P.....032"
.458-500 Gr. Round Nose S. P.....032"

.450 MAGNUM
.458-400 Gr. Round Nose S. P.....049"
.458-400 Gr. Round Nose Solid....049"
.458-500 Gr. Round Nose S. P.....049"
.458-500 Gr. Round Nose Solid....049"
.458-600 Gr. Round Nose S. P.....049"
.458-600 Gr. Round Nose Solid....049"

SIERRA JACKETED BULLETS

Obtainable from Sierra Bullets, Inc., 600 West Whittier Blvd., Whittier, Calif., and from most dealers in reloading components. Prices range from $2.80 to $5.50 per hundred.

.22 CALIBER (.223")
 40 grain Hornet
 45 grain Hornet

.22 CALIBER (.224")
 40 grain Hornet
 45 grain Hornet
 45 grain Semi-Pointed
 45 grain Spitzer
 50 grain Semi-Pointed
 50 grain Spitzer
 55 grain Semi-Pointed
 55 grain Spitzer
 63 grain Semi-Pointed

6MM (.243")
 60 grain Hollow Point
 75 grain Spitzer H.P.
 85 grain Spitzer
 100 grain Spitzer
 100 grain Semi-Pointed

.22 CALIBER (.257")
 75 grain Hollow Point
 87 grain Spitzer
 110 grain Spitzer
 117 grain Spitzer F.B.
 117 grain Spitzer B.T.

6.5MM (.264")
 120 grain Spitzer
 140 grain Spitzer B.T.

.270 CALIBER (.277")
 110 grain Spitzer
 130 grain Spitzer F.B.
 130 grain Spitzer B.T.
 150 grain Spitzer B.T.

7MM (.284")
 120 grain Spitzer
 140 grain Spitzer
 160 grain Spitzer B.T.

.30 CALIBER (.308")
 125 grain Spitzer
 150 grain Spitzer
 180 grain Spitzer F.B.
 180 grain Spitzer B.T.
 180 grain Matchking*

.303 CALIBER (.311")
 150 grain Spitzer
 180 grain Spitzer

8MM (.323")
 150 grain Spitzer
 175 grain Spitzer

GAS CHECKS
 .22, .25, .270, .30,
 .32, and 8MM Caliber

---

*180-grain Matchking, full jacket, Spitzer, boattail bullet is now the preferred bullet for long-range, 1,000 yard match shooting.

SISK JACKETED BULLETS

Obtainable from R. B. Sisk, Iowa Park, Texas, and from most dealers in components.

Name	Grains weight	Diameter	Type Point	Shape Point
.17 Cal.	20	.172″	S.P.	Semi Ptd.
.17 Cal.	25	.172″	S.P.	Semi Ptd.
.17 Cal.	30	.172″	S.P.	Semi Ptd.
Hornet	35	.224″	S.P.F.J.	Blunt
Hornet	40	.223″ & .224″	S.P.F.J.	Blunt
Hornet	45	.223″ & .224″	S.P.F.J.	Blunt
Spitfire	36	.224″	S.P.	Sharp
Lovell	41	.223″ & .224″	S.P.	Sharp
Lovell	50	.223″ & .224″	S.P.	Sharp
Niedner	54	.223″ & .224″	S.P.F.J.	Semi Ptd.
Niedner	63	.223″ & .224″	S.P.F.J.	Semi Ptd.
Express				
(220 Swift)	42	.223″ & .224″	S.P.	Sharp
(220 Swift)	49	.223″ & .224″	S.P.	Sharp
(220 Swift)	55	.223″ & .224″	S.P.	Sharp
(220 Swift)	63	.223″ & .224″	S.P.	Sharp
Savage	40	.228″	S.P.	Blunt
Savage	55	.227″	S.P.	Semi Ptd.
Savage	63	.227″	S.P.	Semi Ptd.
Bench Rest	40	.223″ & .224″	H.P.	Sharp
Bench Rest	55	.223″ & .224″	H.P.	Sharp
Ackley	60	.228″	H.P.	Sharp
Ackley	70	.228″	H.P.	Sharp
Ackley	80	.228″	S.P.	Sharp
Ackely	90	.228″	S.P.	Sharp

S.P. = Soft Point. H.P. = Hollow Point. S.P.F.J. = Soft point, or full jacket

SPEER JACKETED BULLETS

Obtainable from Speer Products Co., Lewiston, Idaho and from most dealers in reloading components. All bullets are expanding.

Caliber & Grains	Shape	Number	Sectional Density	Ballistic Coefficient*
.224″ 40	Spire	.224–40–OS–SP	.114	.143
.224″ 45	Spitzer	.224–45–4–SP	.128	.160
.224″ 50	Spitzer	.224–50–6–SP	.142	.167
.224″ 52	Hollow Pt.	.224–52–6–HP	.147	.195
.224″ 55	Spitzer	.224–55–6–SP	.157	.209
.243″ 75	Hollow Pt.	.243–75–8–HP	.181	.267
.243″ 90	Spitzer	.243–90–8–SP	.217	.323
.243″ 105	Round	.243–105–GP–SP	.254	.256
.243″ 105	Spitzer	.243–105–10–SP	.254	.395
.257″ 60	Spire	.257–60–OS–SP	.129	.161
.257″ 87	Spitzer	.257–87–5–SP	.188	.294
.257″ 100	Spitzer	.257–100–6–SP	.216	.354
.257″ 120	Spitzer	.257–120–6–SP	.258	.425
.263″ 87	Spitzer	.263–87–5–SP	.179	.280
.263″ 120	Spitzer	.263–120–6–SP	.247	.405
.263″ 140	Spitzer	.263–140–6–SP	.289	.482
.277″ 100	Spitzer	.277–100–6–SP	.186	.288
.277″ 130	Spitzer	.277–130–6–SP	.241	.395
.277″ 150	Spitzer	.277–150–6–SP	.278	.463
.284″ 130	Spitzer	.284–130–6–SP	.230	.365
.284″ 145	Spitzer	.284–145–6–SP	.257	.425
.284″ 160	Spitzer	.284–160–6–SP	.284	.469
.3085″ 110	Spire	.3085–110–OS–SP	.166	.261
.3085″ 130	Hollow Pt.	.3085–130–6–HP	.195	.281
.3085″ 150	Flat Pt.	.3085–150–WR–SP	.225	.244
.3085″ 150	Semi Pt.	.3085–150–GP–SP	.225	.218
.3085″ 150	Spitzer	.3085–150–6–SP	.225	.387
.3085″ 180	Round	.3085–180–GP–SP	.270	.288
.3085″ 180	Spitzer	.3085–180–6–SP	.270	.435
.3085″ 200	Semi Pt.	.3085–200–GP–SP	.301	.425
.3085″ 200	Spitzer	.3085–200–6–SP	.301	.502
.311″ 150	Spitzer	.311–150–6–SP	.221	.365
.311″ 180	Semi Pt.	.311–180–GP–SP	.265	.282
.321″ 170	Flat	.321–170–WR–SP	.236	.242
.323″ 125	Spire	.323–125–OS–SP	.171	.225
.323″ 150	Spitzer	.323–150–6–SP	.205	.298
.323″ 170	Semi Pt.	.323–170–SS–SP	.232	.331
.323″ 225	Round	.323–225–GP–SP	.309	.395

Caliber & Grains	Shape	Number	Sectional Density	Ballistic Coefficient*
.333″ 275	Semi Pt.	.333–275–SS–SP	.354	.499
.349″ 180	Flat	.349–180–W–SP	.211	.222
.349″ 220	Flat	.349–220–W–SP	.258	.272
.3585″ 180	Round	.3585–180–R–SP	.201	.223
.3585″ 220	Round	.3585–220–R–SP	.246	.267
.3585″ 250	Spitzer	.3585–250–6–SP	.279	.423
.3755″ 235	Semi Pt.	.3755–235–SS–SP	.239	.257
.3755″ 285	Semi Pt.	.3755–285–SS–SP	.289	.375
.3755″ 285	Rd. FMJ	.3755–285–SS–FMJ	.289	.375

* Ballistic Coefficient, particularly for use with Speer Ballistics Calculator to determine bullet drop, mid-range trajectory, remaining velocity, and bullet energy.

CUSTOM MADE JACKETED BULLETS

In addition to the jacketed bullets supplied by our largest arms companies, Remington-Peters and Western-Winchester, there are a number of companies specializing in making jacketed bullets, and supplying them to the trade and to handloaders. The principal makers of these bullets, and a list of the bullets that they can furnish as of date of publication of this book are given in the lists on the pages that follow. These bullets now range in price from about $2.50 to about $8.00 per hundred, depending on caliber and weight, and they can be obtained, either from the makers direct, or from most retailers of reloading components.

VELOCITIES, ENERGIES, AND TRAJECTORIES OF U.S. FACTORY CARTRIDGES

CARTRIDGE	BULLET Wgt. Grs.	BULLET Style	VELOCITY—FEET PER SECOND Muzzle	100 Yds.	200 Yds.	300 Yds.	ENERGY—FOOT POUNDS Muzzle	100 Yds.	200 Yds.	300 Yds.	MID-RANGE TRAJECTORY 100 Yds.	200 Yds.	300 Yds.
.218 Bee Hi-Speed	46	Mush.	2860	2260	1740	1330	835	520	310	180	0.8	3.5	10.5
.219 Zipper Hi-Speed	56	Mush.	3050	2530	2070	1660	1155	795	535	345	0.6	2.5	8.0
.22 Hornet Hi-Speed	45	Mush.	2650	2080	1580	1220	700	430	250	150	0.8	4.0	12.5
.22 Hornet Hi-Speed	45	S.P.	2650	2080	1580	1220	700	430	250	150	0.8	4.0	12.5
.220 Swift Hi-Speed	48	Pd.S.P.	4140	3490	3040	2570	1825	1300	985	705	0.3	1.5	5.0
.22 Savage Hi-Speed	70	S.P.C.L.	2780	2480	2200	1940	1200	955	755	585	0.6	3.0	7.0
.243 Winchester	80	S.P.	3500	3080	2720	2410	2180	1690	1320	1030	0.4	1.8	4.7
.243 Winchester	100	S.P.	3070	2790	2540	2320	2090	1730	1430	1190	0.5	2.2	5.5
.244 Remington	75	S.P.	3500	3070	2660	2290	2040	1570	1180	875	0.4	1.9	4.9
.244 Remington	90	S.P.	3200	2850	2530	2230	2050	1630	1280	995	0.4	2.1	5.5
.25-20 Winchester	86	Lead	1450	1190	1050	950	400	270	210	175	2.6	11.5	31.5
.25-20 Winchester	86	S.P.	1450	1190	1050	950	400	270	210	175	2.6	11.5	31.5
.25-20 Winchester Hi-Speed	60	M.C.	2210	1700	1300	1060	650	385	225	150	1.1	6.0	18.5
.250 Savage Hi-Speed	100	Mush.	2810	2490	2180	1900	1755	1375	1055	800	0.6	3.0	7.0
.250 Savage Hi-Speed	100	M.C.L.	2810	2490	2180	1900	1755	1375	1055	800	0.6	3.0	7.0
.250 Savage Hi-Speed	87	S.P.	3000	2710	2430	2170	1740	1420	1140	910	0.5	2.5	6.0
.25-35 Winchester Express	117	M.C.	2280	1970	1690	1440	1350	1010	740	540	1.0	4.5	12.0
.25-35 Winchester Express	117	S.P.C.L.	2280	1970	1690	1440	1350	1010	740	540	1.0	4.5	12.0
.257 Roberts Express	117	S.P.C.L.	2630	2330	2050	1790	1800	1410	1095	835	0.7	3.0	8.0
.257 Roberts Hi-Speed	100	M.C.L.	2900	2530	2190	1870	1870	1420	1065	775	0.6	2.5	7.0
.25 Remington Express	117	S.P.C.L.	2300	2020	1760	1510	1375	1060	805	595	0.9	4.5	11.0
.270 Winchester Hi-Speed	150	S.P.C.L.	2770	2490	2220	1970	2560	2065	1645	1295	0.6	3.0	7.0
.270 Winchester Hi-Speed	130	M.C.L.	3140	2820	2530	2260	2850	2295	1850	1470	0.6	2.0	5.5
7mm Mauser Express	175	S.P.	2460	2220	1990	1780	2350	1915	1540	1230	0.8	3.5	9.0
.30-30 Winchester Express	160	M.C.	2200	1910	1650	1420	1720	1295	970	720	1.0	5.0	12.5
.30-30 Winchester Express	170	M.C.L.	2200	1930	1680	1460	1830	1405	1065	805	0.9	4.5	11.0
.30-30 Winchester Express	150	S.P.C.L.	2380	2060	1770	1510	1890	1415	1045	760	1.0	4.5	12.0
.30-30 Winchester Express	170	S.P.C.L.	2200	1930	1680	1460	1830	1405	1065	805	1.0	4.5	12.0
.30 Remington Express	160	M.C.	2200	1910	1650	1420	1720	1295	970	720	1.0	5.0	12.5
.30 Remington Express	170	M.C.L.	2200	1930	1680	1460	1830	1405	1065	805	1.0	4.5	12.0
.30 Remington Express	170	M.C.L.	2200	1930	1680	1460	1830	1405	1065	805	1.0	4.5	12.0
.30-40 Krag Hi-Speed	180	S.P.C.L.	2480	2210	1950	1710	2460	1955	1520	1170	0.8	3.5	9.0
.30-40 Krag Express	220	M.C.L.	2190	1980	1780	1600	2345	1915	1550	1250	1.0	4.5	11.0
.30-40 Krag Express	220	M.C.L.	2190	1980	1780	1600	2345	1915	1550	1250	1.0	4.5	11.0
.30-40 Krag Hi-Speed	180	M.C.L.	2480	2210	1950	1710	2460	1955	1520	1170	0.8	3.5	9.0
.30-06 Springfield Hi-Speed	150	Br.P.	2960	2720	2480	2250	2920	2465	2050	1700	0.5	2.5	6.0
.30-06 Springfield Palma Match	180	M.C.T.H.	2730	2540	2350	2170	2975	2575	2205	1880	0.6	2.5	6.5
.30-06 Springfield Hi-Speed	180	Br.P.	2690	2500	2310	2130	2895	2500	2135	1815	0.6	2.6	7.0
.30-06 Springfield Pointed	150	M.C.	2800	2560	2340	2120	2610	2185	1825	1500	0.7	3.0	6.6
.30-06 Springfield Hi-Speed	180	M.C.L.	2710	2420	2150	1900	2940	2340	1850	1445	0.8	3.5	7.5
.30-06 Springfield Express	220	M.C.L.	2410	2190	1970	1780	2840	2345	1900	1550	0.8	3.5	9.0
.30-06 Springfield Express	220	S.P.C.L.	2410	2190	1970	1780	2840	2345	1900	1550	0.8	3.5	9.0
.30-06 Springfield Hi-Speed	180	S.P.C.L.	2710	2420	2150	1900	2940	2340	1850	1445	0.7	3.0	7.5

Cartridge	Bullet (grs.)	Bullet	Velocity, Muzzle	Velocity, 100 yd.	Velocity, 200 yd.	Velocity, 300 yd.	Energy, Muzzle	Energy, 100 yd.	Energy, 200 yd.	Energy, 300 yd.	Traj. 100	Traj. 200	Traj. 300
.30-06 Springfield Hi-Speed	110	Mush.	3380	2850	2370	1940	2790	1980	1370	920	0.4	2.0	6.0
7.62mm Russian Hi-Speed	150	Br.P.	2810	2570	2330	2110	2620	2220	1810	1485	0.6	2.5	6.5
.300 H & H Magnum Express	220	M.C.L.	2610	2380	2160	1950	3330	2770	2280	1860	0.5	3.0	7.5
.300 H & H Magnum Match	180	M.C.T.H.	2900	2700	2500	2320	3365	2920	2500	2150	0.7	3.0	6.0
.300 Savage Hi-Speed	150	Br.P.	2660	2430	2210	2000	2360	1970	1625	1325	0.7	3.0	7.5
.300 Savage Express	180	M.C.L.	2380	2149	1910	1700	2265	1830	1460	1155	0.8	4.0	10.0
.300 Savage Express	180	S.P.C.L.	2380	2140	1910	1700	2265	1830	1460	1155	0.8	4.0	10.0
.303 British Express	215	S.P.	2160	1940	1740	1550	2230	1795	1445	1145	1.0	4.5	11.5
.303 Savage Express	180	M.C.L.	2120	1840	1590	1370	1800	1360	1010	750	1.0	5.0	13.5
.303 Savage Express	180	S.P.C.L.	2120	1840	1590	1370	1800	1360	1010	750	1.0	5.0	13.5
8mm Mauser Hi-Speed	170	S.P.	2610	2320	2040	1780	2575	2030	1570	1195	0.7	3.5	9.0
8mm Lebal Hi-Speed	170	S.P.	2610	2320	2040	1780	1845	1390	1010	1040	0.7	3.5	8.5
.32-20 Winchester	100	Lead	1280	1060	940	850	365	250	195	160	3.1	15.0	40.5
.32-20 Winchester	100	S.P.	1280	1060	940	850	365	250	195	160	3.1	15.0	40.5
.32-20 Winchester	100	M.C.	1280	1060	940	850	365	250	195	160	3.1	15.0	40.5
.32-20 Winchester Hi-Speed	80	Mush.	2050	1520	1150	980	745	410	235	170	1.4	5.0	23.0
.32 Winchester Special Express	170	M.C.L.	2260	1960	1690	1450	1930	1450	1080	795	1.0	4.5	12.0
.32 Winchester Special Express	170	S.P.C.L.	2260	1950	1690	1450	1930	1450	1080	795	1.0	4.5	12.0
.32 Winchester Self Loading	165	S.P.	1390	1190	1060	980	710	520	410	350	2.6	12.5	31.0
.32 Remington Express	170	M.C.L.	2200	1910	1640	1400	1830	1380	1015	740	1.0	5.0	13.0
.32 Remington Express	170	S.P.C.L.	2200	1910	1640	1400	1830	1380	1015	740	1.0	5.0	13.0
.32-40 Winchester	165	S.P.	1440	1230	1080	1000	760	555	430	365	2.6	12.0	28.0
.33 Winchester	200	S.P.	2180	1870	1600	1360	2110	1555	1135	820	1.1	5.0	13.5
.348 Winchester Hi-Speed	150	S.P.	2520	2380	1930	1550	2765	1890	1240	800	0.6	3.0	8.5
.348 Winchester Express	200	M.C.L.	2520	2160	1840	1560	2820	2075	1505	1080	0.8	4.0	10.0
.348 Winchester Express	200	S.P.C.L.	2520	2160	1840	1560	2820	2075	1505	1080	0.8	4.0	10.0
.35 Winchester Self Loading	180	S.P.	1390	1170	1040	960	775	545	430	370	2.5	13.0	31.0
.35 Remington	200	M.C.	2180	1870	1590	1360	2110	1555	1125	820	1.0	5.0	13.0
.35 Remington Express	200	M.C.L.	2180	1870	1590	1360	2110	1555	1125	820	1.0	5.0	13.0
.35 Remington Express	200	S.P.C.L.	1850	1560	1310	1140	1370	975	685	520	1.5	7.5	19.0
.351 Winchester Self Loading	180	M.C.	1850	1560	1310	1140	1370	975	685	520	1.5	7.5	19.0
.351 Winchester Self Loading	177	S.T.	2530	2210	1910	1640	2840	2160	1610	1190	0.8	3.6	9.4
.358 Winchester	200	S.T.	2250	2210	1780	1570	2810	2230	1760	1370	1.0	4.4	11.0
.358 Winchester	250	S.T.	2740	2460	2210	1990	4500	3620	2920	2370	0.7	2.9	7.1
.375 Magnum	270	S.P.	2550	2280	2040	1830	3460	3160	2770	2230	0.7	3.3	8.3
.375 Magnum	300	S.P.	2550	2180	1860	1590	3160	2300	1680	2230	0.7	3.6	8.3
.375 Magnum	300	M.C.	2550	2180	1860	1590	3160	2300	1680	2220	0.7	3.6	8.3
.38-40 Winchester	180	S.P.	1310	1090	960	870	475	370	305	305	3.2	15.5	37.5
.38-55 Winchester	255	S.P.	1320	1150	1050	980	985	750	625	545	3.0	13.5	32.5
.44-40 Winchester	200	S.P.	1300	1070	940	860	750	390	330	330	3.3	17.5	38.0
.45-70 Government	405	S.P.	1310	1160	1060	990	1545	1210	1010	880	2.8	14.0	32.5
.458 Winchester	500	M.C.	2125	1910	1700	1520	5010	4050	3210	2540	1.1	4.8	12.0
.458 Winchester	510	S.P.	2125	1840	1600	1400	5110	3830	2900	2220	1.1	5.1	13.2

NOTE: The above table shows the height of trajectory at mid-range above the center of the bullet hole in the target. What a hunter usually wishes to know is the height above the line connecting the axis of the bore at the muzzle with the line of aim. Thus, taking the .30-06 Springfield with 180-grain bullet, and a scope with axis 1.5 inches above bore line, one-half this amount, or .75 inch, must be deducted from the figure in the table, making the height of trajectory above line of aim at 100 yards, 1.75 inches instead of 2.5 inches.

TABLE OF VELOCITIES, ENERGIES AND PENETRATION

Modern American Pistol Cartridges
(Courtesy of Remington Arms Co.)

CARTRIDGE	BULLET		Muzzle Velocity Feet per Second	Muzzle Energy Ft. Lbs.	Barrel Inches	Pen. ⅞" Pine Boards
	Wgt. Grs.	Style				
25 (6.35 m/m) Automatic.............	50	M.C.	820	75	2	3
30 (7.65 m/m) Luger..................	93	M.C.	1250	323	4½	11
30 (7.63 m/m) Mauser Automatic......	85	M.C.	1420	380	5½	11
32 Short Colt.......................	80	Lead	800	114	4	3
32 Long Colt........................	82	Lead	800	117	4	3
32 Colt New Police..................	100	Lead	795	138	4	3
32 (7.65 m/m) Automatic Pistol......	71	M.C.	980	152	4	5
32 Smith & Wesson...................	88	Lead	720	98	3	3
32 Smith & Wesson Long..............	98	Lead	795	138	4	4
32 S & W Long Wad Cutter Targetmaster..	98	Lead	770	129	4	—
357 Magnum..........................	158	M.P.	1450	690	8⅜	12½
9 m/m Luger.........................	124	M.C.	1150	365	4	10
38 Smith & Wesson...................	146	Lead	745	179	4	4
38 Smith & Wesson...................	200	Lead	630	176	4	5
38 Special Round-Nose Targetmaster...	158	Lead	870	266	6	6½
38 Special...........................	158	Lead	870	266	6	6½
38 Special...........................	200	Lead	745	247	6	7½
38 Special...........................	158	M.P.	870	266	6	6½
38 Special Wad Cutter Targetmaster...	146	Lead	770	193	6	—
38 Special Wad Cutter...............	146	Lead	770	193	6	—
38 Special Metal Penetrating Hi-Way Master	110	Special	1330	433	5	—

(222)

CARTRIDGE	BULLET Wgt. Grs.	BULLET Style	Muzzle Velocity Feet per Second	Muzzle Energy Ft. Lbs.	Barrel Inches	Pen. ⅞" Pine Boards
38 Special Hi-Speed	158	Lead	1115	436	5	7½
38 Special Flat Point (Colt Special)	158	Lead	870	266	6	6½
38 Colt New Police	150	Lead	695	161	4	4
38 Short Colt	125	Lead	770	165	6	4
38 Long Colt	150	Lead	785	205	6	6
38 Super Automatic Hi-Speed	130	M.C.	1300	488	5	10
38 Automatic	130	M.C.	1070	331	4½	9
380 (9 m/m) Automatic	95	M.C.	970	199	3¾	5½
41 Long Colt	195	Lead	745	241	6	3
44 Smith & Wesson Russian	246	Lead	770	324	6½	7½
44 Smith & Wesson Special	246	Lead	770	324	6½	7½
45 Colt	250	Lead	870	421	5½	6
45 Automatic	230	M.C.	860	378	5	6
45 Automatic Targetmaster	230	M.C.	750	288	5	—
45 Auto. Metal Penetrating Hi-Way Master	173	Special	1140	500	5	—
45 Automatic Rim	230	M.C.	820	343	5½	6
45 Automatic Rim	230	Lead	820	343	5½	6

MATCH CARTRIDGES — Pistol and Revolver

CARTRIDGE	BULLET Wgt. Grs.	BULLET Style	Muzzle Velocity Feet per Second	Muzzle Energy Ft. Lbs.	Barrel Inches	Pen. ⅞" Pine Boards
22 Long Rifle—Police Targetmaster	40	Lead	970	83	6	—
32 S & W Long Wad Cutter Targetmaster	98	Lead	770	129	4	—
38 Special Round Nose Targetmaster	158	Lead	870	266	6	6½
38 Special Wad Cutter Targetmaster	146	Lead	770	193	6	—
45 Automatic Targetmaster	230	M.C.	750	288	5	—

GROOVE DIAMETER AND TWIST OF RIFLING
AMERICAN RIFLES AND HANDGUNS

Caliber and Cartridge	Make	Min.†	Max.	Twist of Rifling inches Turn in
		Groove Diameter		
.218 Bee	Winchester	.224	.2245	16
.219 Zipper	Winchester	.224	.2245	16
.22 Hornet	Winchester	.222	.2228	16
.22 Hornet	Savage	.223	.224	16
.22 Hornet	Z Brno	.224	.2245	16
.22 Short, R.F.	Winchester	.224		20
.22 Short, R.F.	Stevens	.223	.224	25
.22 Short, R.F., Auto.	Remington	.218	.220	24
.22 Short, R.F., Manually Oper.	Remington	.222	.224	16
.22 Long Rifle, R.F.	Winchester	.222	.2228	16
.22 Long Rifle, R.F.	Stevens	.223	.224	16
.22 Long Rifle, R.F.	Remington	.222	.224	16
.22 W.R.F.	Winchester	.226		14
.22 W.R.F.	Stevens	.223	.224	14
.220 Swift	Winchester	.224		14
.22/3000 Lovell 2R	Custom	.2235	.224	16
.222 Remington	Remington	.224	2245	14
.22 Varminter	Gebby	.2235	.224	14
.22-250-3000	Custom	.2235	.2245	14
.22 Savage	Savage	.227	.228	12
6mm Lee Navy	Winchester	.242	.244	7½
.243 Winchester	Winchester	.243		10
.244 Remington	Remington	.243	.244	12
.25 Stevens, R.F.	Stevens	.256	.257	17
.25-20 S.S. & W.C.F.	Winchester	.256	.2575	14
.25-20 S.S. & W.C.F.	Savage	.256	.257	14
.25-20 S.S.	Stevens	.256	.257	13 & 14
.25-35 W.C.F.	Winchester	.256	.2575	8
.25-36 Marlin	Marlin	.257	.2575	9
.25 Remington Auto.	Remington	.256	.258	10
.25 Niedner and .25 Roberts	Niedner	.2565	.2575	10 & 12
.250-3000 Savage	Savage	.257		14
.250-3000 Savage	Winchester	.256	.258	10 & 14
6.5 mm Mannlicher Sch.	Steyr	.263	.264	7½
.256 Newton	Newton	.264	.265	10
.257 Roberts	Winchester	.256	.257	10
.257 Remington Roberts	Remington	.256	.258	10
.270 W.C.F.	Winchester	.277	.2785	10

* We are indebted to the Lyman Gun Sight Corporation for most of this table, but the author has added to and altered it slightly in accordance with his experience.

† Most manufacturers try to adhere to the minimum dimension as standard. Prior to about 1917 many groove diameters slightly exceeded these figures.

Many custom barrels are made intentionally with considerable variations from the above, particularly in twist of rifling.

Caliber and Cartridge	Make	Min.†	Max.	Twist of Rifling inches Turn in
		Groove Diameter		
7mm Mauser	German	.2854	.2874	8.66
7mm Mauser	American	.2845	.2855	10
.280 Ross	Ross	.289	.290	8.66
.30-30 W.C.F.	Winchester	.308	.3085	12
.30-30 W.C.F.	Savage	.308	.3085	12
.50-110-450 Winchester	Winchester	.506		60
.58 Springfield M.L.	U.S. Govt.	.590		68
.30 Remington Auto.	Remington	.308	.3085	12
.30-40 Krag Jorgensen	U.S. Govt.	.3075	.311	10
.30-40 Krag	Winchester	.308	.309	10
.308 Winchester	Winchester	.308	3085	12
.30-06 Springfield	U.S. Govt.	.308	.309	10
.30-06 Springfield	Commercial	.308	.309	10
.30-06 Garand	U.S. Govt.	.308	.309	10
.300 Savage	Savage	.308	.309	12
.300 H & H Magnum	Winchester	.308	.3085	10
8mm Mauser Early	German	.317	.319	9 to 10
8mm Mauser Rimless after 1903	German	.323	.326	9 to 10
.303 Savage	Savage	.308	.309	12
.303 British	English	.312	.314	10
.32 Short & Long R.F.	Winchester	.313	.315	20 to 26
.32 Short & Long R.F.	Stevens	.309	.310	25
.32 Remington Auto.	Remington	.319	.321	14
.32 Ideal	Stevens	.323	.324	18
.32 Winchester Special	Winchester	.320	.3205	16
.32 Winchester Self Loading	Winchester	.320	.3205	16
.32-20 W.C.F.	Winchester	.311	.3115	20
.32-20 W.C.F.	Savage	.310	.311	20
.32-40 Ballard & Marlin	Early	.319	.322	16 to 18
.32-40 Recent	Winchester	.320	.3205	16
.33 W.C.F.	Winchester	.338	.3385	12
.348 Winchester	Winchester	.348	.3485	12
.35 Winchester Self Loading	Winchester	.351	.352	16
.351 Winchester Self Loading	Winchester	.351	.352	16
.35 Remington Auto.	Remington	.357	.359	16
.35 W.C.F. Model 95	Winchester	.358	.3585	12
.35 Whelen	Griffin	.357	.3575	18
.35 Newton	Newton	.359		12
.358 Winchester	Winchester	.358		12
.375 H & H Magnum	Winchester	.375	.376	12
.38 Short, Long & Extra Long	All	.358	.359	36
.38-40 W.C.F.	Winchester	.400	.4005	36
.38-40 W.C.F.	Remington	.398	.400	36
.38-55 W.B.& M.	Early	.379	.382	18 & 20
.38-55 W.B.& M. Recent	Winchester	.379	.3795	18
.38-56 W.C.F.	Winchester	.379	.3795	20
.38-70-255 W.C.F.	Winchester	.379	.3795	24
.38-72-275 W.C.F.	Winchester	.379	.3795	22
.38-90 W.C.F.	Winchester	.379	.3795	26
.40-50 Sharps Straught	Winchester	.403	.405	18
.40-70 S.S. & Ballard	Winchester	.403	.405	20

Caliber and Cartridge	Make	Min.†	Max.	Twist of Rifling inches Turn in
		Groove Diameter		
.40-70-330 Win. M 1886	Winchester	.408		20
.40-72-330 Win. M 1895	Winchester	.406	.407	22
.40-82-260 Win. M 1886	Winchester	.408		28
.40-90 Sharps Straight	Winchester	.403	.405	18
.40-100 Winchester	Winchester	.403	405	28
.40-60 Winchester	Winchester	.4045	.405	40
.401 Winchester S.L.	Winchester	.407	.408	14
.404 Jeffry Magnum	Hoffman	.423	.424	14
.405 Winchester	Winchester	.413	.4135	14
.43 Spanish	Winchester	.439	.440	20
.44-40 W.C.F.	Winchester	.4285	.429	36
.44-40 W.C.F.	Remington	.424	.426	20
.44 Henry R.F.	Winchester	.4285	.4295	36
.45-60 W.C.F.	Winchester	.456	.458	20
.45-70 Springfield, U.S.	U.S. Govt.	.457	.459	22
.45-70 Winchester	Winchester	.456	.458	20
.45-75 W.C.F. Model 1876	Winchester	.456	.458	20
.45-90 W.C.F.	Winchester	.458		32
.45-125 W.C.F.	Winchester	.456	.458	36
.45 Sharps, 3¼″ shell	Sharps	.458	.459	18
.50 Sharps	Sharps	.509		
.50-70 Springfield	U.S. Govt.	.515		24 to 42
.50-95 Winchester	Winchester	.5055		60

TABLE OF GROOVE DIAMETERS OF REVOLVERS

.22	Long Rifle	.222″	9mm Luger		.358″
.25	Automatic	.251	.38-40		.401
.30	Mauser	.311	.41 Colt		.401
.30	Luger	.311	.44-40 Early		.424
.32	Automatic	.312	.44-40 Late		.427
.32-20		.312	.44 Russian		.427
.38	Special, Colt	.354	.44 S & W Special		.427
.38	Special, S & W	.357	.45 Colt Revolver		.452
.357	S & W Magnum	.358	.45 Automatic		.451
.38	Colt Auto.	.356			

TWIST OF RIFLING IN REVOLVERS AND PISTOLS

Smith & Wesson uses right hand rifling with the following twists.

.22 Revolver	1 turn in 10″
.22 Single Shot	1 turn in 15″
.32-20	1 turn in 12″
.32 S & W	1 turn in 18¾″
.357 & .38 Revolvers	1 turn in 18¾″
.44 Special	1 turn in 20″

The Colt Manufacturing Co. makes all revolvers and pistols with left hand twist, 1 turn in 16″ except .22 caliber weapons which have 1 turn in 14″.

HELPFUL BIBLIOGRAPHY

Ideal Handbook. Lyman Gun Sight Corporation, Middlefield, Conn. $1.00.

Belding & Mull Handbook. Belding & Mull, Phillipsburg, Penna. $1.00.

Reloading Information (2 volumes). National Rifle Association, 1600 Rhode Island Avenue, N.W., Washington 6, D.C. 75c per volume.

The Ultimate in Rifle Precision. The Stackpole Company, Harrisburg, Penna. $6.00.

Speer Handloaders Manual. Volume 1: *Standard Cartridges;* Volume 2: *Wildcat Cartridges.* Speer Products Co., Lewiston, Idaho. $2.00 per volume.

Speer Ballistics Calculator. Speer Products Co., Lewiston, Idaho. $1.00.

Complete Guide to Handloading, by Philip B. Sharpe. Funk & Wagnalls Company, 153 East 24th Street, New York 10, N.Y. $10.00.

The American Rifleman. Monthly magazine of the National Rifle Association. All back and current issues. This magazine is included in NRA membership, which costs $5.00 per year. All handloaders should be members of the NRA.

DIRECTORY OF MANUFACTURERS AND DEALERS IN HANDLOADING TOOLS, SUPPLIES, COMPONENTS AND SERVICES

A general list of the goods each firm can supply is given. Many firms also handle other goods for shooters and sportsmen. When corresponding with these firms please mention this book.

P. O. Ackley, Box 185, Murray, Utah.
Custom rifles, barrels, dies, supplies.

Acme Industries, Inc., 625 W. Lawrence St., Appleton, Wisc.
Shot-shell loading tools.

C. V. Allen, 995 Heather Lake, Salem, Oregon.
Custom handloads, components.

American Rifleman. See National Rifle Association

Alcan Company, Inc., Alton, Illinois.
Shot-shell reloading tools, powder, primers, wads, shot, and handloading components.

Apex Rifle Co., 7570 San Fernando Road, Sun Valley, Calif.
Custom rifles, loading tools, services.

Ashton & Co., 1511 N. Gardner St., Hollywood, Calif.
Norma and hard-to-get ammunition for foreign rifles.

Aurand's, 229 E. 3rd St., Lewistown, Penna.
Reloading tools and components.

Badger Shooters' Supply Co., Owen, Wisc.
Tools, components, supplies.

J. W. Baldwin, 5 Milk Street, Westboro, Mass.
Precision-grade .22 caliber match bullets.

Barlow's Gun Shop, 5565 S. Howell Ave., Milwaukee 7, Wisc.
Gunsmithing, tools, components. Oldest rifle shop in U.S., since 1829.

Fred N. Barnes, 318 S. Redlands Road, Grand Junction, Colo.
Jacketed bullets, all calibers and weights.

Bean's Gunshop, 806 Alice St., Modesto, Calif.
Shooters' and handloaders' supplies. Decapping pins for primers hard to eject.

Belding & Mull, 102 N. Fourth St., Phillipsburg, Penna.
B&M reloading tools, powder measure, components, supplies. B&M Reloading Handbook.

Biehler & Astles, 1597 Ridge Road W., Rochester, N.Y.
Dies and swages for jacketed bullets.

G. Bjornstad, 1626 Fargo Ave., Chicago 26, Ill.
Ammunition, jacketed bullets, components.

Sam Bond, New Philadelphia, Ohio.
Ammunition and shooters' supplies.

Brad's Gunshop, 204 Caladium Ave., Lake Jackson, Texas.
Flexible plastic cartridge boxes.

Brown & Ball, 1205 G Ave., LaGrange, Oregon.
Powder Dispenser—one grain at a time.

Bob Brownell, Main & Third, Montezuma, Iowa.
Shooters' and gunsmiths' supplies, tools, components.

Carbide Die & Mfg. Co., Box 226, Corvina, Calif.
Carbide Pistol Cartridge Dies.

Cascade Cartridge Co., Lewiston, Idaho.
Rifle and pistol primers (Speer).

Central Gun Co., (Formerly Lindahl's), Box 326, Lincoln, Nebr.
Tools, accessories, powder, components.

Christopher, Box 2062, Fort Pierce, Florida.
Custom handloads.

Colt's Patent Fire Arms Mfg. Co., 150 Huyscope Ave., Hartford 15, Conn.
Colt revolvers and pistols, supplied through dealers.

H. Cook, 3rd & Central, Albuquerque, N.M.
Jobbing reloading equipment for dealers and gunsmiths.

Cramer Bullet Mould Co., 11625 Vanowen, North Hollywood, Calif.
Cramer bullet moulds and Cramer Lubri-sizer.

Custom Gunsmithing Service, 10329 Stagg St., Sun Valley 3, Calif.
Custom handloading and components.

Dunbar Tool & Die Co., Box 542, Staunton, Virginia.
Dunbar reloading tool, powder measure, dies.

Roy F. Dunlop, 2319 Ft. Lowell Road, Tucson, Ariz.
Rifle gunsmith, stocks, tools, supplies.

Easton Engineering Co., 1116 S. State St., Salt Lake City 4, Utah.
Easton Giant Loading Press.
Federal Cartridge Co., Minneapolis, Minn.
Federal cartridges, primers, components supplied through dealers.
Firearms International Corp., Washington 22, D.C.
F.N., Saco, and other imported rifles and shotguns, barrelled actions, and actions only supplied through dealers.
Femco Specialty Mfg., 1115 N.E. 60th Ave., Portland 13, Ore.
Micro adjustable headspace gages.
Forslund Mfg. Co., 12270 Montague St., Pacoima, Calif.
Mepos lubricator and sizer, Mepos reloader.
Forster Bros. Mfg. Co., 86 E. Lanark Ave., Lanark, Ill.
Forster precision case trimmer, headspace gages.
Frank Foster, Box 983, Clovis, New Mexico.
Primer catchers for Pacific and other tools.
Al Freeland, 3737 14th Ave., Rock Island, Ill.
Shooters' supplies, bench rest, pedestals, scope stands.
Ray Gavoni & Son, 31 Star St., Whitman, Mass.
Custom handloading.
E. L. Gardiner, 422 Sixth St., Rockford, Ill.
Custom jacketed bullets, and jackets.
Earl Gibbs, 1620 Sheridan Blvd., Denver 14, Colo.
Gibbs reloading press, dies, and bullets.
Gopher Shooters Supply, Faribault, Minn.
Tools, components, supplies.
Griffin & Howe, Inc., 202 East 44th St., New York 17, N.Y.
Riflemakers, tools, supplies, special cases.
Grigsby Engineering Mfg. Co., 125 West Ave. 29, Los Angeles 31, Calif.
Reloading equipment, case trimmers.
G&H Die Co., 5011 E. Washington Blvd., Los Angeles 22, Calif.
Chrome-plated dies, reloading tools.
Gunderson Instrument Co., 1824 Queensbury Road, Pasadena, Calif.
Electronic power scales.

Guns Magazine, 8150 N. Central Park Blvd., Skokie, Ill.
Monthly magazine devoted to guns, rifles, and shooting.

Gun Digest Publishing Co., 227 W. Washington St., Chicago 6, Ill.
The Gun Digest, published annually, contains many helpful articles.

Guns Products Division, 4114 Fannin, Houston, Texas.
Inertia bullet pullers, powder funnels.

Gun Specialities, Box 31, College Park, Georgia.
Lewis lead remover for revolvers.

Hanson's Custom Loading, 119 Oak St., Bonner Springs, Kansas.
Custom handloads.

H&M Tool Co., 24062 Orchard Lake Road, Farmington, Mich.
Chambering reamers and gages for all cartridges.

Wilbur J. Hauck, Route 1, West Arlington, Vt.
Custom-rifle maker, components, supplies.

Hensley & Gibbs, 2692 E Street, San Diego 2, Calif.
Bullet moulds, dippers, sprue cutting mallets.

E. C. Herkner & Co., Boise, Idaho.
Echo reloading tools.

Herter's Inc., Waseca, Minn.
Herter's complete line of reloading tools, bullets, components.

High Standard Mfg. Corp., Hamden, Conn.
High Standard pistols and revolvers supplied through dealers.

Milo Hill, Caledonia, Ohio.
Jacketed bullets.

B. E. Hodgdon, Merriam, Kansas.
Powder, —4831, 4895, H.240, Western Ball, etc., components, tools.

Hollywood Gun Shop, 6116 Hollywood Blvd., Hollywood 28, Calif.
Hollywood reloading tools, components, supplies.

Ted Holmes Gun Shop, Route 2, Mattoon, Ill.
Rifle gunsmithing, tools, components, bullets.

J. W. Hornady, 324 W. Fourth St., Grand Island, Nebr.
Jacketed bullets of all calibers and weights, gas checks.

E. A. James, Box 381, Naples, Texas.
Handloads for most German and foreign calibers.

Jordan Precision Bullet Co., Raynham, Mass.
Soft-swaged bullets, .22 and .25 cal.

Kerr's, 9582 Wilshire Blvd., Beverly Hills, Calif.
All makes reloading tools and components.

Kenru Reloading Service, 166 Normandy Ave., Rochester 11, N.Y.
Kenru soft-swaged .22 bullets and jackets.

Kuharsky Bros., 2425 W. 12th St., Erie, Penna.
Primer pocket cleaners.

Kunkel's, Davenport, Iowa.
Reloading tools, ammunition, components, supplies.

Lachmiller Engineering Co., 6445 San Fernando Road, Glendale 1, Calif.
Lachmiller reloading tools, dies, swages.

Llanerch Gun Shop, 2800 Township Line, Upper Darby, Pa.
Shooters' and reloading supplies and components, gunsmithing, targets of all kinds.

Lyman Gun Sight Corp., Middlefield, Conn.
Ideal reloading tools, powder measures, dies, moulds, lubricant, lead alloy, sights.

Marlin Firearms Co., New Haven, Conn.
Rifles and shotguns supplied through dealers.

Philip Jay Medicus, 18 Fletcher St., New York 38, N.Y.
Cartridges, new and old.

J. W. McPhillips, 285 Mastick Ave., San Bruno, Calif.
Custom handloading, including most foreign cartridges. Case forming service.

Minneapolis Shooters' Supply, 3155 40th Ave. So., Minneapolis, Minn.
Reloading tools, components, custom loading.

Frank Mittermeier, 3577 E. Tremont Ave., New York 65, N.Y.
Micrometer and vernier calipers, gunsmiths' supplies.

Masters Machine Works, Box 185, Brookville, Pa.
Jordan Multiple Reloading Press.
Mitchell's Gun Shop, Hanover, N.H.
Custom handloading, supplies, case-forming service.
Moulton & Armstrong, Box 72, San Lorenzo, Calif.
Custom handloading and supplies.
Multiplex Co., Box 283, Logan, Ohio.
Multiplex reloaders and dies.
National Bench Rest Shooters Association.
P. H. Teachout, Sec., Lyndonville, Vt.
National Rifle Association, 1600 Rhode Island Ave., Washington 6, D.C.
Annual membership $5.00 includes subscription to *The American Rifleman.* Every shooter should be a member.
Fred Ness, Red Wing, Minnesota.
Shooters' supplies, components.
Norma Precision, South Lansing, N.Y. & 731 Market St., San Francisco 3, Calif.
Norma imported ammunition, bullets, cases, primers.
National Target Co., 1255 25th St., N.W., Washington, D.C.
Official N.R.A. targets and spotters.
H. C. Neilson, 630 Congress St., Neenah, Wisc.
Special loading blocks.
Nitro Press Mfg. Co., Lafayette, N.Y.
Reloading tools and dies.
Nosler Partition Bullet Co., 382 Wightman St., Ashland, Ore.
Nosler Partition Bullets.
Pacific Gun Sight Co., 2901 El Camino Road, Palo Alto, Calif.
Full line of Pacific reloading tools and scales. *Pacific Reloading Handbook.*
P. J. O'Hare, 552 Irvington Ave., Maplewood, N.J.
Shooters' supplies of all kinds.
C. W. Paddock, 1589 Payne Ave., St. Paul 17, Minn.
Pasteboard boxes for rifle, pistol, and shotgun cartridges.
Perfection Die Co., 916 W. London, El Reno, Okla.
Tungsten-carbide pistol resizing dies.

Potter Engineering Co., 10 Albany St., Cazenovia, N.Y.
Potter reloading tools, electric furnaces, kettles, ingot moulds, lead testers, revolver machine rests.

Precision Shooting, 53 Eastern Ave., St. Johnsbury, Vt.
Monthly magazine devoted to rifle and bench rest shooting, and handloading. $3.00 a year. Very helpful.

Thurman Randle & Co., 1321 Dragon St., Dallas, Texas.
Ammunition, components, supplies, N.R.A. targets.

Raton Gun Shop, 110 N. First, Raton, N.M.
Chambering reamers.

R.C.B.S. Gun & Die Shop, Box 729, Oroville, Calif.
R.C.B.S. reloading tools, dies, powder measures, components, supplies.

Redding-Hunter, Inc., Cortland, N.Y.
Redding powder scales and power measures.

Redford Reamer Co., Box 4863, Redford Station, Detroit 19, Mich.
Chambering reamers and gages.

Ray Riling, 6844 Gorsten St., Philadelphia 19, Pa.
Gun books, new and old.

Rochester Lead Works, Rochester 8, N.Y.
Lead wire for bullet jacket cores.

Remington Arms Company, Bridgeport, Conn.
Rifles, shotguns, ammunition, and components supplied through dealers.

Seaco, 2451 E. Colorado, Pasadena, Calif.
Thermo controlled furnace for bullet casting, precision powder measure.

S&L Machine Co., 6058 Dennison St., Los Angeles 22, Calif.
Tungsten-carbide dies for pistol cartridges.

T. G. Samworth, Georgetown 7, S.C.
Small Arms Technical Publishing Co. Up-to-date books on arms and ammunition. Send for folder.

Savage Arms Corp., Chicopee Falls, Mass.
Savage and Stevens rifles and shotguns supplied through dealers.

(234)

Schmitt Reloading Tools, 459 Sexton Bldg., Minneapolis 15, Minn.
Schmitt reloading tools, and primer pocket re-forming set.
Sharpe & Hart Associates, Inc., Emmitsburg 5, Md., and 4437-A Piedmont, Oakland 11, Calif.
Distributors of Schultz & Larson (7 X 61 Sharpe) rifles, ammunition, and empty cases.
Sierra Bullets, 600 W. Whittier Blvd., Whittier, Calif.
Complete line of Sierra bullets, jackets.
Sportsmans Press (an activity of Association of the U.S. Army), 1529 18th St., N.W., Washington 6, D.C.
Military, gun and sporting books.
Shenandoah Gun Co., Berryville, Va.
Rifle gunsmithing, tools, components, chronograph testing.
Shooters' Accessory Supply, Box 205, North Bend, Oregon.
Little Dipper, Mez-U-Rite, Multi-Mezur, and Mark III Big Dipper powder measures.
G. T. Smiley Co., Box 54, Clipper Gap, Calif.
Smiley case-reaming tools, and primer pocket reamers.
Smith & Wesson, Springfield, Mass.
S&W revolvers and pistols supplied through dealers.
Speer Products Co., Lewiston, Idaho.
Complete line of Speer bullets, .22 to .375 cal., Speer manuals, and Speer Ballistics Computor.
R. W. Sprowls, 1600 7th Ave., S.E., Cedar Rapids, Iowa.
Reloading tools, components, supplies.
Star Machine Works, 418 10th Ave., San Diego, Calif.
Star progressive loading tool, Star lubricator and sizer.
Stoeger Arms Corp., 507 5th Ave., New York, N.Y. (Sales) and 45-18 Court Square, Long Island City 1, N.Y.
Shooters' arms, supplies, equipment, tools, components. *Shooters Bible,* $2.00.
Sturm, Ruger & Co., Inc., Southport, Conn.
Ruger pistols and revolvers supplied through dealers.
Thalson Company, 682 Mission St., San Francisco, Calif.
Shotgun reloading tools.

Glenn J. Thomas, 53 Terminal Place, Bend 3, Oregon.
De luxe cartridge boxes and loading blocks.

Robert S. Thomas, Box 81, Silver Spring, Md.
Reloading supplies, components, "Tommy Dots."

Ray O. Thompson, Box 216, Grand Marais, Minn.
Moulds for gas-check revolver bullets.

Turley's Sporting Goods, Brigham, Utah.
Reloading tools, dies, bullets, components.

W. S. Vickerman, 208 S. Ruby, Ellensburg, Wash.
Vickerman bullet seaters.

L. R. (Bob) Wallack, Northville, N.Y.
Rifle gunsmith, supplies, components, barrels, bench rest equipment.

Wagner's Gun Room, Ashland, Ohio.
Custom handloading, Wagner's handloads.

Warner & Co., 2510-12 Pleasant Ave., Altoona, Pa.
Gas checks in all calibers.

Warshals, 1st & Madison Sts., Seattle 4, Wash.
Reloading tools, components, shooters' supplies.

Was Den, Northampton 1, Pa.
Shooters' supplies, components, bench rest targets.

Weatherby's, Inc., 2779 Firestone Blvd., South Gate, Calif.
Weatherby's rifles and ammunition, sporting goods, tools, components.

Western Alloy Co., Box 643, North Hollywood, Calif.
Kirksite bullets.

Western Gun & Supply Co., 2324 O St., Lincoln 8, Nebr.
Reloading tools, components, accessories.

Jim Wilkinson, Rifle Ranch, Prescott, Ariz.
Reloading tools, components, supplies.

L. E. Wilson, Box 636, Cashmere, Wash.
Case trimmers, primer pocket and inside neck reamers, full length resizing dies, headspace gages, case gages, precision tools.

Winchester Repeating Arms Co., New Haven, Conn.
Rifles, shotguns, ammunition, components supplied through dealers.

Wisler Western Arms Co., 205 Second St., San Francisco 5, Calif.

Equipment, supplies, components, and targets.

Yankee Specialty Co. (W. Rohrbacker, successor) 513 Sanford Place, Erie, Pa.

Yankee reloading tools and moulds.

E P B M We hope you enjoyed this title from Echo Point Books & Media

---

Before Closing this Book, Two Good Things to Know

1. Buy Direct & Save

Go to www.echopointbooks.com (click "Our Titles" at top or click "For Echo Point Publishing" in the middle) to see our complete list of titles. We publish books on a wide variety of topics—from spirituality to auto repair.

Buy direct and save 10% at www.echopointbooks.com

2. Make Literary History and Earn $100 Plus Other Goodies Simply for Your Book Recommendation!

At Echo Point Books & Media we specialize in republishing out-of-print books that are united by one essential ingredient: high quality. Do you know of any great books that are no longer actively published? If so, please let us know. If we end up publishing your recommendation, you'll be adding a wee bit to literary culture and a bunch to our publishing efforts.

Here is how we will thank you:

- A free copy of the new version of your beloved book that includes acknowledgement of your skill as a sharp book scout.
- A free copy of another Echo Point title you like from echopointbooks.com.
- And, oh yes, we'll also send you a check for $100.

Since we publish an eclectic list of titles, we're interested in a wide range of books. So please don't be shy if you have obscure tastes or like books with a practical focus. To get a sense of what kind of books we publish, visit us at www.echopointbooks.com.

If you have a book that you think will work for us, send us an email at editorial@echopointbooks.com